Financial Analysis for Decision Making

SECOND EDITION

Curtis J. Blecke

Daniel L. Gotthilf

PRENTICE-HALL, INC.   Englewood Cliffs, NJ

Prentice-Hall International, Inc., *London*
Prentice-Hall of Australia, Pty. Ltd., *Sydney*
Prentice-Hall of Canada, Ltd., *Toronto*
Prentice-Hall of India Private Ltd., *New Delhi*
Prentice-Hall of Japan, Inc., *Tokyo*
Whitehall Books, Ltd., *Wellington, New Zealand*
Prentice-Hall of Southeast Asia Pte. Ltd., *Singapore*

© 1980 by

Prentice-Hall, Inc.
Englewood Cliffs, N.J.

Library of Congress Cataloging in Publication Data

Blecke, Curtis J
    Financial analysis for decision making.

    Includes index.
    1. Corporations--Finance. 2. Controllership.
3. Cost control. 4. Financial statements. I. Gotthilf, Daniel L.,   Joint author. II. Title.
HG4026.B58 1980   658.1'5   79-24709
ISBN 0-13-315234-0

Printed in the United States of America

To my wife, Millie, and my son, Jim,
for their encouragement and assistance
in writing this book

Curtis J. Blecke

To my partner

Daniel L. Gotthilf

The
Authors

Curtis J. Blecke most recently held the position of Operations & Financial Analyst on the controller's staff of the Consumer and Technical Products Division of Owens-Illinois, Inc., Toledo.

While at Owens-Illinois, Mr. Blecke served with several divisions of that company, where a wide range of assignments placed him in subsidiaries and plants in several states. For seven years he served with the company's Administrative Division—five years in Corporate Planning and two years in Methods and Procedures.

Prior to Owens-Illinois, Mr. Blecke was a cost accountant for the American Can Company.

The author majored in accounting at Northwestern University. He has also done special post-graduate work at the University of Pennsylvania and has attended numerous seminars and study groups.

Presently retired and living in Florida, Mr. Blecke continues his accounting and financial writing. His articles have appeared in *The Financial Executive, N.A.A. Management Accounting,* and *International Management Digest.*

Daniel L. Gotthilf, CPA, is Senior Vice President/Finance, and a Director of Savin Corporation. Mr. Gotthilf's areas of responsibilities with Savin, for the past fifteen years, have included accounting services, data processing, budgeting, and systems and procedures.

His early business years were spent in public accounting practice and as an internal operational auditor. Prior to joining Savin he served as Controller for Universal Laboratories and as Treasurer and Controller for Technical Tape Corporation.

Mr. Gotthilf was an honor graduate of the University of Michigan School of Business in 1948 and subsequently obtained a Certificate in Programming and Data Processing Analysis from New York University.

The author is a frequent lecturer before the American Management Association on a wide range of financial subjects and has written numerous articles for business and financial journals. His book, *Treasurer's and Controller's Desk Book,* is on the Prentice-Hall list of business best-sellers.

What This New Edition Will Do For You

The original book, published in 1966, was well received by the management people to whom it was directed—so much so, in its first ten years it went through ten printings. Because today's business climate requires much more financial information quickly relayed to the corporate decision makers, the time is ripe for a totally updated and expanded Second Edition of the original work. In fact, the extent of the updating and the amount of new material suggests this is more a new book than a second edition.

This new edition is written to provide a basic information reporting format, both graphic and tabular, from which almost any company can tailor effective management reporting techniques to fit its special requirements. These basic financial indicators, and supporting definitions and explanations will serve as useful guides for decision-making line executives, as well as financial staff and accountants. The book also presents in practical, hands-on terms, the methods to implement and monitor the performance of this information system.

A new era in business today mandates tough financial controls and quicker and better decisions from the chief executive officer. New government regulations and disclosure requirements force corporate management to take a hard look at company finances, operations, products and strategies. Businessmen are becoming aware that their decisions must take into account the general social, political, environmental, legal, and economic climate of the community, country and world.

New terminology is in vogue such as "executive liability," "vicarious responsibility," and "public oversight," which means top management has to answer for illegal or unethical dealings even by subordinates far down the corporate ladder. The corporate hierarchy, therefore, must become familiar with every facet of the company's business and the regulations governing it. One way the executive suite can protect itself is to insist on prompt, meaningful, accurate, and comprehensive intelligence from its accounting and financial people.

Financial transactions, more than ever, affect the success and survival of a business enterprise, whether large or small. Top and middle management people, from line to staff, have to be thoroughly familiar with the financial "facts of life" even when their primary responsibilities, experience, and training are restricted to sales, production, marketing, engineering, or industrial relations.

CRITICAL NEW ANSWERS IN THE NEW EDITION

Specifically, this new edition is a treasury of answers and data for today's financial executive who is no longer isolated in his function but, necessarily, involved in the full gamut of operations as they affect fiduciary responsibility. In addition to re-arrangement of key chapters for easier application, four new chapters have been added:

- Computer Utilization for Decision Making
- Cost of Capital and Debt
- Financial Analysis through Budgeting
- Organizing for Financial Management

The suggested methods of information presentation to management are explained in simple terms and implemented by sample forms and formats designed for immediate adaptation with very little revision or expansion. In some cases, the material in the new edition could very well lead management to a decision as to what kind of information system it should have.

WHAT THIS BOOK OFFERS

To the chief executive officer of a company and his top management team: This book will suggest to you the kind of corporate control information you should be receiving to aid in making decisions. If you are presently receiving this type of intelligence from your staffs, it may help you to more clearly understand the background and techniques employed in the preparation of the material.

To the financial staff people who are charged with the responsibility of furnishing line management with information upon which they can base key decisions: This book contains a comprehensive blueprint of just what kind of management information should be brought to executive attention and to what depth and presents a workable procedure to follow.

To middle management personnel, both line and staff: This book should provide a clear picture of the kind of performance and understanding you might be held accountable for. It also shows how actions at whatever level or segment of the business under your control can affect the total overall corporate well-being.

To the engineer, marketing specialist, sales staff, industrial relations people, and other non-accounting executives: This book affords an opportunity to quickly and easily grasp the scope of the entire company's functions and problems. It should give you better insight into your own role in the total corporate picture and certainly improve your communications lines and general rapport with both top management and operating management, as well as the financial people.

To all management people whose personal responsibilities, background and education pertain to non-accounting functions: This book might be an opportunity to circumvent a great deal of time-comsuming reading and studying of a wide range of material by using this concise but extensive outline.

To the statistical and system-oriented staff specialist: This book should suggest methods by which conclusions, recommendations, and information can be translated into traditional and universal business language to gain ready understanding and acceptance.

To the accountant: This book will not only show what happens to the operating data collected, calculated, and tabulated, but also the importance of the accountant's responsibility in providing accurate information in order to furnish the best possible bases for the decision-making areas.

This approach to financial analysis can be adopted immediately by a company regardless of what accounting systems or electronic data processing equipment it may presently use.

You may be sure this is not the kind of book that is read and then relegated to a library shelf or bookcase, but, rather, a working tool to be read and then kept readily at hand for frequent reference.

Specifically, this book is constructed of fourteen sections of concentrated information, ideas, examples, and action programs related to financial analysis for decision-making. Some of the highlights are covered in the following check-list:

1. The first chapter presents a suggested format for a capsule type monthly situation report. This report is constructed so that it covers balance sheet statistics, sales and profit data, manufacturing and operating costs, selling and administrative costs, research expenditures, capital expenditures, and working fund position. Performance statistics such as profit percentages and asset turns are included. Time periods covered are current month, year to date, prior year, and original plan. This key report is contained on a one page letter-size form. Accounting for inflation effects is discussed.

2. The techniques, forms, and reports contained in Chapter 2 are designed to assist management in controlling both asset and liability items which can have serious impact on the business if permitted to get out of control. It presents management on a monthly basis with a device to appraise inventory levels, fixed asset balances, accounts receivable, etc., by various yardsticks and comparisons. Included in this chapter is a method of balance sheet forecasting which ties in to the overall concept of planning future activities, as well as historical analysis. The corporate performance yardstick of "return on investment" is explained and illustrated in this chapter. Improved asset utilization through control and analysis of inventories and receivables is obtained.

3. Chapter 3 describes in non-technical terms how discounted cash flow techniques can be used to decide capital spending. It explains the time value of money concept in the rating of investment opportunities through simple definitions and examples. The next step describes the construction of the annual capital budget and its continuing control. For major capital expenditures, there are forms and procedures for post-completion audits, including performance verification and financial analyses. The calculation for return on investment for an entire business is presented.

4. The fourth chapter defines the term "cash flow" and explains how cash position is affected by increases and decreases in all balance sheet items. It describes how cash forecasts are made and includes forms, work sheets, and illustrative charts. This chapter combines with Chapters 2 and 3 to form a complete basic outline on the subject of company asset management.

5. Chapter 5 examines the matter of direct and absorption cost accounting methods. A procedure is explained and illustrated which combines the two concepts and utilizes the advantages of both.

6. Definitions and examples of distribution costs versus production costs are covered in Chapter 6. It includes sales analyses by order size versus sales volume, and number of customers versus sales volume. Special emphasis is placed on the small order problem. Profitability review by products, product groups, production facilities and sales branches is explained using Direct Cost techniques.

7. Profit improvement through cost reduction is covered in Chapter 7. Specific ideas and programs are outlined and discussed. The use of budgets for cost control is explained and illustrated.

8. Chapter 8 critiques the various borrowing devices, and methods are presented to compare the alternatives. Formulas are presented to measure the cost of equity, bank debt, and straight debt. Convertible securities and leases are considered, and the sources of debt are enumerated.

9. Chapter 9 offers an understandable explanation of the computer—how it works and its application in financial analysis. A glossary of computer terms is included, and binary calculations are simply reviewed. The data processing department's organization and control techniques are evaluated.

10. A method of rating research and development projects by financial analysis is developed in Chapter 10. The chapter proposes a method of determining how your company rates with your competition. It suggests what data to obtain and how to obtain it. A form is illustrated on how to present the comparison figures, both tabular and graphic, to your company management. The value of this information and knowledge and how it can be used to reveal possible weak areas in your own company is discussed. The chapter also presents a program for long-range forecasting and planning. It is believed that a good sound planning program can make a definite contribution to management's most important goals—profits and growth. The possible need of management for special staff

assistance to supplement the financial and operating information systems is covered. Included are explanations and applications of various problem-solving techniques.

11. Chapter 11 deals with reasons for mergers and a method for evaluating merger prospects. Models of financial statements are included to predict the total corporate effect of a proposed merger before consummation. The price for the acquisition is calculated, and determining the method of payment is thoroughly examined.

12. Budgeting concepts are explored, including how to involve managers in the budget and how to communicate the goals throughout the entire organization. The methods of constructing reports and performing mid-stream remedial actions are described.

13. The tools and framework necessary to position responsible financial managers to make profitable decisions are presented, step-by-step. This involves organizing the entire company properly, publishing position descriptions, policies and procedures, and auditing the results.

Hundreds of innovative and business-tested ideas are at your fingertips in this answer-filled guide. Put them to work in your own situation as catalysts for *dramatic and on-going increment to the bottom line.*

Curtis J. Blecke

Daniel L. Gotthilf

Contents

What This New Edition Will Do For You • 8

Critical New Answers In the New Edition, 9; What This Book Offers, 9

1 Using The Monthly Financial Analysis Report As A Prime Financial Tool • 21

Construction of the Key Report, 22; Balance Sheet Data, 22; Sales and Income Data, 23; Performance Statistics, 23; Planning, 23; Source Data, 25; Suggested Accompanying Reports, 25; Timing and Frequency, 27; Comments and Explanations, 28; Taking Inflation Effect Into Account, 28; Utilizing the Skills of the Staff Specialist, 31; Assignment of Responsibility, 31; Aids for Analysis, 32

2 Balance Sheet Analysis: Making Your Working Capital Work Hard For You • 33

Various Decision Areas, 34; Supporting Statements, 34; Management of Working Assets, 34; Financial Position, 35; Accounts Receivable, 35; Inventory Management, 38; Inventory Quantity Levels, 41; Inventory Turnover, 42; Cash, 45; Fixed Asset Balances, 50; Return On Gross Assets, 51; Balance Sheet Budgeting, 53; The Capital Budget, 56; Capital and Debt Analysis, 58; Balance Sheet Management, 59

3 Capital Investment Decisions • 61

Discounted Cash Flow Method, 62; Other Methods, 62; Acceptance By Management, 64; Non-Technical Approach, 65; Return On Investment (The Profitability Rate), 65; Suggested Work Sheets, 67; Estimated Investment Requirements, 70; Calculation of Depreciation, 71; Sum of The Years Digits, 71; Cash Income and Payback Period, 72; Calculation of Return on Investment for Individual Projects, 74; Determining an Acceptable Profitability Rate (ROI), 76; Capital Expenditure Request, 77; Supporting Detail, 77; Calculation of Return on Investment For An Entire Business, 77; Calculating the Return On Investment, 81; Converting the ROI For the Entire Business Into A Stock Value, 82; Post-Installation Evaluation of Major Capital Appropriations, 83; Purposes of Post-Completion Audits, 86; Timing of Post-Audits, 89; Types of Projects Audited, 89; Problems of Post-Audits, 90; Responsibility for Making Post-Audits, 90; Form and Content of Post-Audits, 90; Evaluation of Capital Investments, 90

4 Statement of Changes In Financial Position: The Funds Statement as a Control and Planning Mechanism • 95

Funds Flow Defined, 96; Cash Forecasting, 99; Cash Management, 102; Cash Analysis Pointers, 103

5 Direct Versus Absorption Costing • 104

Selection of a Cost Accounting Method, 105; Understanding of Common Terminology, 105; Explanation of Direct Costing, 111; Advantages of Direct Costing, 115; Disadvantages of Direct Costing, 116; Absorption Costing In a Nutshell, 117; Application of Full Absorption Costing Using a Conventional Standard Cost System, 119; Advantages of Absorption Costing, 120; Disadvantages of Absorption Costing, 120; Conclusions, 121; Recommendations, 122; Cost Control Concepts, 124

6 Distribution Cost and Profitability Review by Products • 125

Definition of Distribution Costs, 126; Distribution Cost Reduction, 126; The Small Order Problem, 127; Analyzing Small Order Costs, 127; Distribution Expense Applied to Standard Costs, 129; Selling Expense, 133; Specialization In Small Volume Business, 135; Product Analysis, 136; Quality of Sales Mix, 136; Tabulation of Data, 136; Sales and Cost Analysis, 137; Profit Contribution Analysis, 138; Profit Analysis By Product and Plant, 138; Profit Analysis By Product and Sales Branch, 138; Remedial Action Programs, 142; Corporate Surgery, 143; Maximizing Profit Through Product Discrimination, 143; Product Profitability Pointers, 144

7 Financial Analysis for Cost Reduction • 145

The Cost Reduction Concept, 146; Participation in Cost Reduction Programs, 146; Cost Reduction Opportunities, 147; Organizing For Cost Reduction Programs, 155; Profit Improvement Pointers, 157

8 Successful Management of Cost of Capital and Debt • 159

Equity, 160; Bank Debt, 162; Straight Debt, 163; Debt With Equity, 165; Accounting for Convertible Debt and Debt with Stock Purchase Warrants, 167; Installment Loans and Leases, 168; Leverage Leasing, 169; Sale and Lease Back, 171; Make or Buy Decisions, 171; Lease and Lease Back Versus Ownership, 172; The Captive Finance Subsidiary, 173; Acquisitions, 175; Costing Capital and Debt, 175

9 Computer Utilization: Prime Tool for Modern Financial Decision Making • 177

What It Is and How Does It Work, 178; Glossary, 182; Organizing For Data Processing, 185; Computer Reports and Applications, 186; Controlling The System, 188; Selecting Between Alternative Systems, 189; The Computer and Financial Analysis, 191

10 Decision Making for Tomorrow • 193

Evaluation of Research and Development Projects, 193; Economic Value of Research and Development Output, 194; Quantitative Evaluation of R & D Projects, 196; Qualitative Evaluation of R & D Projects, 197; Annual Performance Rating With Competition, 199; Value of Comparison Analysis, 199; Sources of Data, 201; Time Periods Studied, 202; Practical Performance Bench Marks, 203; Case Histories and Examples, 204; Long-Range Profit Planning, 206; Definition and Function of Planning, 206; Necessity for Long-Range Planning, 206; Advantages of Formalizing a Planning Procedure, 207; A Suggested Planning Procedure, 207; Basic Purpose and Objectives, 208; Marketing Plans, 208; Manufacturing Plans, 209; Research, Development and Engineering Plan, 210; Capital Investment Planning,

211; Financial Projections, 211; Assignment of Responsibility for the Plan, 212; Periodic Comparison of Plan Versus Actual Performance, 213; Operations Research and Analysis, 213; Operations Analysis Versus Operations Research, 213; Advantages of An Operations Analysis Staff, 214; Suggested Procedure for An Operations Research Assignment, 214; Limitations of the Operations Research Approach, 215; Value Analysis, 215; Profit Protection Techniques for Tomorrow, 217

11 Key Factors and Proven Techniques in Evaluation of Mergers and Acquisitions • 219

Compliance with Regulatory Government Agencies, 221; Selection of a Partner, 222; Statistical Analysis to Evaluate a Merger Program, 222; Checklist of Information for Evaluation of a Company Under Consideration for Acquisition, 223; Purchase or Pooling of Interests, 229; Determination of Acquisition Price, 229; Determining the Method of Payment, 232; Possible Results of a Merger, 239; Acquisition Aids, 239

12 Fine Tuning Financial Analysis Through Modern Budgeting Techniques • 241

The Budgeting Concept, 242; The Profit Plan, 242; The Budget, 244; Communicating the Budget, 244; Budget versus Actual (BVA) Performance, 248; Reporting System Features, 249; Budgeting Pointers, 252

13 Streamlined Organizing For Systematic Financial Management • 253

Organizational Charts, 254; Chart of Accounts, 257; Accounting Manual, 258; Position Descriptions, 259; Standard Operating Procedures, 260; Operating Policies, 261; Personnel Policies, 262; Publication Control, 262, Exercise of Authority, 264; Philosophy of Management, 264; Management by Objectives, 265; Internal Auditing, 267; Organizational Concepts for Financial Control, 268

Glossary of Selected Technical Financial Terms • 269

Index • 283

List of Exhibits

Exhibit 1
Financial Analysis Report As of June 30, 19XX • 26

Exhibit 2
Total Company or Division • 36

Exhibit 3
Credit Department Monthly Report • 38

Exhibit 4
Accounts Receivable Status Report • 39

Exhibit 5
Total Company or Division • 40

Exhibit 6
Inventory Turnover Measurement by Month • 43

Exhibit 7
Inventory Analysis Data • 44

Exhibit 8
Control of Profits Chart • 52

Exhibit 9
Total Company of Division • 53

Exhibit 10
Ledger Card • 55

Exhibit 11
Balance Sheet Budget • 57

Exhibit 12
Plan for Future Capital Expenditures • 59

Exhibit 13
Return on Investment • 68

Exhibit 14
Estimated Investment Requirements • 69

Exhibit 15
Depreciation Schedule • 70

Exhibit 16
Cash Flow Back • 73

Exhibit 17
Project Evaluation Calculation of Return on Investment • 75

Exhibit 18
Present Value Tables Periodic Factors • 76

Exhibit 19
Capital Expenditure Request • 80

Exhibit 20
Checklist for Investment Justification • 81

Exhibit 21
Do-It-Yourself Calculation for Determining Return on Investment and Stock Value from Annual
Report Information • 85

Exhibit 22
Post Installation Evaluation Major Capital Appropriations • 91

Exhibit 23
Post Installation Evaluation Major Capital Appropriations • 92

Exhibit 24
Diagram of Cash Flow • 97

Exhibit 25
Illustration of Cash Flow • 98

Exhibit 26
Funds Statement Work Sheet • 100

Exhibit 27
Illustration of Financial Position • 102

Exhibit 28
Simple Break-Even Chart • 113

Exhibit 29
Comparison of Absorption vs. Direct Costing as Affected by Changes in Sales Volume • 114

Exhibit 30
Cost of Production Statement March 19XX • 118

Exhibit 31
Standard Cost Card • 123

Exhibit 32
Sales Analysis Order Size vs. Sales Volume • 128

Exhibit 33
Sales Analysis Number of Customers vs. Annual Volume • 129

Exhibit 34
Standard Cost Determination • 130

Exhibit 35
Standard Cost Determination • 131

Exhibit 36
Analysis of the Market • 135

Exhibit 37
Analysis of Sales Commission to Sales Potential and Profit Contribution • 135

Exhibit 38
Sales and Cost Analysis by Product and Product Group • 137

Exhibit 39
Gross Profit Analysis by Product and Product Group • 139

Exhibit 40
Profit Analysis by Product and Plant • 139

Exhibit 41
Profit Analysis by Product and Sales Branch • 140

Exhibit 42
Territorial Return on Investment • 141

Exhibit 43
Territory Marketing Targets • 142

Exhibit 44
Operating Budget Detail • 156

Exhibit 45
Budget Statement • 157

Exhibit 46
The Functional Relationships of a Programmed Computer • 179

Exhibit 47
Binary Table • 181

Exhibit 48
Organization of a Centralized EDP Control Function (in a Decentralized Company) • 186

Exhibit 49
Research Project Authorization Request • 195

Exhibit 50
R & D Constraint Analysis Chart • 198

Exhibit 51
Financial Comparison, 19-- • 200

Exhibit 52
Return On Gross Assets • 201

Exhibit 53
Inventory Turnover • 202

Exhibit 54
Checklist of Information for Evaluation of a Company Under Consideration for Acquisition • 223

Exhibit 55
Merger of Company "A" Company "B" Pro-Forma Income Statement • 226

Exhibit 56
Merger of Company "A" and Company "B" Pro-Forma Balance Sheet • 228

Exhibit 57
Methods of Determining the Purchase Price • 231

Exhibit 58
Prior Year to December 31, 19XX • 243

Exhibit 59
Organizational Chart • 256

Exhibit 60
Chart of Accounts • 257

CHAPTER 1

Using The Monthly Financial Analysis Report As A Prime Financial Tool

This report is the starting point in evaluating the status of a business.

Intelligence available from management sciences and techniques, as well as the more familiar but still highly important financial production and marketing transactions, must obviously be communicated to decision-making management. A controlled information system should be constructed for maximum knowledge of the key factors which most influence profitability and competitive strength. Firstly, it should be confined to a relatively few basic significant indicators designed to expedite decision-making and control. Secondly, it should be formulated in the general language of business and employ conventional yardsticks of corporate performance. Thirdly, it will include the framework for the business organization which will permit communication of objectives to all levels. This will enable all levels of management to clearly understand the facts relative to their individual responsibilities.

CONSTRUCTION OF THE KEY REPORT

This report is constructed so that it covers balance sheet statistics, sales and income data, manufacturing and operating costs, operating profit, net profit, research expenditures, capital expenditures, and working capital position. It covers current month, year to date, prior year, latest forecast, and original plan. It is contained on a one-page form, size 8½ x 11. (Exhibit 1)

The back-up reports which contribute to the "end result," as exemplified in this top management summary, are discussed further on in this chapter and in succeeding chapters. All this back-up material or selected reports from it can accompany the monthly status report. The graphic charts and illustration suggested can be made into visuals and projected onto a screen at meetings; or, flip cards can be prepared. In either case, 8½ x 11 copies of reports and charts should be distributed to key management people for further use, rather than expect them to remember statistics disseminated at a management meeting.

This same total company performance and financial analysis report can also be used for product divisions, individual plants, or whatever is desired, depending upon the size and diversification of the company concerned. It can either employ the management by exception concept or tell the whole story and identify those segments and areas of the company where they are performing unusually well or poorly. Responsibility should then be readily ascertained and appropriate action programs initiated.

Although this capsule information report was designed for the top executive, it should also cover division managers, plant managers, etc., either in whole or in part. Comments and explanations on both superior and sub-standard performance should be attached to this report because "why something happened" is just as important as "what happened." However, top management should not be deluged with reams of data, such as daily plant efficiency reports and the like; these should be dealt with by other levels of management on a routine basis.

The monthly financial analysis report (Exhibit 1) is composed of three sections: balance sheet data, sales and income data, and performance statistics. It is constructed so that all this information is contained on one 8½ x 11 page. As many pages can be used as are desired. However, as the first page covers only the total company, additional pages using the same form can then be prepared by plants, sales lines, products, territories, branch sales offices, and geographic regions, depending upon how much depth management needs for analyses. It is not likely that every heading could be used for many of the detail reports, especially in the balance sheet section. This aspect does not lessen the analytical value of the form.

BALANCE SHEET DATA

The top section reveals the status of the company's assets and liabilities as of the last day of the current month. Naturally we cannot analyze the month of June until some time after July 1st, in any aspect of the business. Under the heading, "Current Year to Date Average," we use the average month-end asset and liability balances for as many months as have elapsed at the given time for the current year. The third heading shows the asset and liability balances as of December 31st of the previous year, and the last heading covers the projected balances as of December 31st of the current year plan or prediction. The various categories of assests and liabilities are accumulated and condensed into only the major classifications. For example, this internal management report shows one heading for "Accrued Wages and Expenses." This might be broken down into much more detail in a company's formal financial statement. Omitted entirely from this report are reserve amounts, stockholders' equity and retained earnings, and the allowance for depreciation usually found as a reduction from fixed assets in the asset section. These omissions were made in the interest of brevity, and because this particular report advocates the use of gross assets in the determination of the corporate performance measurement of "return on investment."

SALES AND INCOME DATA

The headings here are conventional and traditional, and the time periods are self-explanatory. Here again, the reader is encouraged to follow his own inclinations and needs in designing a form for his own company.

PERFORMANCE STATISTICS

We have tried to select here those indices of a company's well-being which are not only significant but are easily understood. *This report is the starting point in evaluating the status of a business,* and should not be too broad in scope. The details should be covered in the supporting data in whatever depth is necessary.

PLANNING

The financial community, including bankers and stockholders, are inclined to appraise a company by its past performance, and also against its competition and business in general. However, most large publicly held corporations are more and more queried as to future plans and prospects. Therefore, management reporting can hardly be confined to financial statements showing the results of current and prior months, year to date, prior year, past ten years, etc., but should also include action plans for next month, next year, etc. The historical data is useful to depict the progress, or lack of it, in a business and serves as a base for improvements and trend projections. However, I submit that it might be rewarding to spend more time analyzing the wisdom of future plans concerning capital expenditures, research projects, acquisitions, etc. and less time analyzing and regretting past actions and results. A more careful examination of various alternative courses of future business actions could result in fewer costly mistakes in judgment. This would also provide stockholders, the owners of the business, with useful information on which to base investment decisions. To encourage this, the Securities and Exchange Commission has established "safe-harbor" rules for companies making public projections.

You will note that the proposed key financial status report includes the heading "Original Current Year Annual Plan." We are assuming here that most companies have some sort of short-term and long-range planning procedure. Planning will not eliminate problems but can help to minimize them. Acceptance of this fact and the seemingly increasing number and scope of problems have prompted many managements to adopt a formal planning program as a major corporate function.

Essential to good planning is forecasting—forecasting the economy, industry volume, company sales, markets, prices, cost—both for the short term and over an extended period. Implemented by such data, the vital financial projections evolve, together with their supporting schedules, as the basis for key decisions plus a yardstick for actual performance. Forecasts are part of the budgeting system. Comparing actual results to the forecast permits management to take corrective action in mid-stream. It facilitates the attainment of objectives.

An effective planning system must begin with the development of objectives in detail rather than in aggregates. If you do not plan in detail, you cannot control in detail. If you do not control in detail, you do not control effectively. How much detail is required, of course, is a matter of judgment which must be determined in the light of the specific problems which face the company and the seriousness or urgency with which those problems are viewed. These details, of course, are intended to support the overall corporate objectives, the broad corporate goals sent down from the board of directors and the president. Planning starts at the highest level, and is communicated down through the organization where the detailed plans are established which assure that the top corporate goals will be achieved.

We should recognize at the outset that perfect planning cannot possibly be realized except as a stroke of luck. In other words, we can predict but we cannot foretell. It is more realistic for management to accept the limitations inherent in any long-range plan than to be too rigid in its goals. As a matter of fact, planning in itself is not a guarantee of corporate success or survival. On the other hand, there is a definite relationship between responsible planning and corporate profits in a keenly competitive and fast-changing economic climate. Constant comparison of original plan with actual performance on a current basis will surely and gradually improve the quality of the planning function.

Planning is not merely an extension of budgeting. It does not diminish the importance of landing today's contract or of keeping current costs or inventories in line. It may not have much effect on this year's profit and loss statement, but it may have a profound effect on the profit picture in the coming year or years.

SOURCE DATA

It is neither the intent nor the function of this book to compare or recommend any particular system of accounting methods and management techniques. It is assumed that every company has enough data already in existence to prepare simple profit and loss and balance sheet statements. It also is assumed that there is adequate information gathering ability to prepare sales analyses and profit contribution statistics. If this is not the case, the type of management information reporting covered in this book may help a company to decide what system of general accounting, cost accounting, problem solving or budget programs they would prefer to adopt.

All companies, whether large or small, obviously have some system of finanacial reporting to management. The size and resources of a company pretty much dictate the degree of sophistication which can be employed in the various methods of problem solving, information gathering, analysis, and planning.

SUGGESTED ACCOMPANYING REPORTS

The type of reports, both tabular and graphic, which might support and augment the key report (Exhibit 1) is limited only by the needs of the business and the imagination of the staff analyst.

The array of facts and information should resemble a pyramid so that the peak provides a capsule or flash report and the detail can be delved into in as much depth as is felt necessary. Much of this detail in depth can be retained by the staff department, although a certain amount of it should accompany the main report. For example, a single report would cover the performance of an entire company. Similar reports could then be prepared, broken down by plants, sales lines, products, territories, branch sales offices, and whatever is necessary to give top management the information they need to determine problem areas, and in what matters remedial action might be indicated. This data should separate the important components so that it points out which segment of the business is responsible and the reason for the possible unsatisfactory performance.

One of the detailed supporting analyses might consist of a breakdown of sales by product, sales division, geographic area, channel of distribution, and any other pertinent or revealing category. It could be presented as a trend and cover current performance

FINANCIAL ANALYSIS REPORT AS OF June 30, 19XX

Division ————————————

(In Thousands of Dollars)

BALANCE SHEET DATA

	Actual Current Month End Balance	Actual Current Year To Date Average	Actual Prior Year Balance	Original Current Year Annual Plan
CURRENT ASSETS	6/30/19--	1st 6 Mos.	19--	19--
Cash	1,900	1,950	2,000	2,000
Securities (Short Term)	845	923	1,000	1,505
Receivables	2,400	2,200	2,000	2,200
Inventories	2,150	2,075	2,000	2,100
TOTAL CURRENT ASSETS	7,295	7,148	7,000	7,805
CURRENT LIABILITIES				
Payables	500	400	300	325
Accrued Wages & Expenses	390	380	370	400
Accrued Federal Tax	900	850	800	900
TOTAL CURRENT LIABILITIES	1,790	1,630	1,470	1,625
WORKING CAPITAL	5,505	5,518	5,530	6,180
CURRENT RATIO	4.08	4.39	4.76	4.80
GROSS FIXED ASSETS	8,400	8,200	8,000	8,600
DEFERRED CHARGES, DEPOSITS, ETC.	1,100	1,100	1,100	1,100
TOTAL GROSS ASSET BALANCE	16,795	16,448	16,100	17,505
AVERAGE GROSS ASSETS TO DATE	16,448	16,448	15,530	16,803

SALES AND INCOME DATA

	Current Month Actual	Current Year To Date Actual	Prior Year Actual 12 Months	Current Annual Plan 12 Months
NET SALES	1,000	6,000	10,000	11,000
Inventory Value of Sales	600	4,250	6,100	6,800
Manufacturing Variance	50	250	450	400
All Other Cost of Sales	50	300	650	700
Research and Development	35	200	300	350
Selling and Administrative	50	450	900	850
NET PROFIT AFTER TAX	108	275	800	950

PERFORMANCE STATISTICS

% GROSS PROFIT TO SALES	30.0	20.0	28.0	28.2
% NET PROFIT TO SALES	10.8	4.6	8.0	8.6
% RETURN ON ASSETS (Annualized)	7.9	3.3	5.1	5.6
ASSET TURNOVER (Annualized)	.73	.73	.64	.65
RECEIVABLES TURNOVER (days' sales)	72.8	66.4	73.0	73.0
INVENTORY TURNOVER (Annualized)	5.58	5.78	5.0	5.37
CASH PROVIDED (Applied)	(45)	(255)	700	505
NET ADDITIONS TO FIXED ASSETS	50	200	400	600
DEPRECIATION ACCRUAL	20	100	200	300

Exhibit 1

compared to past history compared to future plans or predictions. A similar report could be prepared showing the profit contribution by the same breakdown employed in the sales volume analysis. This could be gross profit or net profit, depending upon the type of accounting system employed, the availability of the information, and the desires of management.

Many companies prepare management information which only uses the concept of management by exception. However, sometimes it is just as important to know where exceptionally good performance exists and unusually high profits are being made in order to know where trouble may exist. For example, it may be that some product lines are so profitable that prices could easily be lowered, and if this is not done, the company may be inviting competition in the very area where they might be most solidly entrenched. There is sometimes as much risk in selling at too high a price as at too low a price. At too low a price, there obviously will be little or no profit, and at too high a price, other companies would be able to come in and compete on a price level which could still allow them a handsome profit, but which might deprive you of a very profitable segment of your business. Where selling prices are pretty much set by industry, it is still valuable knowledge to know just what the profitability situation is by various product lines. In a sick company sometimes diversification is the answer, perhaps through acquisitions. In other cases, even divestiture of some areas or segments of the business might be advisable from an overall profit standpoint. At any rate, from a management standpoint *knowledge is power*. Intelligent decisions cannot be made without full possession of all the facts. When all the facts are available it can be decided whether competition in a certain business is indicated or not. Corporate facilities, production schedules, sales strategies, and personnel can then be geared to handle whatever kind of business it is decided to compete in.

Although the primary reports should be formalized in a printed form, supporting data and comments need not be restricted to printed forms. Here considerable flexibility can be obtained by using columnar forms with desired headings filled in. It could happen that there may be something important to report, but if there is not a heading for it on some formal printed report or enough space allowed, the information may not be included. The number of formal printed forms should be kept to a minimum, and instead ordinary columnar paper and tabular forms by month and year, with blanks across the top which can be filled in, should be used. This provides flexibility. Typed reports should only be made when important or especially meaningful information is revealed, and top management attention is indicated. The technique of establishing a reporting system is described in the chapter titled Financial Analysis Through Budgeting.

TIMING AND FREQUENCY

The financial status report is defined and designed as a monthly report. It should be prepared as soon after the end of the month as the information can be made available.

Naturally, management at all levels will be concerned and occupied with all kinds of problems and decisions as they arise on a daily basis. However, it is advocated here that the total performance and analysis report be considered only once a month. If this report is analyzed comprehensively, there would be neither time nor value in evaluating this amount of intelligence more often. As an alternative, selected pieces of information can be updated on a daily basis. Responsible managers, using on-line CRT devices or time-sharing terminals, may call forth selected information on demand. For example, cash or sales could be updated daily. There is less meaning for a daily update of payables or performance statistics.

COMMENTS AND EXPLANATIONS

The correlation of comments, explanations, and recommendations to financial reports is usually mandatory. These comments should become a definite part of the reports. All this information should be retained for historical and trend determination purposes. Every occurrence within a company which causes a significant variation in its progress or financial situation is no doubt known by one or more management persons at the time. Unless this intelligence is recorded, however, the facts will be obscured or forgotten in time, and thus have no value to the decision-making function. Significant variations in a company's performance should be explained at the time the figures are published. Various staff and line people could prepare comments on those phases of the business for which they are responsible on a continuing basis. For example, sales managers might explain surges or slumps in sales during the current month. Plant managers might provide brief explanations regarding major variances in costs and manufacturing losses. It is suggested that a brief diary or log might be maintained by these individuals to record exceptions or unusual happenings as they occur. If this were done, these comments could be forwarded to the Comptroller's Department immediately after the end of the month, which should provide plenty of time to incorporate them into the monthly financial analysis report. A review of the accumulation of this information in prior periods should also help to sharpen the planning and forecasting abilities.

TAKING INFLATION EFFECT INTO ACCOUNT

The question arises as to whether the effects of inflation should be reflected in the financial statements and, accordingly, in the Monthly Financial Analysis Report, and, if so, in what manner.

The SEC, in its accounting rule ASR 190, mandated disclosures of replacement costs in footnotes to the financial statements. Consequently, the accounting system must be designed to permit calculation of replacement costs. The rule applies to public companies with certain assets in excess of $100 million and comprising more than 10% of total assets. In brief, the replacement costs affect inventories, plant, and equipment on the balance sheet. For the income statement, sales are recalculated at year-end prices, and depreciation is recomputed based on the replacement cost of the assets. This technique is future oriented, in that it shows stockholders and investors whether the current level of sales is sufficient to generate the cash which will be needed to replace inventories and plant and still earn a profit. The method of calculation is flexible in that the SEC permits different companies to use different methods of estimating replacement costs. One may estimate that a plant will be replaced with exactly the same type of plant; another company may conceive of a completely new plant which requires an estimate of construction cost and productivity. Replacement cost disclosures are, perhaps, more useful for investors than for company management.

One large accounting firm has proposed the use of Current Value accounting as an alternative. This is similar to the replacement cost method, except that it is applied to the entire set of financial statments and is used for tax reporting. Each item in the financial statement would be revalued at replacement cost or current market value after taxes.

The Financial Accounting Standards Board, in an early Exposure Draft, proposed the Gross National Product deflator to reflect price advances applied to sales, assets and liabilities. The GNP deflator, unlike the future-oriented replacement cost method, looks back over past performance and permits investors and management to measure the company's performance against the decline in the purchasing power of the dollar. A deficiency in this method is that the GNP deflator would be the same for all companies, thus ignoring the varying impact of inflation on different industries. This can be compensated for by the individual company through adjustments to the GNP deflator based on conditions affecting that company. This formula will penalize a company having a large investment in plant without correspondingly large debt. This is a fair penalty, however, as a standard inflation strategy should include the incurring of more long-term debt. The GNP deflator, then, permits management to make the best assessment of its performance in the face of inflation, as measured by the decline in the dollar's purchasing power.

Some companies estimate the effect of inflation in their budgets. They anticipate price and cost increases in the profit planning process. This is readily done in evaluating capital expenditures and expected cash flows. ROI analyses should, therefore, recognize the effect of dollar erosion on the calculated return. More than estimates of future effects, however, are possible. The Monthly Financial Analysis Report in Exhibit 1 can be restated, both balance sheet and income statement items, to reflect the published Gross National Product Implicit Price Deflator (GNP Deflator). GNP Deflators are published by the U.S. Department of Commerce, Bureau of Economic Analysis. For example, a current GNP Deflator index of 170 means that the current general level of prices is 70% higher than the general level in the base year of 1958. Expressed another way, the general purchasing power of the dollar has declined about 41% (70/170) since 1958. By applying the index to the index in the year of acquisition, in the case of fixed assets, assets can be restated to the current year's general purchasing power. For example, $1,000 of plant purchased in 1964, when the index was 108.8, can be restated to $2,070 of the general purchasing power of the dollar at the end of 1978 (index = 225) by multiplying the $1,000 cost by 225/108.8 =2.07.

The techniques for restating the financial statements using the GNP Deflator were published by the FASB in December, 1974 in a proposed statement titled Financial Reporting in Units of General Purchasing Power. This statement was subsequently withdrawn and was not published as a formal Financial Accounting Standard, primarily due to the SEC's publication of its replacement cost accounting requirements in ASR 190. Then, in December, 1978, the FASB published a second Exposure Draft, Financial Reporting and Changing Prices. This draft, like the 1974 proposal, continued to espouse the use of general purchasing power accounting—this time using the consumer Price Index for All Urban Consumers, published by the Bureau of Labor Statistics of the U.S. Department of Labor—in presenting supplementary financial data in "constant dollars." In an effort to meet the needs of interested parties other than management (investors, creditors, the public, and governmental agencies), however, the Board recognized that "current cost" information (akin to replacement cost or net realizable value), plus information on holding gains or losses (the change in values due to holding inventory or plant and equipment during inflationary or deflationary periods) would be useful in supplementary form, particularly in those enterprises having large investments in inventory, property, plant and equipment—or which have experienced price changes significantly different from the general level of inflation. The FASB, therefore, proposed presentation of either type of information, but encouraged presentation of the latter. This draft was subsequently adopted as FASB Statement No. 33, and the SEC then withdrew its requirements for ASR 190 replacement cost disclosures.

Nevertheless, the tenets set forth in the earlier proposed statement are valid and, in the authors' opinions, the most useful to financial management for the restatement of financial statements to reflect the effects of inflation on the dollars reported. In general, balance sheet items are classified as monetary or non-monetary items. Monetary items are cash, liabilities, and preferred stock. Restatement does not change monetary items, and they are stated at identical numbers in terms of units of money and units of general purchasing power at the balance sheet date. Non-monetary items are all other balance sheet items, like marketable securities, inventories, prepaid expenses, fixed assets, deferred charges, intangibles, deferred credits, common stock, paid-in capital, and retained earnings. Non-monetary items are restated to units of general purchasing power at the most recent balance sheet date. Income statement items are similarly restated at the most recent balance sheet date.

In addition to converting current earnings and balance sheet position to a general purchasing power basis and to considering replacement of capital items on a replacement cost basis, there are accepted inflation strategies most companies could employ.

1. Use LIFO costs in valuing inventories, to more closely reflect replacement costs.
2. Carry larger inventory levels when prices are increasing.
3. Place long-term commitments, at today's prices, for future inventory requirements.

4. Increase long-term debt for as much and as long as possible to pay off in cheaper future dollars.

5. Retain residual value rights or purchase options in leasing transactions, as the replacement cost of the equipment will appreciate.

6. Purchase and rehabilitate used plant and equipment, at lower cost than replacement new.

7. Expand capital investments in plant and equipment as a hedge against future increasing replacement costs.

8. Avoid designing energy-sensitive products which will surely increase in cost.

UTILIZING THE SKILLS OF THE STAFF SPECIALIST

The staff executive whose function it is to provide management with decision-making information is a specialist. He is a specialist in the same way that a medical diagnostician is a specialist. The diagnostician or internist must have an accurate and detailed knowledge of the human anatomy. In addition to this knowledge he possesses experience, training, and skill. However, in making decisions regarding medication, surgery, and treatment, he relies heavily on charts, observations, laboratory reports, and other paper work meticulously maintained by nurses, orderlies, and technicians on a daily, and sometimes even an hourly basis. This information includes such things as blood pressure, temperature, pulse, etc. Although paper work in business performs much the same function for the corporate decision-maker, here is where the metaphor ends. To a doctor, all these indicators add up to what he needs to know to make a decision. In business, the indicators must be collected, processed, translated, and summarized into a form which the decision-maker can readily use. The doctor analyzes and interprets the detail himself. In corporate life, however, this is defeated by sheer size. Interpretation, selection, and analysis of the more pertinent facts must be done by staff people. It becomes obvious then that the prime responsiblity of the staff specialist is the selection and the treatment of the mass of facts and statistics available to him. The staff specialist resembles the diagnostician in another respect. It is his duty to inform management what he really finds and not merely what he thinks management would like to hear. It is the responsibility of the staff specialist to present the facts to management as they are and not as viewed through rose-colored glasses. Further, it is also his responsibility to present these facts to management in everyday language and easy to understand form.

ASSIGNMENT OF RESPONSIBILITY

Although many different sources are drawn upon for information, it will fall mainly to the accounting area to provide the data needed. For this reason, it would seem that the company controller is likely to be responsible for the preparation of most of the report forms advocated in this book. Indeed, the Financial Executives Institute has defined the job responsiblities of the controller, one of which is stated to be "reporting and interpreting the results of operations."

In most companies today, the controller is the key figure in every aspect of the business because he is the information center. How he collects, accumulates, analyzes, and reports a vast fund of knowledge and data must certainly have a profound effect on the general conduct and success of the total business. For example, an effective corporation controller today might have on his staff, in addition to the usual accounting complement, a mathematician, a budget director, a methods and procedures analyst and a data-processing specialist. In addition, he would establish close rapport with marketing, sales, industrial engineering, research, development, operating engineering people, and plant management. The controller's staff, therefore, might not only consist of an accounting department, but, for all practical purposes, an operations research team as well. The degree of success in integrating these various functions will be reflected in the character of the management reporting.

In order to best achieve this purpose, every possible technique, new and old, provided it is liberally laced with good common sense, should be exploited. It seems that there are different styles in business management techniques, and many of them revolve in cycles. The accountant, the mathematician, the methods and procedures analyst, the industrial engineer, and the data processing person all have a real contribution to make to the art of financial analysis for decision making. The trick is to utilize the best of each, and whenever possible to organize them to complement each other. The integration of these functions also tends to circumvent the purist in any one field who feels that his approach is the only one. This is sometimes called the "bias of the specialist." In addition, while the tools and formulas of many of these specialists, such as equations, flow charts, tabulating tapes, etc., are valuable aids, they should be translated into conventional statements and illustrations before they are presented to top management. For example, if a sophisticated management tool like "PERT" (Program Evaluation and Review Technique) is employed, it is not recommended that the details of the network construction and charts should find their way into the line executive's office. Rather, it is suggested that only the solutions and recommendations accruing from these procedures progress to executive attention and decision.

AIDS FOR ANALYSIS

1. A top management information system should be limited to basic and significant factors, presented in a form to expedite decision making and control.

2. Traditional and recognizable business language and terms should be employed to communicate the resultant information to the operating executives.

3. A suggested flash or snapshot report consisting of key performance statistics is illustrated in Exhibit 1.

4. This report pinpoints the highlights of the profit and loss statement and the balance sheet for the current period with comparisons with past performance and future predictions.

CHAPTER 2

Balance Sheet Analysis: Making Your Working Capital Work Hard For You

Analysis of the balance sheet could indicate the degree of skill in the management of working capital.

A balance sheet is the basic statement of financial position for all businesses and industries. There are executives who feel that the profit and loss statement is the most basic form of information about a company, and that the balance sheet is too static. It deals with assets, debts, net worth, and other types of information which, they believe, do not relate to the day-to-day operations of a business. In actual practice, however, there are probably more top management decisions which affect the balance sheet than affect the profit and loss statement. Moreover, the key management decisions which relate to Return on Investment use both Balance Sheet and P & L figures.

In Chapter 1, we found that 50% of the total gross assets are gross fixed assets, which usually consist of land, buildings, and equipment. Current assets are approximately 43%, and the balance of 7% covers miscellaneous deferred charges, deposits, etc. Percent return on assets, asset turnover, and particularly inventory turnover, often obtain equal attention with percent profit to sales in measuring a company's performance and profitability.

In this chapter, we will relate accounts receivable balances, inventory balances, and total gross assets to sales, and we will compare the ratios between annual periods to obtain benchmarks and trends (see Exhibits 2, 5 and 9). Management of fixed assets will be covered in Chapter 3.

This chapter also contains suggested procedures to control some of these key factors on a month-to-month basis and in more detail. The high ratio of inventories and/or receivables to total current assets in the majority of all business and industry warrants special attention in this balance sheet.

VARIOUS DECISION AREAS

Decisions on capital expenditures and acquisitions, for example, are usually made by top management and exert a profound influence on the balance sheet and the profit and loss situation. Decisions relating to production scheduling, labor problems, sales problems, and machine breakdowns have an immediate effect on the P & L, but are usually handled by other levels of management on a routine basis.

SUPPORTING STATEMENTS

The traditional format of the balance sheet should be augmented by more dynamic statements and exhibits. Auxiliary statements and analyses of the formal balance sheet should compare the actual financial condition of the business to a budget or a plan. Comparisons to prior years and predictions for future years can be prepared. They can reveal whether there are adequate funds to run the business on the level which the actual operating statements and budgets indicate will soon be reached. They can also measure, through ratio analysis, the effectiveness of how excess funds are invested, and how the assets are divided and balanced between cash, equipment, inventories, etc.

MANAGEMENT OF WORKING ASSETS

Analysis of the balance sheet could indicate the degree of skill in the management of working capital. In the current asset section of the balance sheet, probably the three most important items for analysis and control would be the cash position, the accounts receivable, and the inventory situation. Another important measurement of balance sheet management is the concept of return on investment. This is expressed in terms of average total gross assets related to profits and sales, as demonstrated in the Financial Analysis Report, Exhibit 1, Chapter 1. This is illustrated, further, in Return on Investment and Earnings Per Share, Exhibit 58, Chapter 12, titled Financial Analysis Through Budgeting. Another important treatment of the balance sheet is the practice of balance sheet budgeting. One important benefit accruing from a sound balance sheet budget program is the predetermined effect on the cash position resulting from the projected capital budget, inventory policy or other spending plans.

FINANCIAL POSITION

Cash flow or statement of changes in financial position and cash forecasts, both short-term and long range, are one of management's most important control information needs. Because of the scope and complexity of this key business factor, this subject will be covered in depth in Chapter 4.

ACCOUNTS RECEIVABLE

In many companies the accounts receivable balance represents a very large amount of capital. Although it is an asset, it is tied up and cannot be spent until it is collected. It is important that top management receive information which measures the effectiveness of its credit and collection performance. The accounts receivable balance can be measured in different ways. It can be related to sales, either as a percentage of sales or a turnover of sales, or a trend report of the daily number of sales represented by the total accounts receivable balance. This would show the average collection period currently being experienced in relation to either a specific goal or to collection periods for prior years or months. Another control measure might be a report which ages the outstanding receivables. In other words, it would break down the total receivables into categories of open accounts up to 30 days, 30 to 60 days, 60 to 90 days, and more than 90 days. The obvious next step from this type of report would be a list of outstanding receivables by individual customers. Exhibit 2 graphically depicts in bar charts the amount of receivables and sales, primarily to demonstrate a trend situation between selected time periods. The trend line at the top relates the receivable balance to sales volume between selected time periods.

The number of days' sales represented by accounts receivable is obtained by dividing the receivables by the sales. The resultant percentage times the number of days over which the sales were computed provides the result. In calculating the days' sales in receivables, there may not be an even flow of sales or a uniformity of collections during the year. Uneven flows will distort the days' sales figure. This is resolved by calculating sales on a quarterly basis or some other period approximately thirty days longer than the expected result. For example:

Sales per quarter	$3,000 (a)
Receivables at end of quarter	$2,400 (b)
Percent of quarter's sales un-collected at end of quarter (b ÷ a)	80% (c)
Average number of days' sales uncollected (91* × c)	73

*Use actual number of days in the quarter.

This calculation could be expressed in months by assuming three months in the quarter. Then 3 x (c) equals 2.4 months as the average number of months' sales uncollected.

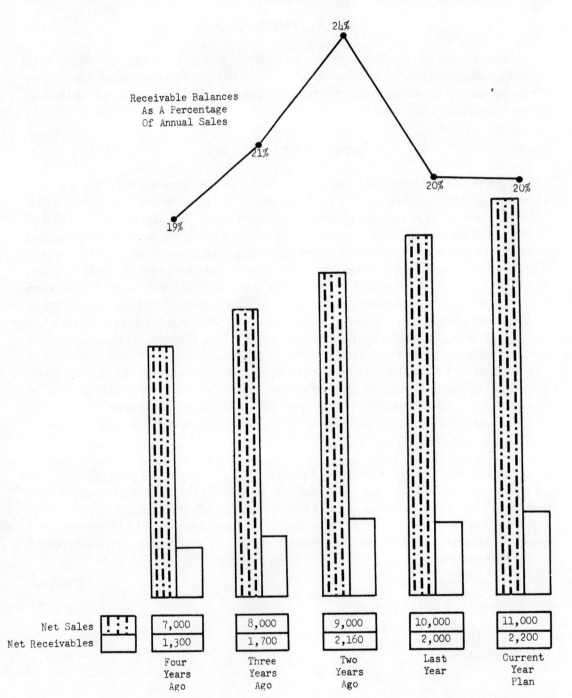

Receivable Balances
As A Percentage
Of Annual Sales

Net Sales		7,000	8,000	9,000	10,000	11,000
Net Receivables		1,300	1,700	2,160	2,000	2,200
		Four Years Ago	Three Years Ago	Two Years Ago	Last Year	Current Year Plan

Exhibit 2

Total Company or Division

Although accounts receivable are practically impossible to reduce beyond a certain point, they should be closely watched. Many companies offer a cash discount to their customers to encourage prompt payment of billings. Customary is a 2% discount if payment is made within 10 days from date of invoice. However, it is not very practical for a large and active account to make out a check for every invoice, as there could be twenty or thirty invoices rendered to the same customer in one month. In these cases, it is sometimes agreed that the customer be permitted to accumulate all the invoices received for one calendar month and pay the total with one check by the 10th of the following month and receive the 2% discount. A particularly large invoice received on the last day or so of a month would be paid under this arrangement in about 10 days or so. However, if this same particularly large invoice would be issued on the first day or so of a month, the customer would have as much as 39 days to pay it and still legitimately receive his cash discount. The timing, therefore, of shipments and invoices could cause a considerable swing in the amount of current assets tied up in receivables at any given time, particularly at the month's end. Breathes there a financial officer who has never agonized over whether or not to allow such discounts to the company's own customers. Here are some of the arguments in favor of allowing discount terms of say, 2/10/eom:

1. Customers who can afford to pay sooner do not, unless discount terms are made available to them.

2. Customers who cannot afford to pay sooner will do so, diverting funds from other vendors not offering discounts.

3. A 2% discount for payment within 10 days gives the vendor the use of 98% of the money for an extra 20 days.

4. While this has a cost of 37% per annum ($2 for 20 days = $36 for a 360-day year, or 37% on $98), the company probably earns close to this on its invested capital.

5. A faster turnover on trade accounts receivable gives the balance sheet a better look and is the mark of a well managed company. Banks and investors have more confidence.

6. Less credit need be used to carry receivables, allowing the company to borrow for more important needs, such as capital expenditures or research and development.

7. Vendor's sales are probably increased when discounts are allowed, as customers tend to purchase in larger amounts to achieve greater savings. This, at least, is valid in the first fiscal period in which the discount is initiated.

8. In the case of customers who are able to take discounts but do not, there is no certainty that payment will be made on the net due date, 30 days after shipment. There is no incentive to make payment on the net due date and no penalty for failure to do so. Consequently, if a more attractive alternative appears, funds may be diverted.

9. On an after tax basis, the 2% discount is really a 1% discount for most companies, assuming a 50% tax rate, and the 37% effective rate is really half that.

There are two control procedures, however, that can be followed in order to keep a receivable situation from getting out of hand. Exhibit 3 is an example of a simple monthly report to management showing the accounts receivable status. It relates the receivable balance and collections to sales and furnishes a report of the number of past due accounts and the amount involved. A certain amount of past due accounts is to be expected, but constant vigilance by the credit department can keep this situation within reasonable limits.

JUNE 30, 19xx

	CURRENT MONTH	*PRIOR MONTH*
Accounts Receivable Balance	$3,000,000	$3,150,000
Total Collections	$2,850,000	$3,100,000
Total Net Sales	$2,600,000	$2,950,000
Current Receivables % to Current Sales		115.4%
Cash Collections % to Prior Months Sales		96.6%
Cash collections % to Prior Months Receivables		90.5%

PAST DUE STATUS	*NUMBER OF ACCOUNTS*	*TOTAL AMOUNT*	*% TO CURRENT RECEIVABLES*
1 to 30 days	82	$115,000	3.8%
30 to 60 days	29	42,000	1.4
60 to 90 days	14	8,000	.3
90 days or longer	5	11,000	.4
	130	$176,000	5.9%

Exhibit 3

Credit Department Monthly Report

Exhibit 4 is a graphic illustration of how sales, receivable balances, and collections relate to each other. In this particular example, there is a high degree of stability, as evidenced by a consistent and normal relationship. In some companies there might be seasonal factors which would reflect quite a different pattern. Different companies and different industries would have quite different ratios between receivable balances, collections, and sales. There is no universal ideal or standard for accounts receivable turnover. Each company must evaluate its own situation and watch the "trend" within its own operations, plus take into account the experience of other companies in the same industry when possible.

INVENTORY MANAGEMENT

The importance of inventory control in modern business operation can hardly be overstressed. It is far more than just another figure on a month-end or year-end balance sheet. Inventory position in management reaches into almost every aspect of a business.

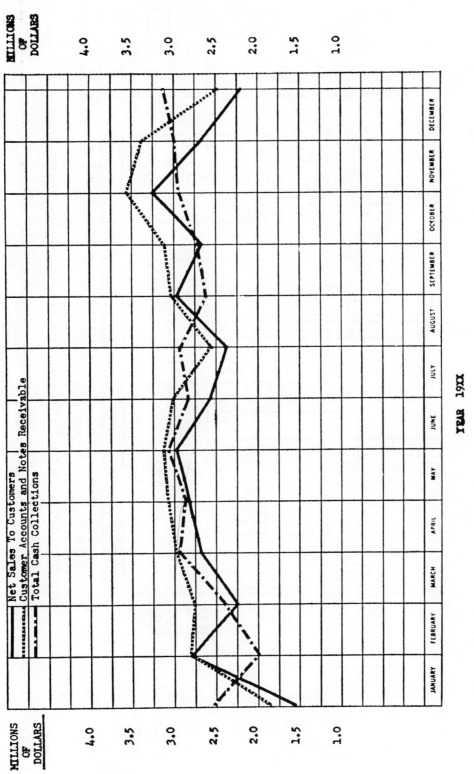

Exhibit 4

Accounts Receivable Status Report

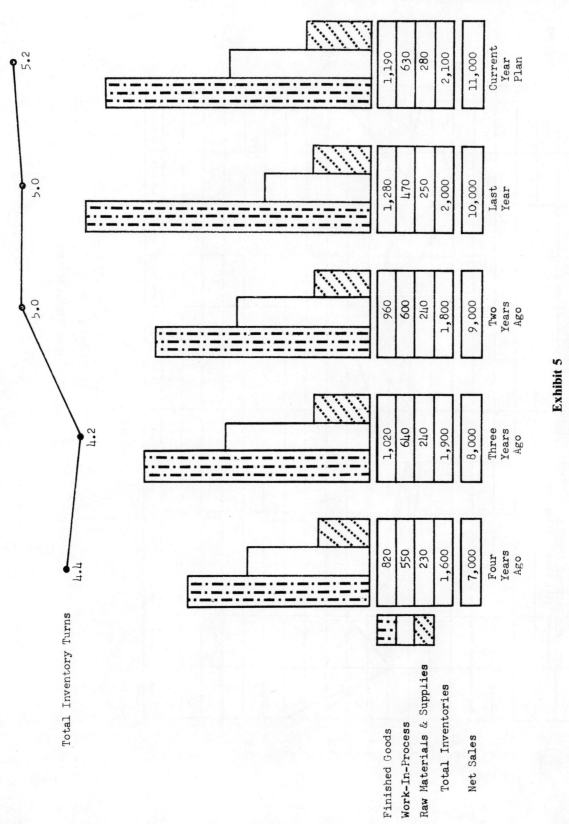

Exhibit 5

Total Company or Division

In most manufacturing companies, the main part of the day-to-day problem is correlating sales with production. Excessive inventories or obsolete and slow-moving products can greatly increase the risk factor, because inventories often represent a substantial percentage of the total current assets. In preparing management control information on inventories, not only should the actual inventory balance figures be presented, but they should also be related to sales or activity and be expressed as an inventory turnover rate. Exhibit 5 shows the trend of inventory quantities between time periods by category. The trend line at the top relates the total inventory balances to sales volume expressed in inventory turns between selected time periods. It is a common practice, in some companies, based on both economics and employee relations, to build inventories during low sales volume periods before resorting to idling machines and shutting down departments and even factories. As a result, inventories sometimes fluctuate inversely with the general business activity. This is particularly common in industries where sales volume is traditionally seasonal.

INVENTORY QUANTITY LEVELS

Inventory control, or good inventory management, does not necessarily mean less inventory. The most economical size of an inventory, nevertheless, poses a continual question. The sales manager might feel we should never keep a customer waiting, and the production manager would prefer production runs long enough to realize the lowest production costs. The comptroller, on the other hand, might contend that abnormally large inventories strain the cash resources that otherwise could be put to better use in increasing profits. The economic manufacturing quantity is that which results in the lowest unit cost of production after considering two sets of cost factors—carrying charges and job change costs. The carrying charges increase as the manufactured lot increases; whereas the job change costs decrease as the quantity increases. The crossover of these two cost factors represents the economic manufacturing quantity.

The application of the operation's research techniques to inventory control helps management to carefully consider the advantages of high stocks and the penalties of carrying them. Also, many companies are utilizing the advantages of computers to gain better stock control. Many software companies offer "canned" inventory programs to produce Economic Order Quantity (EOQ) levels for purchasing and Materials Requirement Planning (MRP) reports to control inventories.

Inventory control is contingent upon numerous factors, all of which should be placed in appropriate perspective. For example, the sizes of inventories are sometimes tied closer to the number of items in the sales line than to total dollar sales volume.

Although from an accounting standpoint inventories are considered as current assets, they actually represent frozen money for a certain time period. Some items are much more fluid than others, and it is very advantageous to know which is which. To some extent, this can be done by aging the inventories by item, as in aging accounts receivable by customer. For example, suppose an item is inventoried at an open balance of $4,500. The inventory card shows that the item was manufactured and entered into inventory three years ago at a total dollar value of $6,000. An analysis of the sales of this item for the past five years reveals that sales have levelled off to a historical and also predictable average of $500 annually. This means that three years ago a twelve year supply of this item was produced, and there is still apparently nine years supply on hand.

The size of a company's investment in plant inventories of raw materials, work in process, and finished goods, may vary considerably from month to month. It should not be assumed that an increase in inventory indicates a lack of efficiency, when in fact it might be a desirable situation at that particular time. Therefore, it is recommended that the inventory situation be prepared in the form of "inventory turns," in addition to the total figures.

INVENTORY TURNOVER

Whether or not inventories are high is, of course, a relative thing. The size of investment in inventories, in relation to sales volume, is of prime significance. Some companies may prefer to use inventory value of goods sold, or standard cost value of goods produced, instead of sales. We have used sales here for convenience of illustration, not to express a preference or recommendation. In addition to showing inventory balances each month, we are also showing their "turnover," or number of times per year they are consumed per annual business volume. For example, if the twelve month total sales divided by the average finished goods inventory balance at the end of that period equals four "turns," it means roughly that we are carrying an investment of three months stock of finished goods. If this could be reduced to two months supply without jeopardizing customer service, it would increase the turnover from four to six and thus improve the overall return on total gross assets employed.

Exhibit 6 is a graphic illustration of this inventory turnover measurement by month. The turnover is illustrated by both a solid line and scatter dots. The solid line represents a twelve month moving average, and is employed in order to smooth out the peaks and valleys of seasonal or unusual month-to-month variances. This solid line is the trend indicator. The scatter dots depict the performance of each individual month without reflecting any influence from preceding months. The placement of these dots, however, is an indicator of the direction the solid (trend) line will probably be following. If the direction is an adverse one, suitable remedial action should be taken before any situation gets serious.

Exhibit 7 is a tabular report from which Exhibit 6 is prepared. In addition to number of "turns," the last column on this report also converts the size of the inventory into "number of months supply." This is a simple arithmetical calculation of dividing the number of turns into twelve months. It is included here only because some managers prefer to think of stocks in terms of supply periods, rather than as turnover.

It is believed that inventory balances as of the last day of any particular month are not really as factual or indicative as average inventories over longer periods. Inventory balances should not only be related to sales activity, but also to other inventory balance time periods. The basic nature and inventory demands of a particular business or industry should be considered, particularly when seasonal factors exist.

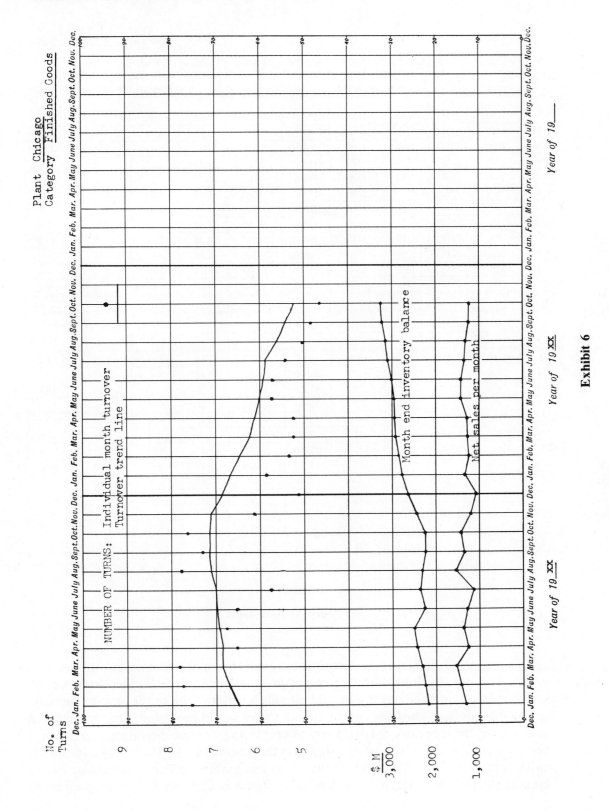

Exhibit 6

Plant   <u>Chicago</u>
Category   <u>Finished Goods</u>

19XX	Inventory Balance	Monthly Average	Moving 12 mo. Average	Net Sales Per Month	Moving 12 mo. Tot. Sales	Monthly Sales Annualized	Monthly Inventory Turnover	"Trend" Inventory Turnover	"Trend" No. of Mos. Supply	19XX
JAN	2190	2135	2092	1350	13620	16200	7.59	6.51	1.84	JAN
FEB	2253	2221	2092	1440	14070	17280	7.78	6.73	1.78	FEB
MAR	2300	2276	2098	1560	14420	18720	8.22	6.87	1.75	MAR
APR	2410	2355	2119	1280	14560	15360	6.52	6.87	1.75	APR
MAY	2500	2455	2153	1390	14870	16680	6.79	6.91	1.74	MAY
JUN	2280	2390	2167	1300	15100	15600	6.53	6.97	1.72	JUN
JUL	2400	2340	2189	1130	15310	13560	5.79	6.99	1.72	JUL
AUG	2310	2355	2207	1530	15660	18360	7.80	7.10	1.69	AUG
SEP	2230	2270	2228	1380	15880	16560	7.30	7.13	1.68	SEP
OCT	2240	2235	2254	1420	16070	17040	7.62	7.13	1.68	OCT
NOV	2450	2345	2304	1200	16150	14400	6.14	7.01	1.71	NOV
DEC	2610	2530	2348	1080	16060	12960	5.12	6.84	1.75	DEC
TOTAL				16060						TOTAL

19XX										19XX
JAN	2780	2695	2397	1320	16030	15840	5.88	6.69	1.79	JAN
FEB	2860	2820	2447	1250	15840	15000	5.32	6.47	1.85	FEB
MAR	2910	2885	2498	1270	15550	15240	5.28	6.22	1.93	MAR
APR	2950	2930	2543	1290	15560	15480	5.28	6.12	1.96	APR
MAY	2980	2965	2583	1410	15580	16920	5.71	6.03	1.99	MAY
JUN	3000	2990	2643	1420	15700	17040	5.70	5.94	2.02	JUN
JUL	3100	3050	2702	1380	15950	16560	5.43	5.90	2.03	JUL
AUG	3150	3125	2772	1310	15730	15720	5.03	5.67	2.12	AUG
SEP	3210	3180	2853	1280	15630	15360	4.83	5.48	2.19	SEP
OCT	3250	3230	2937	1250	15460	15000	4.64	5.26	2.28	OCT
NOV										NOV
DEC										DEC
TOTAL										TOTAL

Exhibit 7

Inventory Analysis Data

In Exhibit 7, the first column reports the actual last day inventory balance for each month. The second column merely averages the month end figures for the current month and the preceding month, as this should provide a closer figure to the amount on hand during the month in which the current month's sales would be related. The third column smooths out the inventory balance trend by employing a twelve month moving average. For example, the total of the balance figures in the first column for the first twelve months on the exhibit is 28,173. This figure (which means nothing in itself) divided by twelve months equals 2,348, which is the December figure in Column 3. This total figure of

28,173, minus the last January balance of 2,190, plus the new January balance of 2,780, equals 28,763, which divided by 12 equals the January figure in Column 3 of 2,397. Column 5 is the moving twelve month total of the monthly sales figure in Column 4. For example, the total annual sales for the first twelve month period on the Exhibit is $16,060. Deduct last January ($1,350) and add the current January ($1,320), and the moving twelve month total sales as of the current Janaury is $16,030. Column 6 is merely each sales figure per month multiplied by twelve. This is calculated because the turnover of an asset is usually related to an annual volume amount. In cyclical or volatile companies, quarterly turnovers should be calculated instead of annual. Column 7 is the result of Column 6 divided by Column 2. Column 8 is the result of Column 5 divided by Column 3.

CASH

A certain amount of cash must be carried in the bank and on the books to meet payrolls and pay bills. Excess cash should be working constantly, earning interest or dividends from notes and securities, or increasing profits by purchases of additional production facilities in a company's regular business. In order to accomplish this, money must be kept in productive circulation. When a customer pays a bill, his check could possibly remain in a state of suspension for several days or even weeks while it is being audited and processed by clerks, who might be verifying its correctness with the invoices and posting the receipt to various records. Considerable sums of money can, therefore, be lying idle and contributing nothing. It is easier to maintain minimum cash working balances and to maximize investment of excess cash into interest bearing securities if this float time of checks can be reduced. This may be accomplished through the following types of banking arrangements:

1. *Lock Box Banking*—Companies with customers outside their immediate metropolitan area should explore the flow of customers' checks from the mailing point through the Federal Reserve Banking System. Most banks perform lock box services or will refer you to a bank which does. Setting up a lock box usually involves giving the bank an entire month's receipts, either checks or data processing runs, showing amounts and dates received by territory. If your system does not provide for territory coding, envelopes may be saved for an entire month, date stamped with receipt and check amount. The bank will process these through their lock box computer program and will output a report showing the optimum locations for lock box accounts. This report allows for mailing time and the lag in clearance through the Federal Reserve System. Customers are then instructed, at the time they are invoiced for merchandise, to remit to a special lock box account number at a particular post office address. The bank is authorized to pick up checks at the lock box post office and deposit them in a special box bank account. Funds are then cleared from this special lock box bank account in the company's regular general account on a routine basis. A complete set of lock box instructions will not only provide the mechanics of the operation, but also the internal accounts receivable control which is needed.

Lock Box Banking, in addition to clearing funds more quickly, offers the following advantages:

a. Checks are picked up at the post office on Saturdays, which companies do not normally do.

b. The possibility of employee fraud is eliminated. Only bank employees handle checks and the bank is responsible for defalcations. The company can save the cost of employee dishonesty bonds or similar insurance.

c. The company saves the cost of establishing internal control procedures between accounts receivable and accounting departments since there is no actual handling of cash or checks.

d. Checks are deposited on a timely basis. The company is not concerned with key employee illness or other factors which could delay timely deposits.

Lock Box Banking advantages may usually be obtained without cost to the company. The cost of the bank's services will usually be met by the balances in the lock box account. This enables the company to still obtain greater balances utilization, on an overall basis, plus the foregoing advantages.

2. *Zero Balance Accounts*—These are usually ancillary accounts, in addition to the company's principal or general account, used for petty cash, freight payments on a weekly basis, travel expense accounts, municipal tax payments, payrolls, and other frequently used special accounts. They are, therefore, working bank accounts which are not used to carry balances but are kept at zero. A letter of instructions is given to the bank, authorizing them to make transfers before the close of banking business, each day, in an amount sufficient to cover the checks returned for payment to the zero balance account. A limit is usually placed on the amount which may be transferred, say $5,000, and any larger transfers must be approved by a signatory. Transfers are made from the general account, where balances are normally maintained, and advice of such transfer is forwarded to the treasurer's department on a daily basis. Thus, maximum utilization of cash is the result, as small balances need not be carried in these operating accounts in anticipation of checks being returned.

3. *Imprest and Color-coded Accounts*—Imprest accounts are similar to zero balance accounts in that the amount of the deposit exactly equals the checks written. The difference, however, is that imprest account deposits are made at the time checks are written, or a few days after, when they are expected to be returned for payments. They do not provide quite as much cash utilization as zero balance bank accounts, but in those cases where the bank is not equipped or prepared to make pre-authorized zero balance transfers, the imprest method gives the nearest result.

Imprest bank accounts may frequently be used with color-coded checks. Bank reconciliations are completely unnecessary with imprest or zero balance accounts, since the daily deposit exactly equals the daily disbursements. When used in conjunction with color-coded checks, the amount outstanding from any given month may be easily calculated. Normally, six different color codes will suffice for an account without too much activity, changing color each month. A large national payroll account, serving many branch office locations, could use nine colors to allow for lost checks and late stragglers beyond the six-month period. Each month, the cancelled checks are totaled by color and subtracted from the total of checks originally written. The difference is the amount outstanding to be carried forward to next month. Color-coded checks may then be arranged in numerical order and filed. After two months of no activity in a particular color, the outstanding checks may be canceled, stop payments issued, and the bank balance adjusted. The individual outstanding check should then be investigated to determine why it hasn't been returned. In the case of payroll checks, this may indicate some flaw in the system for handling checks sent to terminated employees at remote offices. The color-coded check, therefore, serves to eliminate the traditional bank reconciliation, substituting instead adding machine tapes, and also as an internal control system review.

   4. *Petty Cash Accounts*—These accounts are best handled on an imprest or zero balance basis. Maximum cash utilization is obtained by well documented procedures on when to use petty cash or to pay through the company's general account. When petty cash is used as a checking account, rather than as a true cash box, bills tend to be paid more promptly than they would through the general account. In the case of a company with a great many field offices and remote locations, there can be hundreds of petty cash checking acounts, all paying vendors bills more quickly than necessary. Here are a few simple rules for controlling petty cash payments, which may be adapted to suit any particular company:

   a.   Invoices in amounts over $50 may not be paid through petty cash fund checks (to avoid too prompt payment of larger invoices).

   b.   Invoices in amounts under $50 must be paid through petty cash fund checks (to avoid the unnecessary expense of purchase requisitions, purchase orders, receiving reports, and vouching for payment).

   c.   Collect freight bills may not be paid through petty cash funds. Vendor shipments should be made freight prepaid and billed back on vendor invoice. Inter-branch shipments should be freight prepaid by the shipping branch. All this avoids duplicate freight payments and the need for checking every freight bill to determine whether it is a proper charge or whether it has been paid by another branch or the headquarters office.

   d.   Expense reports which require higher approvals (above that of the office administering the petty cash fund) may not be paid through petty cash. This keeps proper controls on excess Travel & Entertainment expense spending.

   e.   A petty cash voucher must be made out for each disbursement, and this must be supported by a vendor's receipt. Hence, two documents are needed, one from the approver and one from the vendor.

f.   Petty cash reconciliations must be submitted with each reimbursement request, and these should be home office audited to verify conformity to procedures.

g.   Petty cash reimbursements must be made at least once a month (to avoid a requirement to establish a larger fund than necessary. Like inventory, a faster turnover requires less investment).

5. *Accounts Payable Imprest Accounts*—The company's principal account for bill payments is the Accounts Payable bank account. The volume and activity is such that it may not be operated as a zero balance account. However, operating it on an imprest basis, making daily deposits in the same amount as daily disbursements, will provide maximum cash flow. Deposits into the imprest account can be written and timed, based on the section of the country to which the disbursement was sent.

Investing Short-Term Cash

Proper cash management will occasionally produce excess cash. This may arise due to the timing of long-term debt offerings or equity issues, or simply because of the cyclical nature of the business. Excess short-term funds may be invested in a variety of ways to produce income or reduce costs for the company:

1.   Short-term bank debt may be temporarily reduced to save on interest costs.

2.   Heavier purchases of inventories may be made if there is an expectation of inventory cost increases. This should be examined in the light of the cost of carrying additional inventories. These excess inventories should be planned to liquidate themselves in 90 days.

3.   Marketable securities may be purchased, consonant with the degree of risk you are prepared to assume. This may include tax-free municipal bonds and other Moody's-rated industrial bonds. Commercial paper is also issued by rated businesses at somewhat higher rates of return, with little risk.

4.   Short-term interest-bearing Certificates of Deposit are available from banks for 30-, 60- and 90-day periods.

5.   If the company purchases from overseas markets, excess dollars may be used to purchase currency in forward markets, at today's prices, thereby hedging against currency fluctuations.

6.   Link-financing transactions may be negotiated with other companies. You establish an interest-bearing Certificate of Deposit with a bank specified by the other company. The bank makes prime rate loans to the other company, using your deposit in times of tight money conditions. You receive points or a fee from the other company which, combined with your interest on the CD, gives you a higher rate of return than you could normally obtain. When negotiated with a customer, the device cements a selling relationship. When done with a vendor, it assures a supply of the merchandise you buy and provides additional surety of the receipt of your points or fee through your right to offset against payments due to the vendor.

7. Excess bank balances may be carried with your working banks, at no interest income to you, to compensate them for those times when you may have to operate with less than the required balances.

8. The company may purchase its own securities and resell them at a later date, subject to meeting SEC requirements. The shares may also be issued to employees under incentive or stock option programs. Such a purchase reduces the number of outstanding shares and thus increases earnings per share.

9. Repurchase Agreements (Repo's) may be purchased from banks for as little as one day, at close to 30 day Certificate of Deposit rates.

Other Short-Term Borrowing Techniques

In addition to usual bank financing and the maximum utilization of cash within the company, there are a number of other techniques that may be explored to raise short-run monies. When used in this context, short-run is intended to mean for periods of one year or less. Some of the following methods may also be translated into long-term arrangements with proper contract provisions:

1. *Equipment Lease Financing*—may be done with a variety of equipment lessors to finance furniture and fixtures, materials handling and manufacturing equipment, with monthly payments from 1 to 5 years. Financing rates are quoted as "add-on" rates and range from 6% to 10% add-on, which translates to almost double that for simple interest. The yield to the lessor is highest on a shorter-term lease. The obligation is not reflected on the balance sheet and may usually be in addition to existing bank credit lines.

2. *Commercial Financing*—may usually be done for periods of at least one year, and thereafter may be terminated with little notice. This involves borrowing on trade accounts receivable, usually 80% advances on those receivables which are not more than 90 days past due, at a cost which is 150%-200% of bank prime interest rates. Such a rate can work out to 1% on net sales. Added features of financing can be revolving inventory loans to provide greater borrowing capability.

3. *Factoring*—is a variant on commercial financing, with the major difference being that the receivables are actually sold to the factor, collected by the factor, and rates are somewhat lower than charged by commercial finance companies. Since the receivables are sold with recourse, factoring works best when the receivables are of high quality.

4. *Commercial Paper*—may be issued by the company to obtain funds to supplement bank borrowings. This is generally confined to companies in the $100 million sales level, issuing paper in the aggregate of $10 million in lots of $100,000. The paper may be issued for any number of convenient months and the rates paid depend on the credit of the issuer and the length of time for which issued, but the rates are traditionally in the area of prime.

5. *Letters of Credit*—are guarantees of payment by a bank on submission of proof of shipment or other performance. They avoid the necessity of the company paying cash in advance of shipment and tying up funds that could be used to better advantage in the business. Banks charge a fee and a rate for bankers' acceptances arising after shipment which, in combination, is always approximately the same as prime.

6. *Link Financing*—as previously described may be used on the other end of the transaction to borrow money based on the credit of a customer or supplier. The cost is always in excess of prime, due to the points or fee paid to the supplier of the Certificate of Deposit.

7. *Inventory Reductions*—may be planned for limited periods of time to free funds for short periods of time. A comparison must be made of the risk associated with short inventories and the cost of other short-term fund raising alternatives.

8. *Bank Balances*—may be worked down, provided that banks understand that the shortfall will be made up with excess balances being carried at a later date.

9. *Treasury Stock*—previously acquired, may be resold, subject to SEC regulations, or issued under incentive or stock option programs.

There are other short-run management expedients which may be employed to increase cash availability. These involve the proper deployment of the resources of the company in any given department. Accounts receivable turnover may be increased by mounting a special-effort collection campaign with past due customers owing in excess of specific amounts. A national service department may embark on an overtime program to repair and make salable the company's product, thereby increasing inventory turnover and freeing up cash. The customer service department may "blitz" the issuance of credit memos to customers for returned merchandise and billing adjustments, thereby making it easier for the collection people to enforce prompt payments of trade accounts receivables. Proper cash flow, in other words, is directly affected by the total management approach which is concerned with all facets of the operation of the company.

FIXED ASSET BALANCES

Fixed assets usually consist of land, buildings, and equipment. Increases in fixed assets or capital expenditures really do not show up on the profit and loss statement because only the current year's depreciation is charged against costs. Careful analysis of this item on the balance sheet, therefore, is a must, because it can represent large reductions in operating capital. Care must be taken that additions to fixed assets do not outrun sales potential. Periodically there should be analyses and reports made on facility utilization. Such reports would reveal any cases where idle fixed assets result in overstatement of a company's worth on its balance sheet and penalize the profit and loss statement from a depreciation standpoint. Financial Analysis for Fixed Asset Acquisitions is discussed in the next chapter.

RETURN ON GROSS ASSETS

The most common basis for measuring profits is the ratio of profits to sales. For many years, management people have used this basis as a gauge of performance and will continue to do so in the future. But, more and more, management is looking at the relationship of the profits to the investment required to produce them, or the return on the investment. Ordinarily, when we speak of investment, we think of the relationship of profits to the net worth or invested capital of a business, and this is always important to the stockholders of a company. There is a more effective investment base, however, which can be used to measure performance, and that is the left-hand side of the balance sheet, which represents the assets employed in the business.

Return on investment (or assets) is affected by both profits on sales and turnover of assets as related to sales. Each of these, in turn, is affected by a variety of factors. Control of profits thus involves more than just control of costs. Failure to relate sales volume and profit performance to the assets required to produce them can result in excessive plant investment and abnormally high inventories. To facilitate a quick understanding of the factors involved and their function, we have included a "control of profits" chart. This chart (Exhibit 8) is merely an illustration of the major elements making up the profit and loss statement and balance sheet.

In reading from the top left side of Exhibit 8, we see that inventory value of ware sold (or normal cost of the products), plus manufacturing variance and shipping and delivery costs, makes up the cost of sales. Sales minus cost of sales equals gross profit, and gross profit minus operating expenses (made up of selling, administrative, and engineering costs) minus federal tax equals after tax earnings. The use of after tax versus pre-tax earnings is merely a matter of management preference. Earnings divided by sales equals earnings as a per cent of sales, which is the conventional profit measurement basis noted previously.

Dropping down to the lower section, we can see the major items usually found on the asset side of the balance sheet. Both product and manufacturing inventories, accounts receivable, cash and our fixed asset investment are our total investment. We subtract current liabilities, on the arbitrary assumption that suppliers are not investors. The use of gross fixed assets (net land, buildings, and equipment with accumulated depreciation added back) is again arbitrary for use in this example. Sales divided by total investment equals the annual turnover of the assets. The net earnings as a percent of sales multiplied by the turnover equals the percent return on the gross assets.

Exactly the same answer is obtained by merely dividing the annual profit by the total assets. However, this would not tell us whether our good or bad profit return on assets accrues from high or low sales volume, high or low manufacturing costs, or a combination of both.

You can readily determine from this chart that profits are the result of the mix of cost, sales volume, price, and margin. Turnover is only a relationship of sales and the assets employed. Every one of the elements in this chart is controllable to a certain extent. Good management and good results require that the maximum of control be applied to all the factors depicted on this chart. (See Exhibit 9). The Return on Investment chart, Exhibit 58, in Chapter 12, illustrates the relationship of the factors involved and gives a specific calculation of the ROI. In addition, the ROI for an entire business is calculated in Chapter 3.

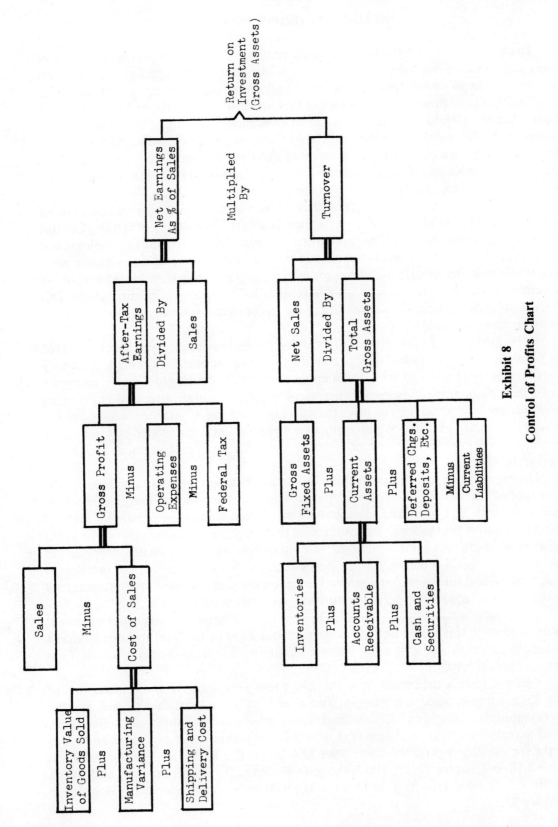

Exhibit 8

Control of Profits Chart

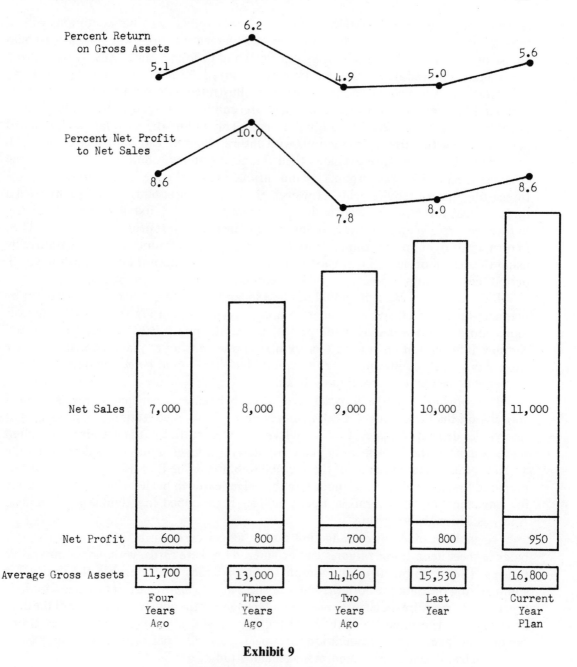

Exhibit 9

Total Company or Division

BALANCE SHEET BUDGETING

The budgeting of sales and profits, both short-term and long-range, is certainly nothing new on the American business scene. Many businesses today have a planning and budgeting system of some sort which projects, in whole or part, a profit and loss statement into the future. More and more companies are finding that they can run a more efficient and profitable operation today if they have some idea what conditions will be next month, next year, and five years from now. Executives are using forecasts to help adjust production, sales, purchasing, and financing to long-term trends. A formalized P & L budget procedure has become an integral part of the accounting function in many companies. This is recognized in the format as illustrated in Exhibit 1, Chapter 1, in the Annual Plan column. Various techniques are employed in projecting technological developments, management judgment, etc. The value of correlating historical performance with current transactions with future planning can hardly be challenged.

Many companies have extended their financial statement budgeting to include the balance sheet. This was brought about primarily by the need for more accurate forecasting of cash requirements. However, the balance sheet budget is more than just a tool to calculate a more accurate cash requirement figure. The first dividend is the ability to forecast a return on gross assets or investment, instead of just profit ratio to sales. This, in turn, leads right into the opportunity to appraise proposals for capital expenditures by using the return on investment yardstick in addition to determining the cash payback period, costs savings estimate, or other methods described in Chapter 3.

Balance sheet budgeting should not be a separate and unique activity carried out by planners far removed from consideration of everyday operating matters. Planning is much more effective if it is made part of the company's normal administration and routine. Information on current factory operations and future plans affecting balance sheet items, such as inventories and capital facilities, should be communicated to the proper staff people on a continuing basis.

It is obvious that the forecast level of each balance sheet item depends, almost entirely, on the P&L Budget. Cash comes from receivables collections, and the level of receivables depends on sales. Inventory levels must be sufficient to support the required sales, as must be the investment in plant. Similarly, the level of purchases determines the amount of payables and most of the accrued liabilities. The P&L Budget must, thus, be prepared first and will serve as input into the ledger cards to be described. The technique for implementing the overall company budget is described in Chapter 12, Financial Analysis Through Budgeting.

To make balance sheet budgeting easy, a ledger card can be kept for each major balance sheet item. Budget figures can be entered on these cards, with past comparative figures. (See Exhibit 10) This simple card provides considerable flexibility for summarizing the data for both the balance sheet and cash forecast. It also has a built-in score card to measure the accuracy of the budget against the actual. The source of the data or method of determination of the budgeted figures will vary between companies. Some factors to take into consideration are past patterns, national economic trends, technological developments, and management's judgment.

The accounts receivable data in this example is taken as a percentage ratio of receivables to sales, based on the company's past experience. The percentage used is reviewed every quarter. The actual figures are taken from the company's formal financial statements. What the forecasters look for, of course, are changes between the beginning and ending balance for a given period. When unusual fluctuations turn up, an analysis is attached to the ledger card.

LEDGER ITEM:			ACCOUNTS RECEIVABLE	
Time Period	Balance As Of	Forecast	Actual	(Over) Under
Prior	12-31-19			
	12-31-19			
	12-31-19			
Years	12-31-19			
	12-31-19xx	1,800	2,000	(200)
Current	Jan.	2,000	2,100	(100)
	Feb.	2,100	2,200	(100)
	Mar.	2,200	2,000	200
Year	Apr.	2,300	2,300	—
	May	2,400	2,200	200
19xx	June	2,500	2,400	100
	July	2,400		
By	Aug.	2,200		
	Sept.	2,300		
Month	Oct.	2,100		
	Nov.	2,100		
	Dec.	2,200		
Future	12-31-19xx	2,400		
	12-31-19xx	2,500		
	12-31-19			
Years	12-31-19			
	12-31-19			

Explanation
Source of Data — Actual Month end balance from Accounts Receivable Dept. Verified later to formal balance sheet.
Source of Data — Budget Based on monthly sales budget used in annual plan. Ratio of receivables to sales based on prior year actual experience plus special current information from Credit Dept.
Comments Amount of variances to date this year have been contained to less than 10% or reasonable limits. See attached analysis sheets for explanation of unusual fluctuations.

Exhibit 10

It is suggested that the ledger card for fixed assets be supported by a list of the proposed capital expenditures, which in some cases might be revised and augmented every month.

Once these cards are organized in an orderly manner, it is very easy to prepare from them a balance sheet budget and/or a cash requirement forecast. A suggested format for the balance sheet budget is depicted in Exhibit 11. Here again, simplicity and flexibility are provided. This report can be prepared monthly, quarterly, or annually, and various combinations of comparisons and projections can be made. The categories should be tailored to the individual company concerned, but it is suggested that they be confined to major items and that the details be restricted to the supporting ledger cards.

The amount of cash that is forecast is a figure which can be arrived at by "backing into it." The same total liabilities and net worth figure are merely written in opposite the heading "Total Gross Assets." From this, then, is deducted all the other balance sheet asset items, and the remainder, therefore, has to be cash, securities, and investments. The minimum operating cash requirement can be put under the "Cash" heading, and the balance considered available for investment in income-producing securities. This figure might represent the amount of capital available for corporate growth opportunities without borrowing.

THE CAPITAL BUDGET

A manufacturing firm's total capital equipment is a high cost asset and is rather inflexible in the short run. It has major effects on present and future strategy, costs, revenues, product acceptance, and almost all other aspects of operations. A capital budget gives specific expression, in terms of plant and equipment, to the objectives of the organization. It can be used to require operating officials to think through their plans and coordinate them with those of other departments and divisions; in turn, it gives top management an opportunity to evaluate and sharpen the direction that the firm is taking through its capital appropriations. The capital budget is also usually the source of the fixed asset figure in the balance sheet budget.

The capital items in an approved budget, even though subject to later individual approval, must also be flexible enough to meet all the circumstances that arise during the course of a budget year. Competition, consumer demand, technology, or any of a host of factors may alter previous needs or give rise to new ones, and the decision process should allow for adaptation to them.

Managements which use budgets as part of their capital expenditure process should not permit over-all budget approval to serve as a green light for individual projects; the

PARTICULARS	NEXT MONTH		PROJECTED TO DECEMBER 31		
	Date: June		Revised	Original	
	Estimate	Actual	Estimate	Actual Fcst.	Actual
	Year Current	Year Prior	Year Current	Year Current	Year Prior
Cash — General & Interest Funds	1,800	1,750	2,100	2,000	2,000
Short-Term Securities	1,000	800	1,330	1,505	1,000
Net Accounts & Notes Receivable	2,500	2,250	2,250	2,200	2,000
Total Inventories	2,200	2,000	2,150	2,100	2,000
CURRENT ASSETS — TOTAL	7,500	6,800	7,830	7,805	7,000
Gross Fixed Assets Incl. Work In Progress	8,500	7,700	8,600	8,600	8,000
Misc. Deposits, Investments & Receivables	800	750	850	850	800
Deferred Charges	200	300	250	250	300
TOTAL GROSS ASSETS	17,000	15,550	17,530	17,505	16,100
Accounts Payable	450	270	350	325	300
Withholdings From Employees	150	80	110	100	90
Accrued Misc. Expenses & Misc. Taxes	120	70	120	100	80
Accrued Salaries & Wages	200	210	220	200	200
Accrued Federal Income Tax	850	790	900	900	800
TOTAL CURRENT LIABILITIES	1,770	1,420	1,700	1,625	1,470
Accum. Depreciation — Fixed Assets	5,150	4,900	5,300	5,300	5,000
Contingencies Reserve	200	200	200	200	200
TOTAL RESERVES	5,350	5,100	5,500	5,500	5,200
Common Stock	4,000	4,000	4,000	4,000	4,000
Earned Surplus	5,880	5,030	6,330	6,380	5,430
NET WORTH	9,880	9,030	10,330	10,380	9,430
TOTAL LIABILITIES & EQUITY	17,000	15,500	17,530	17,505	16,100
TOTAL ASSETS — YEAR-TO-DATE AVERAGE	16,275	15,825	16,815	16,803	15,530
Asset Turnover To Sales	.74	.70	.68	.65	.64
Net Sales—Year-To-Date	6,000	5,500	11,500	11,000	10,000
Profit After Tax—Year-To-Date	450	400	900	950	800
Return on Gross Assets	5.5	5.1	5.3	5.6	5.1
% Profit After Tax To Sales	7.5	7.3	7.8	8.6	8.0
Net Sales For The Month	980	920	Date	By	
Profit After Tax For The Month	80	67	6-1	xx	C.J.B.
% Profit To Sales	8.2	7.3			

Exhibit 11

Balance Sheet Budget

projects should be resubmitted during the budget year, typically with supplementary or new information in justification. (See Exhibit 20, Chapter 3)

The total future goals, objectives, and plans can furnish a framework for capital expenditure budget when evolved in the context of total objectives and plans for the future.

Five years is not an unusual planning period, and plans typically integrate sales and cost projections, operating needs, and capital equipment needs. Equipment plans are, understandably, very general (and in no sense firm) beyond a one-year budget.

Although long-range capital expenditure plans are desirable, fairly specific short-range plans are a requisite for most firms. Capital budgets usually cover estimated needs for annual periods of at least one year in detail, and longer periods in terms of major facilities only.

Top management's long-range objectives can be translated into general statements concerning such areas as:

1. Physical growth objectives of the firm, spelled out in terms of specific years.

2. Expectations as to future size of the market, or markets, and as to the market share that the firm should try to secure.

3. General economic or specific industry trends that are predicted for long-term.

Short-term forecasts are more affected by conditions such as competitive activity or economic and technological conditions. They generally deal with sales forecasts, wage and material cost projections, and current general or regional economic conditions.

Almost all major ideas for capital expenditures come from top management itself, while ideas for smaller projects, such as process or product improvement, new machinery, and the like, stem from managerial personnel at subordinate organizational levels.

Regardless of how the capital budget is categorized and summarized for formal presentation, the work sheet, as illustrated by Exhibit 12, should be helpful. Each form will cover one capital item; or, in the case of small equipment (office furniture, etc.), one form can cover a group or category and represent one entire year's needs.

These cards provide considerable flexibility, as they can be prepared by different levels of management, plants, and locations throughout a company. After they are all collected, they can be sorted into any group or category that is desired. They are especially valuable when more than one type of summary of capital budget is desired. For example, they can be sorted by plant and a summary prepared. They can then be resorted by type of expenditure and a different summary prepared.

CAPITAL AND DEBT ANALYSIS

These balance sheet items are dealt with in a complete chapter titled "The Cost of Capital and Debt."

Plant ___#12—Chicago___   Date Prepared ___October 15, 19xx___

Category (check applicable box)

Expansion ☐
Major replacement or improvement ☐
Normal replacement or improvement ☒

Description of Capital Facility

Automatic Carton Sealer and Conveyor

Estimated date capital facility will be put into use ___March 1, 19xx___

Estimated life of facility ___15___ years. Estimated economic life ___10___ years.

Reason for Request

It is planned to unitize the present "B" and "C" product line. The above equipment will eliminate most of the present manual sealing and trucking labor.

Estimated Dates Capital Appropriations Will Be "Expended"

	1st Year				2nd Year		
Jan.	$20,000	July	$____	1st Qtr. $____	3rd Year $____
Feb.	10,000	Aug.	____	2nd Qtr. ____	4th Year ____
Mar.	____	Sept.	____	3rd Qtr. ____	5th Year ____
April	____	Oct.	____	4th Qtr. ____	
May	____	Nov.	____		
June	____	Dec.	____	Total Amount $30,000	

Division Manager _____   Plant Manager _____

Exhibit 12

Plan for Future Capital Expenditures

BALANCE SHEET MANAGEMENT

1. The balance sheet should actually rate equal billing with the profit and loss statement in both the financial and operating evaluation and control of a business.

2. The balance sheet can be made more understandable and useful if it is augmented by the type of supporting analyses in both tabular and graphic form as suggested and illustrated in this chapter.

3. Many balance sheet items, such as inventories, receivables, cash, and fixed assets, must be carefully controlled, or the consequences will spill over into the profit and loss statement.

4. Adequate inventory levels and acceptable receivable balances can be best determined by relating them to business volume.

5. Cash management requires utilization of a variety of banking techniques and procedures to increase cash float.

6. One of the most effective and meaningful bases by which to measure corporate performance is the ratio of net profit to total assets, because it reflects both profit on sales and asset turnover in one percentage figure. This is a form of return on investment.

7. Balance sheet budgeting is essential for predicting future cash position and requirements based on planned or expected capital expenditures, inventory levels, accounts receivable situations, and all other asset and liability transactions.

8. A sound capital expenditure budget for future facility requirements is often the framework within which a company's total future goals, objectives, and plans, in almost every aspect of their business, must be contained.

CHAPTER 3

Capital Investment Decisions

Return on investment is a presage of higher P/E ratios. As ROI goes, so goes the company.

Capital expenditure decisions are part of the foundation for the future development of a company. They are a major factor in establishing a competitive position. A high batting average in successful investment decisions, therefore, will have a profound effect upon a company's future earnings and growth. Corporate management should be receptive to techniques which will improve this highly important planning function. These techniques apply equally to make-or-buy, lease-or-buy, purchasing of large quantities, and straight investments.

When the budgets are prepared for the coming year, every department in a company of any size usually anticipates its expenditures on the high side. Every supervisor who is in charge of a particular operation sincerely believes that his capital appropriation budget is the most important one in the company. This is normal and desirable; he is the wrong man for the job if he does not feel that way. Yet, the sum total of all the spending plans may exceed the available cash resources. Arbitrary decisions by the top management in the allocation of the capital spending can not only result in great risk of error, but can damage the morale of the supervisors whose plans are curtailed without reasonable explanation. By employing a formalized and disciplined procedure for the evaluation and rating of all major capital spending proposals, this problem can certainly be minimized.

61

DISCOUNTED CASH FLOW METHOD

For illustrative purposes, we have selected a "discounted cash flow" method for measuring the profitability of proposed investments in capital facilities. This is familiarly called Return on Investment (ROI). This technique should not necessarily replace any present traditional and familiar methods of evaluating capital appropriations. Rather, it can supplement other procedures, and its main purpose is to introduce the time value of money concept in the consideration of investment opportunities.

The Discounted Cash Flow Method (sometimes called the Present Value Method) relates the cash inflows for each year and for all years, adjusted for the time value of the money, to the original cash investment. The cash inflows are "discounted" back to the present. The method is difficult to compute manually, but any standard book of accounting tables contains Present Value tables which make the computation easy. Some electronic portable calculators, Hewlett Packard or Texas Instruments for two, contain pre-programmed systems to permit Present Value calculations at your desk. Time-sharing terminals of companies specializing in financial applications commonly offer Present Value programs.

In addition to Present Value tables, this ROI method uses standard mortgage tables to compute the return on cash inflows relating to fixed or wasting assets. When the investment in a project includes plant or equipment which depreciates and which eventually must be replaced, each cash inflow includes a return of principal, as well as interest on the investment. The standard mortgage table shows cash flows as a percentage of original investment when principal is amortized or recovered as a part of cash flow. This technique is exhibited in the ROI example, later in the chapter.

OTHER METHODS

1. *Payback*—measures the net cash inflows against the initial cost to determine how many years of inflows are needed to obtain payback of the initial investment. This is usually expressed as a "two year payback." The method has disadvantages in that it ignores cash inflows after the payback period, and it also ignores the decrease in the value of money due to inflation and the timing of its receipt—that is, its present value. Nevertheless, the method is simple and can be an acceptable yardstick. Its very simplicity encourages its use. A consistent analytical method is better than none at all.

    This method can be best of all, however, when there is uncertainty which makes it difficult to project the future cash inflows—for example, competitive pressures which may obsolete the project, or an uncertain market for the product to be produced. In these cases, a short payback period is preferrable as risks are quickly eliminated and the capital can be reinvested. This method, then, concentrates on near-term earnings as having more value than those of later years. Since this technique is so commonly used, it is discussed in more detail on page 72.

2. *Rate of Return*—is a measure of the percentage of the annual net cash inflows of the original investment. A $10,000 inflow per year, requiring an original cash

outlay of $50,000 results in a 20% ROI. This method does not work well if cash flows are unequal over the useful life, nor does it give consideration to the expected duration of the cash inflows. A 30% ROI for 10 years is obviously more desirable than a 30% ROI for a shorter period, but the simple percentage figure does not express that advantage.

3. *Internal Rate of Return*—is similar to the discounted Cash Flow or Present Value Method described earlier. However, it finds a discount rate for the expected cash inflows, using a trial and error method, which exactly equals the original investment. This rate of return is then compared to the company's standard or required rate of return to determine whether the project is acceptable.

4. *Price/Earnings Ratio (P/E Ratio)*—is the typical yardstick used by securities analysts in evaluating public companies. The *Wall Street Journal* prints this figure daily in its stock market tables. The current price of the company's stock is divided by its earnings, and it is expressed as a "10 times P/E ratio" (a stock priced at $20 per share divided by earnings of $2 per share). The denominator is usually the most recent four quarters, on a rolling basis, after-taxes and pre-extraordinary items. This method is an excellent representation of the value of the company to the stockholder. It is somewhat similar to an ROI approach for the total business, rather than for an individual project. This method ignores the basic investment and does not give effect to the elimination of the financing aspects of the investment, as does ROI, but the relationship of price to earnings is somewhat similar to investment (price) to return (earnings). It is a good rule-of-thumb technique to evaluate a total business.

5. *Return on Equity or Invested Capital*—is a method subject to a variety of interpretations. Return may mean profit, rather than cash flow, usually does not add back non-cash items such as depreciation or deferred taxes. The denominator in the equation, when equity, ignores the effect of leverage obtained through debt financing; when invested capital, it usually means long-term debt plus equity, but fixed assets are considered net of depreciation, and the age of the assets can materially affect the results obtained.

6. *Cash Flow per Share*—relates the inflows not to the investment, as with ROI, but rather to equity or net assets at depreciated values, and it ignores debt or leverage. Capital intensive companies with high fixed asset values will have much greater cash flows, due to depreciation, than companies with large investments in current assets like receivables and inventories. But this extra cash flow from depreciation must be allocated to eventual replacement of the facilities if the company is to remain in business. It must, too, be reduced for the effect of inflation at the time of replacement. Only a proper ROI calculation takes care of these various factors.

7. *Book Value per Share*—completely ignores the return or cash flow element of the ROI formula. It relates, instead, the per share amount of the stockholder's investment to the market value of each share. Some investors look for bargain

stocks whose market value is below book value, on the theory that the company could be liquidated for its book value. This is a specious view. Companies are not bought to be liquidated and, as a rule, in liquidation they usually bring less than book value. The return on the investment cannot be overlooked.

ACCEPTANCE BY MANAGEMENT

Informal discussions with accountants and other staff people from a cross-section of various companies and industries revealed that many of them have been studying various discounted cash flow techniques for quite some time but have withheld actual installation. There were mostly two reasons for their hesitation. First, some accounting people were having difficulty in deciding exactly which method to adopt. Their difficulty stemmed from the many variations that have been proposed and discussed in accounting and business journals. Some thought that the differences between some of these techniques were not great enough to affect the results, as long as the method selected is kept consistent. It is more important to initiate some sound program and get it into action than to attempt to first find the perfect method, anticipating every possible contingency before its actual installation.

The second reason for hesitation is that the manner in which this has evidently been presented by some companies to administrative, production, engineering, and sales management people was too technical in its financial aspects for non-accounting personnel. Perhaps wider acceptance of this concept or philosophy of capital investment could be obtained if the presentation to these groups stressed the role they are to play, rather than emphasizing the finer points of financial discount tables or the mechanics of the actual rate calculation.

The calculation of return on investment obviously falls into the area of the accountant's responsibility. It is, of course, desirable that the management group understand the basic concept of this method, even though they may not be fully acquainted with every detail of its procedures. The successful application of this method, however, depends greatly upon the information the accountants must obtain from responsible engineering, production, and marketing people in the preliminary analysis of a proposed capital expenditure—the amount of cash income and investments (including working capital), their relative timing, the risk factor of the investment, and the estimated economic life of the project.

Since the determination of some of these characteristics must necessarily be based upon estimates, some businessmen feel the scientific approach is not scientific at all, and they might as well continue to rely on management hunch. The point missed here is that if a company's officers reach a decision without first accumulating the necessary data required in the more scientific approach, it is certainly implied that some kind of estimate must have been made. Is is not better to identify and itemize these estimates so they can be examined objectively?

NON-TECHNICAL APPROACH

The following explanation is suggested as the basis for an approach which might have more appeal to engineering, production, and sales management than a highly technical presentation that might be an interesting intellectual exercise for accounting and financial people, but which might result in a deferment of overall management acceptance of the discounted cash flow method.

Cash income, or cash flow, is broadly defined as profit after tax plus depreciation on fixed assets. Depreciation on fixed assets is a non-cash expense because it is an amount of money charged to costs (and hence reducing profit) year after year, although the actual cash outlays were made at some prior time. To reflect the actual cash flow for the period, depreciation and other non-cash expense items must be added to the profit after tax cash income. Actually, cash flow involves increases and decreases in all balance sheet items, both assets and liabilities. For example, an increase in inventory levels is a direct reduction of cash, while decreased inventories (sales), or increased accounts payable (purchases), result in an increase in cash.

In presenting this program to management it might be well to provide some background for the financial facts of life which led to this cash flow consideration. The growth and expansion of any business requires cash. It can be obtained through earnings, borrowing, stock issues, etc. To do the most effective job, considerable vigilance is required in the area of cash position and cash flow. The balance sheet, and particularly the balance sheet budget, must be analyzed just as carefully as the income and expense statements. Capital investment decisions should be made with full consideration of both current and forecast cash position.

For example, in any given period, the expenditures for capital facilities could exceed the profit after tax plus depreciation or cash flow. This could happen if a purchase of $200,000 worth of equipment was made in a given year, and costs for that year included only the first year's depreciation—$25,000. The profit and loss statement might still look very favorable, but the bank balance could drop below the minimum operating requirement.

The importance of cash flow to the conduct of a business dictates careful consideration of this factor in the selection and approval of capital appropriations. Therefore, all proposed capital expenditures of an appreciable amount which are "profit-adding," through volume expension or cost reduction, must be viewed in light of their effect on company cash, in addition to the more familiar considerations of degree of risk and potential profit. Capital projects which are "profit-maintaining" must be considered by their effect on cash position, but are not evaluated through cash flow. This type of capital expenditure is controlled through the budget program.

RETURN ON INVESTMENT (THE PROFITABILITY RATE)

The "ranking" or selection of a group of profit-adding capital expenditure proposals can be aided by the consideration of their profitability rates as calculated via the discounted cash flow method. The long-term effect on the cash position is expressed by this profitability rate. This procedure recognizes the time value of money. The actual receipts and expenditures connected with a proposed project will be predicted for each year over the economic life of the project. Then they will be discounted back to a present worth equal to the present value of the money to be invested. The rate required to obtain this recovery of the investment is the *profitability rate* or Return on Investment (ROI).

A dollar received today is worth more than a dollar to be received at a future date because of the earnings that dollar can generate in the interim. Conversely, a sum of money to be paid today is a greater burden than the sum to be paid at a future date because of the earnings which must be foregone in the meantime. The following example illustrates this point.

Year	*(1)* *How $1.00 left at 15%* *compound interest will* *grow.*	*(2)* *What $1.00 due in the* *future is worth today at* *a discount rate of 15%.*
0	1.0000	1.0000
1	1.1500	.8696
2	1.3225	.7561
3	1.5209	.6575
4	1.7490	.5718
5	2.0114	.4972
6	2.3131	.4323
7	2.6600	.3759
8	3.0590	.3269
9	3.5179	.2842
10	4.0456	.2472

The above rates are taken from published Financial Compound Interest and Annuity Tables. This is merely an illustration of the considerable appreciation or depreciation of the cash income inherent in an investment with a 15% profitability rate. In Illustration (1) we see that $1.00 grows to $4.00 in ten years @ 15% compound interest. Illustration (2) is just the reverse—here we see that $1.00 loaned out today is only worth 25¢ if we couldn't recover it until the end of ten years. Conversely, 25¢ invested today @ 15% would grow to $1.00 in ten years.

To apply this investment fact of life to a capital expenditure, let us assume that we invest $500 in a facility which obtains an annual cash flow of $100 per year for ten years. The financial statement method of accounting tells us that our cash pay back period is five years, and the total return for the ten years is $1,000. In order to find the return on investment, however, we must discount the annual returns on a compound interest basis. In this case, the return on investment is 15%, with the annual rates taken from the tables illustrated in the previous paragraph.

$100.	@	.8696	equals	$87
100.	@	.7561	"	75.
100.	@	.6575	"	66.
100.	@	.5718	"	57.
100.	@	.4972	"	50.
100.	@	.4323	"	43.
100.	@	.3759	"	37.
100.	@	.3269	"	32.
100.	@	.2842	"	28.
100.	@	.2472	"	25.
$1000.				$500.

The total of the discounted receipts is exactly the amount of the original investment. In actual practice, of course, we have no way of knowing what the rate is, so we calculate two or more discount rates by trial and error until we "bracket" the amount of investment, and then obtain the exact amount by common arithmetical interpolation.

Once an acceptable rate is determined (see page 75), any calculated percentage under this minimum acceptable rate is rejected and the project is abandoned.

In the example we gave, a $100 cash inflow per year based on an original investment of $500 would represent a return of 20%. This would be the true ROI were all of the assets current or non-wasting. This would be the case if the only required assets were inventory or accounts receivable. The return on this type of asset is the same return obtained from depositing money in a bank at compound interest. The cash inflows would represent pure interest, or return on your deposit. There is no repayment of principal involved. In the example we gave, however, we have assumed that an investment was made in a fixed or wasting asset, say a machine which is going to be depreciated over a period of 10 years. In such a case, where a fixed asset is assumed, each cash inflow represents not only interest, but the repayment of principal. Our example recognizes this as is evident by the calculated return of 15%. This point is more evident when looking at a simple amortization table of the type used for mortgages. This is illustrated in Exhibit 13, showing the true ROI (the column headings) for various cash flows as a percentage of original investments. If the cash flow continues for 10 years at 20% of the original investment ($100 returned on a $500 investment), the true ROI is seen to be 15%. Our present value tables, obviously, recognize this wasting aspect of the fixed asset. We will need to use this amortization mortgage table in evaluating the ROI of an entire business, as we will see shortly.

SUGGESTED WORK SHEETS

In the first part of this chapter we have gone to some length to explain the concept and purpose of this particular procedure. Assuming that there is understanding and acceptance of this technique, the next step is to prepare work sheets which will lead to its implementation. Exhibits 14 to 17 should be comprehensive enough to be used as guides for whatever forms you will need to fit your own company's particular requirements. It should go without saying that this formalized procedure should be limited to proposed capital expenditures of substantial size and importance only.

Return on Investment: Cash Flows and Lives Associated with Various Returns When Principal is Amortized as a Part of Cash Flow*

Year	0%	1%	2%	3%	4%	5%	6%	7%	8%	9%	10%	12%	15%	18%	21%	24%	25%	30%	40%
5	.200	.206	.212	.218	.225	.231	.237	.244	.250	.257	.264	.277	.298	.320	.342	.364	.372	.411	.491
6	.167	.173	.179	.185	.191	.197	.203	.210	.216	.223	.230	.243	.264	.286	.308	.331	.339	.378	.461
7	.143	.149	.155	.161	.167	.173	.179	.186	.192	.199	.205	.219	.240	.262	.285	.308	.316	.357	.442
8	.125	.131	.137	.142	.149	.155	.161	.167	.174	.181	.187	.201	.223	.245	.268	.292	.300	.342	.429
9	.111	.117	.123	.128	.134	.141	.147	.153	.160	.167	.174	.188	.210	.232	.256	.280	.289	.331	.420
10	.100	.106	.111	.117	.123	.130	.136	.142	.149	.156	.163	.177	.199	.223	.247	.272	.280	.323	.414
11	.091	.096	.102	.108	.114	.120	.127	.133	.140	.147	.154	.168	.191	.215	.239	.265	.273	.318	.410
12	.083	.089	.095	.100	.107	.113	.119	.126	.133	.140	.147	.161	.184	.209	.234	.260	.268	.313	.407
13	.077	.082	.088	.094	.100	.106	.113	.120	.127	.134	.141	.156	.179	.204	.229	.256	.265	.310	.405
14	.071	.077	.083	.089	.095	.101	.108	.114	.121	.128	.136	.151	.175	.200	.226	.252	.262	.308	.404
15	.067	.072	.078	.084	.090	.096	.103	.110	.117	.124	.131	.147	.171	.196	.223	.250	.259	.306	.403
16	.063	.068	.074	.080	.086	.092	.099	.106	.113	.120	.128	.143	.168	.194	.220	.248	.257	.305	.402
17	.059	.064	.070	.076	.082	.089	.095	.102	.110	.117	.125	.140	.165	.191	.219	.246	.256	.304	.401
18	.056	.061	.067	.073	.079	.086	.092	.099	.107	.114	.122	.138	.163	.190	.217	.245	.255	.303	.401
19	.053	.058	.064	.070	.076	.083	.090	.097	.104	.112	.120	.136	.161	.188	.216	.244	.254	.302	.401
20	.505	.055	.061	.067	.074	.080	.087	.094	.102	.110	.117	.134	.160	.187	.215	.243	.253	.302	.400
22	.045	.051	.057	.063	.069	.076	.083	.090	.098	.106	.114	.131	.157	.185	.213	.242	.252	.301	.400
24	.042	.047	.053	.059	.066	.072	.080	.087	.095	.103	.111	.128	.155	.183	.212	.241	.251	.301	.400
26	.038	.044	.050	.056	.063	.070	.077	.085	.093	.101	.109	.127	.154	.182	.211	.241	.251	.300	.400
28	.036	.041	.047	.053	.060	.067	.075	.082	.090	.099	.107	.125	.153	.182	.211	.241	.250	.300	.400
30	.033	.039	0.45	.051	.058	.065	.073	.081	.089	.097	.106	.124	.152	.181	.211	.240	.250	.300	.400
32	.031	.037	.043	.049	.056	.063	.071	.079	.087	.096	.105	.123	.152	.181	.210	.240	.250	.300	.400
34	.029	.035	.041	.047	.054	.062	.070	.078	.086	.095	.104	.123	.151	.181	.210	.240	.250	.300	.400
36	.028	.033	.039	.046	.053	.060	.068	.077	.085	.094	.103	.122	.151	.180	.210	.240	.250	.300	.400
38	.026	.032	.038	.044	.052	.059	.067	.076	.085	.094	.103	.122	.151	.180	.210	.240	.250	.300	.400
40	.025	.030	.037	.043	.051	.058	.066	.075	.084	.093	.102	.121	.151	.180	.210	.240	.250	.300	.400
45	.022	.028	.034	.041	.048	.056	.065	.073	.083	.092	.101	.121	.150	.180	.210	.240	.250	.300	.400
50	.020	.026	.032	.039	.047	.055	.063	.072	.082	.091	.101	.120	.150	.180	.210	.240	.250	.300	.400

Exhibit 13

NOTES: Figures in body of table are annual cash flows as a percent of investment.
"Year" indicates expected life of investment.
Column headings show percent ROI under these conditions,
interest being compounded annually.

*Reprinted by permission of the publisher from *R.O.I.: Practical Theories and Innovative Applications,* by Robert A. Peters, © 1974 by AMACOM, a division of American Management Association.

No.   E-123

PROJECT   HQ Machine to Manufacture Product "D"
ESTIMATED INVESTMENT REQUIREMENTS

Year	19__	19__	19__	19__	
Annual Period	-2nd	-1st	0	1st	TOTAL
CAPITAL					
Land					
Buildings					
Manufacturing Equipment			10,000		
Other (explain)					
Total Capital			10,000		
EXPENSE					
Pre-Operating			1,000		
Other (explain)					
Total Expenses			1,000		
TOTAL IMMEDIATE INVESTMENT			11,000		11,000

Estimated Starting Date of Operation _____

ADDITIONS TO WORKING FUNDS

Year	19__	19__	19__	19__	
Annual Period	1st Year				TOTAL
Accounts Receivable	1,000				1,000
Raw Material Inventory					
Stores Inventory					
Finished Goods Inventory	2,000				2,000
W.I.P. Inventory					
Other (explain)					
Total Required	3,000				3,000

TIME SCHEDULE OF EXPENDITURES AND INVESTMENT

Annual Period At End	CAPITAL		Expensed Items	Working Funds	Total Investment
	Land	Facilities			
-2nd					
-1st					
0		10,000	1,000		11,000
1st				3,000	3,000
2nd					
3rd					
4th					
5th					
TOTAL		10,000	1,000	3,000	14,000

Exhibit 14

ESTIMATED INVESTMENT REQUIREMENTS

Exhibit 14 is in three sections. The top section provides headings for the category of capital and expense costs and the year they will be incurred. The calendar years are also classified as minus 2, minus 1, zero, and first. The first year represents the period in which the facility is expected to commence actual production and gainful use. This first year usually has some left-over investment costs occurring in it, although the bulk of the investment will probably occur in the zero and minus years. This timing is as important in discounting or compounding the investment cash outflow as it is in discounting the income, or payback cash inflow. The middle section is also self-explanatory and is used to estimate how much additional cash will be tied up as working capital. This is limited to a maximum of four years, commencing with the year the actual production is scheduled to

Year	Annual Period At End	*DEPRECIATION OF ASSETS BY S.Y.D. METHOD*				Total Depreciation
		Buildings @____Yrs. AMT.____	Mgf. Equip. @ 10 Yrs. ____ AMT. 10,000	@____Yrs. AMT.____	@____Yrs. AMT.____	
	-2nd					
	-1st					
	0					
	1st		1,818			1,818
	2nd		1,636			1,636
	3rd		1,455			1,455
	4th		1,273			1,273
	5th		1,091			1,091
	6th		909			909
	7th		727			727
	8th		545			545
	9th		364			364
	10th		182			182
	11th					
	12th					
	13th					
	14th					
	15th					
Remaining Book Value						
TOTAL			10,000			10,000

Exhibit 15

Depreciation Schedule

begin. If more years are needed, the form should be revised slightly. A good rule-of-thumb is to provide for 90 days of inventory and receivables. The bottom section is merely a summary of the first two sections to facilitate using the totals in the next steps.

CALCULATION OF DEPRECIATION

Exhibit 15 is merely a work sheet to calculate the total depreciation of the proposed facility over the life of the project. Depreciation on fixed assets is cash income because it is an amount of money charged to costs (and hence reducing profit) year after year, although the actual cash outlays were made at some prior time. The money was only taken out of the bank once, but the charges to costs are amortized over the years of the estimated useful life of the asset. The method of calculating depreciation for this form should be the same one as used by your company for their formal property records accounting.

(Depreciation charges can be categorized by general type of asset if desired. An average life can be used for each classification when there are various types of assets and different book lives. The charge for depreciation is on an annual basis with the first full year's charge shown opposite 1st annual period. These annual depreciation charges are calculated on the basis of the book life of the asset. When the book life is greater than the economic life, the book value remaining at the end of the economic life is charged in the final year of the project.)

SUM OF THE YEARS DIGITS

This is one of several approved methods of calculating accelerated depreciation. The major advantage of this method, or the double declining balance method, is the reduction of risk in capital venture money by writing off the cost faster than the straight line method, which is merely the number of years of estimated life of a facility divided into the total cost. Under the Sum of The Years Digits method, the deduction for each year is computed as follows:

Determine the estimated useful life and total the digits contained in this figure. Suppose the estimated life is five years and the cost $1,000. The sum of the digits for a five year life is 15 (5 + 4 + 3 + 2 + 1). Then divide each digit by the total of 15 as follows: 5 ÷ 15 is .3333, 4 ÷ 15 is .2667, 3 ÷ 15 is .2000, etc. Then multiply the cost of $1,000 by each of these factors. The depreciation allowed for the first year would be $1,000 times .3333, or $333. The second year $267, third year $200, fourth year $133 and the fifth year $67. These five depreciation rates total exactly $1,000 or 100% recovery of the original investment. Any company using the sum of the years digits method obviously would not make all of the above calculations as demonstrated above every time they figured depreciation.

Tables of decimal factors would no doubt be prepared to expedite and simplify this procedure. The following table covers three time periods: 5 year, 10 year, 15 year life, merely as an example. In actual practice, the tables of factors would probably cover a much wider range of time periods.

SUM-OF-DIGITS DECIMAL FACTORS

YEAR	FACTOR	YEAR	FACTOR	YEAR	FACTOR
1	.3333	1	.1818	1	.1250
2	.2667	2	.1636	2	.1167
3	.2000	3	.1455	3	.1083
4	.1333	4	.1273	4	.1000
5	.0667	5	.1091	5	.0917
	————	6	.0909	6	.0833
	1.0000	7	.0727	7	.0750
		8	.0545	8	.0667
		9	.0364	9	.0583
		10	.0182	10	.0500
			————	11	.0417
			1.0000	12	.0333
				13	.0250
				14	.0167
				15	.0083
					————
					1.0000

Sum-of-the-digits tables, similar to the above, may readily be constructed using the arithmetic formula:

$$\frac{n \times (n + 1)}{2}$$

where n is the number of periods. To illustrate, with a 5 year life, this equals:

$$\frac{5 \times (5 + 1)}{2} = 15$$

There are, thus, 15 periods and the factors for each period are determined in reverse order. In the first year, 5/15 or .3333 is the result; in the second year, it is 4/15 or .2667; in the third year, 3/15 or .2000, and so on.

CASH INCOME AND PAYBACK PERIOD

Exhibit 16 is a work sheet with the top section designed to record the estimated cash flow, or cash income, by year. The total cash flowback consists of profit after tax, expensed costs after tax, (for any items of expense incurred prior to the start of operations) total depreciation (a non-cash expense), and, finally, at the end of the last year of the project, the return of the $3000 of working funds. The bottom section is designed for the calculation of the cash recovery period.

In figuring the "payback period," we do not discount the cash flow. This procedure is used merely to measure the "risk" factor of the investment by calculating how soon we will actually recover the original capital outlay. There is, of course, no point in making investments which just give us our money back. Therefore, the payback calculation must be used in conjunction with the profitability rate figure in order to consider both profitability and risk in making an investment decision.

Annual Period	Expense Items	Op. Profit After Tax	Deprec.	Total
-2nd	After			
-1st	Tax			
0	500			500
1st		1,182	1,818	3,000
2nd		1,364	1,636	3,000
3rd		1,545	1,455	3,000
4th		1,727	1,273	3,000
5th		1,909	1,091	3,000
6th		2,091	909	3,000
7th		2,273	727	3,000
8th		2,455	545	3,000
9th		2,636	364	3,000
10th	3,000*	2,818	182	6,000
11th				
12th				
13th				
14th				
15th				
Total	3,500	20,000	10,000	33,500

*Return of working funds

CALCULATION OF CASH RECOVERY PERIOD
(Number of years from start of operation for cash flow back to repay expenditure)
Based on immediate investment of $14,000 (includes working funds)

CASH FLOW BACK			
Annual		Cumulative	
Year	Amount	Years	Amount
19--	500	0	500
19--	3,000	1	3,500
19--	3,000	2	6,500
19--	3,000	3	9,500
19--	3,000	4	12,500
19--	3,000	5	15,500
		6	
		7	
		8	
		9	
		10	

$14,000 minus $12,500, 4 year total, equals $1,500.

$1,500 divided by $3,000, the amount of the 5th year, equals .5 years.

4 years plus .5 years equals 4.5 years payback period.

Exhibit 16

Cash Flow Back

The mechanics of this calculation are explained in the following example: Assume an investment of $1,000 with cash income of $400 per year for five years.

Year	Per Year	Cumulative
1	400	400
2	400	800
3	400	1200
4	400	
5	400	

At the end of three years we have more than recovered our investment. At the end of 2 years we have recovered less than the investment. Investment $1,000, less $800 two year total, equals $200; three year total $1,200, less two year total $800, equals $400.

$200 ÷ $400 equals .5   .5 plus two years equals 2.5
The payback period is 2½ years.

CALCULATION OF RETURN ON INVESTMENT FOR INDIVIDUAL PROJECTS

Exhibit 17 is a suggested form to facilitate the mechanics of determining the "profitability rate." The function and purpose of this figure is explained earlier in the chapter.

Exhibit 18 is merely a table of cash discount factors for every percentage from 1% to 10%, every other percentage from 10% to 30% (including the 15% column from page 66), and every 5th percentage from 30% to 50%. It is included in this book for the convenience of the reader who may wish to apply a wider range of rating percentages than provided for in Exhibit 17.

If the discounted cash flow approach to evaluating and rating capital expenditure is adopted, it should be formal and accurate. However, it should not be permitted to become stereotyped and perfunctory. It should not be used to justify expenditures for which the need is obvious. Management should be informed enough to discriminate between when not to use it and when to use it. Any technique, no matter how good, loses value when used foolishly or unnecessarily. The discounted cash flow measurement of a capital investment proposal is a valuable aid to management decision making, but is not a substitute for it.

No.   E-123

PROJECT   Purchase and install one HQ Machine to manufacture product "D" items to augment our product "C" line.

CASH OUTFLOW

Annual Period At End	Trial 1 0% Int. Rate Total Investment	Trial 2 5% Int. Rate		Trial 3 10% Int. Rate		Trial 4 15% Int. Rate		Trial 5 25% Int. Rate		Trial 6 40% Int. Rate	
		Fac-tor	Present Value	Fac-tor	Present Value	Fac-tor	Present Value	Fac-tor	Present Value	Fac-tor	Present Value
-2nd		1.103		1.210		1.323		1.563		1.960	
-1st		1.050		1.100		1.150		1.250		1.400	
0	11,000	1.000		1.000		1.000	11,000	1.000	11,000	1.000	
1st	3,000	.952		.909		.870	2,610	.800	2,400	.714	
2nd		.907		.826		.756		.640		.510	
3rd		.864		.751		.658		.512		.364	
4th		.823		.683		.572		.410		.260	
5th		.784		.621		.497		.328		.186	
	14,000						13,610		13,400		

CASH INFLOW

Annual Period At End	Total Cash Flow Back	Fac-tor	Present Value	Fac-tor	Present Value	Fac-tor	Present Value	Fac-tor	Present Value	Fac-tor	Present Value
-2nd		1.103		1.210		1.323		1.563		1.960	
-1st		1.050		1.100		1.150		1.250		1.400	
0	500	1.000		1.000		1.000	500	1.000	500	1.000	
1st	3,000	.952		.909		.870	2,610	.800	2,400	.714	
2nd	3,000	.907		.826		.756	2,268	.640	1,920	.510	
3rd	3,000	.864		.751		.658	1,974	.512	1,536	.364	
4th	3,000	.823		.683		.572	1,716	.410	1,230	.260	
5th	3,000	.784		.621		.497	1,491	.328	984	.186	
6th	3,000	.746		.564		.432	1,296	.262	786	.133	
7th	3,000	.711		.513		.376	1,128	.210	630	.095	
8th	3,000	.677		.467		.327	981	.168	504	.068	
9th	3,000	.645		.424		.284	852	.134	402	.048	
10th	6,000*	.614		.386		.247	1,482	.107	642	.035	
11th		.585		.350		.215		.086		.025	
12th		.557		.319		.187		.069		.018	
13th		.530		.290		.163		.055		.013	
14th		.505		.263		.141		.044		.009	
15th		.481		.239		.123		.035		.006	
16th		.458		.218		.107		.028		.005	
17th		.436		.198		.093		.023		.003	
18th		.416		.180		.081		.018		.002	
19th		.396		.164		.070		.014		.002	
20th		.377		.149		.061		.012		.001	
	33,500						16,298		11,534		

INTERPOLATION

@ 15% 16,298 minus 13,610 =   2,688
@ 25% 13,400 minus 11,534 =   1,866
                                4,554

4,554 × 10% (difference between 15% and 25%) = 455
2,688 ÷ 455 = 5.9% plus 15% equals 20.9% Return on Investment
*Includes return of working funds

Exhibit 17

Project Evaluation
Calculation of Return on Investment

YEARS HENCE	1%	2%	3%	4%	5%	6%	7%	8%	9%	10%	12%	14%	15%
−2	1.020	1.040	1.061	1.082	1.103	1.124	1.145	1.166	1.188	1.210	1.254	1.300	1.323
−1	1.010	1.020	1.030	1.040	1.050	1.060	1.070	1.080	1.090	1.100	1.120	1.140	1.150
0	1.000	1.000	1.000	1.000	1.000	1.000	1.000	1.000	1.000	1.000	1.000	1.000	1.000
1	.990	.980	.971	.962	.952	.943	.935	.926	.917	.909	.893	.877	.870
2	.980	.961	.943	.925	.907	.890	.873	.857	.842	.826	.797	.769	.756
3	.971	.942	.915	.889	.864	.840	.816	.794	.772	.751	.712	.675	.658
4	.961	.924	.888	.855	.823	.792	.763	.735	.708	.683	.636	.592	.572
5	.951	.906	.863	.822	.784	.747	.713	.681	.650	.621	.567	.519	.497
6	.942	.888	.837	.790	.746	.705	.666	.630	.596	.564	.507	.456	.432
7	.933	.871	.813	.760	.711	.665	.623	.583	.547	.513	.452	.400	.376
8	.923	.853	.789	.731	.677	.627	.582	.540	.502	.467	.404	.351	.327
9	.914	.837	.766	.703	.645	.592	.544	.500	.460	.424	.361	.308	.284
10	.905	.820	.744	.676	.614	.558	.508	.463	.422	.386	.322	.270	.247
11	.896	.804	.722	.650	.585	.527	.475	.429	.388	.350	.287	.237	.215
12	.887	.788	.701	.625	.557	.497	.444	.397	.356	.319	.257	.208	.187
13	.879	.773	.681	.601	.530	.469	.415	.368	.326	.290	.229	.182	.163
14	.870	.758	.661	.577	.505	.442	.388	.340	.299	.263	.205	.160	.141
15	.861	.743	.642	.555	.481	.417	.362	.315	.275	.239	.183	.140	.123
16	.853	.728	.623	.534	.458	.394	.339	.292	.252	.218	.163	.123	.107
17	.844	.714	.605	.513	.436	.371	.317	.270	.231	.198	.146	.108	.093
18	.836	.700	.587	.494	.416	.350	.296	.250	.212	.180	.130	.095	.081
19	.828	.686	.570	.475	.396	.331	.277	.232	.194	.164	.116	.083	.070
20	.820	.673	.554	.456	.377	.312	.258	.215	.178	.149	.104	.073	.061
21	.811	.660	.538	.439	.359	.294	.242	.199	.164	.135	.093	.064	.053
22	.803	.647	.522	.422	.342	.278	.226	.184	.150	.123	.083	.056	.046
23	.795	.634	.507	.406	.326	.262	.211	.170	.138	.112	.074	.049	.040
24	.788	.622	.492	.390	.310	.247	.197	.158	.126	.102	.066	.043	.035
25	.780	.610	.478	.375	.295	.233	.184	.146	.116	.092	.059	.038	.030

Exhibit 18

**Present Value Tables
Periodic Factors**

YEARS HENCE	16%	18%	20%	22%	24%	25%	26%	28%	30%	35%	40%	45%	50%
−2	1.346	1.392	1.440	1.489	1.538	1.563	1.588	1.638	1.690	1.823	1.960	2.103	2.250
−1	1.160	1.180	1.200	1.220	1.240	1.250	1.260	1.280	1.300	1.350	1.400	1.450	1.500
0	1.000	1.000	1.000	1.000	1.000	1.000	1.000	1.000	1.000	1.000	1.000	1.000	1.000
1	.862	.847	.833	.820	.806	.800	.794	.781	.769	.741	.714	.690	.667
2	.743	.718	.694	.672	.650	.640	.630	.610	.592	.549	.510	.476	.444
3	.641	.609	.579	.551	.524	.512	.500	.477	.455	.406	.364	.328	.296
4	.552	.516	.482	.451	.423	.410	.397	.373	.350	.301	.260	.226	.198
5	.476	.437	.402	.370	.341	.328	.315	.291	.269	.223	.186	.156	.132
6	.410	.370	.335	.303	.275	.262	.250	.227	.207	.165	.133	.108	.088
7	.354	.314	.279	.249	.222	.210	.198	.178	.159	.122	.095	.074	.059
8	.305	.266	.233	.204	.179	.168	.157	.139	.123	.091	.068	.051	.039
9	.263	.225	.194	.167	.144	.134	.125	.108	.094	.067	.048	.035	.026
10	.227	.191	.162	.137	.116	.107	.099	.085	.073	.050	.035	.024	.017
11	.195	.162	.135	.112	.094	.086	.079	.066	.056	.037	.025	.017	.012
12	.168	.137	.112	.092	.076	.069	.062	.052	.043	.027	.018	.012	.008
13	.145	.116	.093	.075	.061	.055	.050	.040	.033	.020	.013	.008	.005
14	.125	.099	.078	.062	.049	.044	.039	.032	.025	.015	.009	.006	.003
15	.108	.084	.065	.051	.040	.035	.031	.025	.020	.011	.006	.004	.002
16	.093	.071	.054	.042	.032	.028	.025	.019	.015	.008	.005	.003	.002
17	.080	.060	.045	.034	.026	.023	.020	.015	.012	.006	.003	.002	.001
18	.069	.051	.038	.028	.021	.018	.016	.012	.009	.005	002	.002	.001
19	.060	.043	.031	.023	.017	.014	.012	.009	.007	.003	.002	.001	
20	.051	.037	.026	.019	.014	.012	.010	.007	.005	.002	.001	.001	
21	.044	.031	.022	.015	.011	.009	.008	.006	.004	.002	.001		
22	.038	.026	.018	.013	.009	.007	.006	.004	.003	.001	.001		
23	.033	.022	.015	.010	.007	.006	.005	.003	.002	.001			
24	.028	.019	.013	.008	.006	.005	.004	.003	.002	.001			
25	.024	.016	.010	.007	.005	.004	.003	.002	.001	.001			

Exhibit 18 (cont.)

For those substantial capital-spending proposals which require the use of this procedure, a searching analysis should be made of every aspect. This includes informed estimates of the out-of-pocket investment amount, working capital tied up in inventories and receivables, economic life of the project, and the forecast additional income or savings.

These estimates require engineering, production, marketing, and financial analysis as well as a high degree of management judgment. The project's characteristics ultimately determine its profitability, and it is in assessing them that management judgment plays its most vital role. The more penetrating the analysis at this point, the better will be the final decision.

Much of the hitherto unavoidable guesswork has been taken out of the appraisal of a capital investment opportunity by the development of the discounted cash flow approach. This method correlates the combined thinking of all areas of management, and if it is presented in a thoughtful, orderly manner, it should result in more intelligent and profitable decisions.

DETERMINING AN ACCEPTABLE PROFITABILITY RATE (ROI)

A Federal Trade Commission publication, the *Quarterly Financial Report,* indicates that the Return on Investment of U.S. Manufacturers of Durable Goods has declined from 10.09% to 7.36% from 1965 to 1972. The declining trend is continuing in recent years, perhaps because manufacturers are being too attentive to Price/Earnings ratios or Profits to Sales ratios, ignoring ROI.

Return on Investment is a presage of higher P/E ratios or percentage of Profits to Sales ratios—not the other way around. As ROI goes, so goes the company. The sum of all the individual ROI's, for all the individual projects, will equal the overall corporate ROI. It should be obvious, therefore, that a 7 to 8% ROI is not acceptable. You can obtain that on a two year time-savings deposit. Better to close down the project or the business and put the cash in the bank.

The desired return invoices an evaluation of the amount of risk for each particular company, the alternatives available to it (there may be none, so higher risk cannot be avoided), and the timing considerations which are influenced by managerial judgments. These factors notwithstanding, the financial community provides us with a variety of signals: a) the rate for long-term, low risk government securities b) mortgage rates c) industrial and utility bond rates d) time-deposit savings bank rates e) speculative tax shelter and leveraged lease rates.

If a 7 to 8% return, then, is not acceptable, what is? As a rule-of-thumb, anything above 8 to 11% should be considered satisfactory; rates above 11% to 13% are very satisfactory; rates above 13% to 15% may be viewed as just below excellent, and returns above 15% are excellent. Increase these rates more during times of high inflation.

Remember to temper these parameters with judgments based on the factors enumerated in the third paragraph preceding. A 15% ROI may be unsatisfactory for an emerging company, with a small capital base and high earnings, which has returned 30% for the past several years. An industry study, using the ROI techniques for an entire business, described later, may be prepared from published annual reports, thereby providing a ranking basis.

CAPITAL EXPENDITURE REQUEST

When a project is to be started, the usual means of securing authority to proceed is to submit an appropriation request for management approval. This is usually a standard printed form and is confined to basic and summarized information. Exhibit 19 is an example of what might be included on such a form and is intended to provide the reader with a starting point in designing a form for his own company.

SUPPORTING DETAIL

The amount of supporting detail will probably be dictated by the size and importance of the project, plus the requirements and desires of the management. Where profitability analyses are made, perhaps copies of these work sheets could be attached to the request. Another supporting document might be a checklist or justification memo. A sample of what this might include is illustrated in Exhibit 20.

CALCULATION OF RETURN ON INVESTMENT FOR AN ENTIRE BUSINESS

The same Profitability Rate determination or Return on Investment utilized for measuring individual projects just described may be used to measure the total business. The method is not mathematically perfect in each detail, but it is substantially correct for all except the most extreme cases. Certain arbitrary assumptions must be made to evaluate the balance sheet, as we shall see following, but it is better to be arbitrary and somewhat imperfect than not to use the ROI device at all. Moreover, attempts to sophisticate and refine the measuring devices will become so laborious that there will be a tendency to use management judgment alone in making investment decisions. This would be a mistake. Both return on investment analysis and considered management evaluation must always be the dual ingredients of investment decision making. A short-cut and simplified ROI technique is therefore presented to evaluate a total business. It may be used for acquisitions, to evaluate separate divisions of a business, for investment purposes, or for industry comparisons.

Company or Division	Request No. _____
	Request Date _____
	Requested By _____
	Approved By _____
	Date _____

Date	Plant	Department	Total Estimated Cost $11,000

Description	Amount of Investment	
New manufacturing facility	Land	_____
	Buildings	_____
	Bldg. Facilities	_____
Purpose Produce new product	Mfg. Equipment	10,000
	Total Capital	10,000
Reason Demand of market for this new product	Total Expense	1,000
	Add'l Working Funds Required	3,000
	Total Investment	14,000
Present Situation Cannot produce this new product on existing facilities	Economic Justification Additional Sales Volume	
	Annual Units _____	
	Annual Value _____	
	Cost of Sales _____	
	Est. Net Profit	
Possible Alternatives Forego profit on new product and possibly also lose prestige and position in industry	Cost Reduction Estimate Annual Savings	
	Labor _____	
	Material _____	
	Repairs	
General Comments	Economic Life	
	Market _____ Years	
	Facilities _____ Years	
	Estimated Timing	
	Starting Date _____	
	Completion Date _____	
	Production Date _____	
(Additional Data or Detailed Schedules Should be Attached)	Begin Savings Date _____	

Discounted Cash Flow 20.9%   Net Profit on Sales_____%   Cash Payback 4.5 Years

Profit Adding ☒   Profit Maintaining ☐

☐ Cost Reduction   ☒ Additional Facility

☐ Expansion of Existing Operation or Product   ☐ Replacement

☒ Expansion into New Operation or Product

Exhibit 19

Capital Expenditure Request

Number, Location, and Date

1. Appropriation Number
2. Plant and Department
3. Date of Request

Request

1. Amount
    a. Requested for Expenditure Approval
    b. Working Funds Needed
2. Purpose

Discussion

1. Present Situation
2. Reasons for Proposed Project
3. Alternatives

Economic Justification—(for profit adding expenditure requests only)

1. Volume Expansion Proposals
    a. Sales Volume in Units
    b. Sales Revenue
    c. Total Cost of Sales
    d. Availability of Labor
2. Cost Reduction Proposals
    a. Labor Savings
    b. Materials Savings
    c. Repairs Savings
    d. Power, Fuel Savings
    e. Other Savings
3. Economic Life of Proposed Project
    a. Market Analysis
    b. Obsolescence
    c. Other Information

Execution

1. Date Project Spending Will Begin
2. Estimated Date of Production Start-up

Recommendation

1. Yardsticks—(for profit adding expenditure requests only)
    a. Profitability Rate
    b. Payback Period
    c. Percent Margin—Volume Expansion Proposals
2. Comments on Other Characteristics Than Financial or Economic, such as Industry Position, Customer Accommodation, etc.

Exhibit 20

Checklist for Investment Justification

The Investment—is determined from an evaluation of the balance sheet. Assume the following:

Balance Sheet
As at 12/31/xx

Current Assets	$100,000	Current Liabilities	$40,000
		7% Long-term Debt	70,000
Fixed Assets	150,000		
Depreciation Reserve		Equity (2,000 sh. common)	90,000
	50,000		
Net Fixed Assets	$100,000		
Total Assets	$200,000	Total Liabilities & Equity	$200,000

The Return—is determined from the Income Statement, as follows:

Income Statement
For the Year Ending 12/31/xx

Revenues		$400,000
Less:		
Cost of sales, selling, general and administrative expenses, excluding interest and depreciation	$340,000	
Interest on long-term debt	5,000	
Depreciation	15,000	360,000
Net income before taxes		40,000
Provision for taxes		20,000
Net income after taxes		$20,000

The Investment is $210,000, consisting of $60,000 of current assets minus liabilities and $150,000 of gross fixed assets before depreciation. We arbitrarily assume that current liabilities are not a part of capitalization, that suppliers do not normally consider themselves as investors, and that they result from the temporary use of vendors' capital. They are, thus, netted against the current assets to obtain a net current investment figure.

We also make the assumption that the asset life is 10 years ($150,000 in gross original fixed assets divided by $15,000 per year of depreciation expense). Depreciation is straight line for both book and tax purposes, and the investment reflected on this balance sheet is assumed to be typical. Management must review all calculations based on this premise and make subjective adjustments where needed. In addition, we are using assets at year end, rather than average assets. This, therefore, assumes no large infusion of new assets toward the end of the year. Obviously, the asset figure could be adjusted to obtain a more representative result, or one could even use beginning of the year assets. It is important to keep the calculations simple and convenient, so that the very use of the ROI procedure does not become burdensome and fall into disuse. To this end, the following simplified and arbitrary rules should be used to classify the balance sheet's assets into current or fixed (wasting) assets as a necessary prelude to calculation of the Return on Investment:

Current Assets—These may normally be always classified as current, based on the independent accountant's evaluation.

Long-term Receivables—These should be reclassified to current, as they are identical to current receivables except for the time lag.

Investments and Deposits—These should be considered current, as there is no wasting aspect to their value.

Property, Plant, and Equipment—Land is not wasting and should be reclassed as current. All else is considered fixed or wasting.

Word of Caution: If the assets are undervalued due to inflation or being natural assets such as timber or mineral deposits, the investment should be written up for this calculation to current, replacement, or fair market value. A capital investment company, say a steel mill, with heavy investment in wasting assets may have old equipment, almost fully depreciated, with a very high replacement cost. Not recognizing the effect of inflation will produce abnormally high returns on investment. The day of reckoning will come when the new equipment must be bought and installed. ROI's will then tumble if they are based on the old returns.

Assets carried at net of depletion or amortization (oil, gas, patents, capitalized R&D, tooling)—these normally would be considered as wasting, but most balance sheets do not show the original gross investment. As a convenience, then, it is easier to classify these as current at the end of each balance sheet period. They are, too, usually not consequential in amount. Since they will be classified as current, any cash flow included in the income statement under amortization or depletion will have to be excluded from the cash flow used in the ROI calculation. This maintains a consistent procedural approach.

Deferred Charges—Reclass these as current, similar to prepaid expenses.

Goodwill—These should be reclassed to current assets and any write-offs should be excluded from cash flow. This applies whether the goodwill is being amortized or not. The rationale for this is the same as for assets carried net of depletion. As a matter of convenience, and because the original amount of goodwill is usually not shown on the balance sheet, classify it as current.

Other Assets—Since original amounts are not shown and there is no evidence that they are being depreciated, classify them as current.

Current Liabilities—These are usually carefully classified as current by the independent accountants. If short-term debt is considered as permanent financing, say with a finance company, it may be combined with long-term debt.

Reserves and Deferred Credits—These should be considered current and thus enter into the calculation as a deduction from current assets. They are not usually a part of capitalization or permanent financing and are logically considered current.

Minority Interest—Include this with current liabilities for the sake of convenience. Some companies offset this, prorata, against current and fixed assets, but the simplified approach is preferred.

Preferred Stock—Treat this the same as long-term debt, except that the preferred dividend is recognized on an after-tax basis and is not deducted as an expense of doing business.

Convertible Preferred or Debt—Usually assume conversion and calculate ROI on a fully diluted basis, unless the conversion terms are so unattractive as to make conversion practically impossible.

These classifications may be simply accomplished on the work sheet at Exhibit 21.

The Return for the business is $38,000, consisting of $20,000 of net income after taxes, $15,000 of depreciation (being a non-cash expense), and $3,000 for the after-tax effect of interest on long-term debt. In the example, the interest is $5,000 and the actual tax would be $2,500. The figure of $3,000 is rounded up. The theory for adding back the interest cost of debt is to ignore the effect of the type of financing from the ROI calculations. If equity were used, net income would be higher (although earnings per share would probably be lower due to more shares being out). In addition to the adjustment for interest, the Return should be adjusted for the cash flow effect of accelerated depreciation which might have been used for tax purposes. If a Source & Use

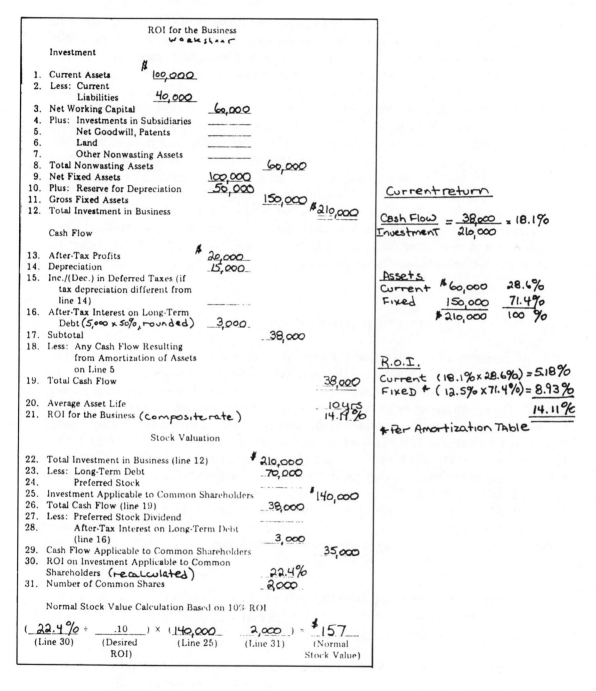

ROI for the Business
Worksheet

Investment

1. Current Assets $ 100,000
2. Less: Current Liabilities 40,000
3. Net Working Capital 60,000
4. Plus: Investments in Subsidiaries _____
5.   Net Goodwill, Patents _____
6.   Land _____
7.   Other Nonwasting Assets _____
8. Total Nonwasting Assets 60,000
9. Net Fixed Assets 100,000
10. Plus: Reserve for Depreciation 50,000
11. Gross Fixed Assets 150,000
12. Total Investment in Business $ 210,000

Cash Flow

13. After-Tax Profits $ 20,000
14. Depreciation 15,000
15. Inc./(Dec.) in Deferred Taxes (if tax depreciation different from line 14) _____
16. After-Tax Interest on Long-Term Debt (5,000 x 50%, rounded) 3,000
17. Subtotal 38,000
18. Less: Any Cash Flow Resulting from Amortization of Assets on Line 5
19. Total Cash Flow 38,000

20. Average Asset Life 10 yrs
21. ROI for the Business (composite rate) 14.11%

Stock Valuation

22. Total Investment in Business (line 12) $ 210,000
23. Less: Long-Term Debt 70,000
24.   Preferred Stock _____
25. Investment Applicable to Common Shareholders $ 140,000
26. Total Cash Flow (line 19) 38,000
27. Less: Preferred Stock Dividend _____
28.   After-Tax Interest on Long-Term Debt (line 16) 3,000
29. Cash Flow Applicable to Common Shareholders 35,000
30. ROI on Investment Applicable to Common Shareholders (recalculated) 22.4%
31. Number of Common Shares 2,000

Normal Stock Value Calculation Based on 10% ROI

(22.4% ÷ .10) × (140,000 ÷ 2,000) = $ 157
(Line 30) (Desired ROI)   (Line 25)   (Line 31)   (Normal Stock Value)

Current return

$$\frac{Cash\ Flow}{Investment} = \frac{38,000}{210,000} = 18.1\%$$

Assets
Current $ 60,000   28.6%
Fixed   150,000   71.4%
         $ 210,000   100 %

R.O.I.
Current (18.1% x 28.6%) = 5.18%
Fixed * (12.5% x 71.4%) = 8.93%
                          14.11%

* Per Amortization Table

Exhibit 21

**Do-It-Yourself Calculation for Determining Return
on Investment and Stock Value
from Annual Report Information**

of Funds Statement, or a Statement of Changes in Financial Position is available, the effect of accelerated depreciation will be readily visible. If not, obtain book depreciation from the Income Statement or the footnotes to the Financial Statements and compute additional depreciation, for tax purposes, as the increase in the Deferred Tax Liability account from last year on the balance sheet. The Deferred Tax account might occasionally show a decrease, meaning less cash flow, and this should also be adjusted in the calculation of the Return. Such a decrease would be likely to result where the fixed asset investment had not been replaced and the older assets had been substantially depreciated in past years leaving a smaller current charge for tax than for book depreciation. In a similar area, where Investment Tax Credits are deferred rather than "flowed-through," the Return should be adjusted to include the flow-through effect of the ITC. The idea is—show cash flow as it really happened. The Return, in summary, is the cash flow resulting from net income after taxes as reported in the financials, plus depreciation and investment tax credits adjusted for any tax variances, plus the after-tax effect of any interest charges on long-term debt.

CALCULATING THE RETURN ON INVESTMENT

The first step is to determine the annual cash flow ($38,000) to the Investment ($210,000). This is 18.1%, but it is not the final ROI. If the Investment were all current, the 18.1% would be the true ROI, somewhat related to drawing interest on a bank savings deposit. The return would be all interest, and your principal would have remained intact. Conversely, if all the assets were fixed or wasting, your return would be the rate required to pay off a mortgage of $210,000 over 10 years at the rate of $38,000 each year. Exhibit 13 indicates that this return is between 12 and 15%, or approximately 12.5%. (Follow the 10 year line over to the right seeking an 18.1% or .181 annual cash flow. This falls between .177 and .199, under the 12% to 15% columns. Obtain the exact percentage through interpolation—.181 minus .177 = .004 ÷ (.199 minus .177) = .1818 × (15% minus 12%) = .005 plus 12% = 12.5%). However, since both current and wasting assets have been utilized, the portion of each must be weighted as follows:

1. Determine annual cash flow to assets employed:

$$\frac{\text{Cash Flow (Return)}}{\text{Assets Employed (Investment)}} = \frac{\$38,000}{\$210,000} = 18.1\%$$

2. Determine proportion of current and wasting assets to the total of the two:

Net current assets	$ 60,000 =	28.6% of total assets
Gross fixed assets	150,000 =	71.4% of total assets
Total assets	$210,000 =	100.0%

3. Calculate a composite or weighted ROI:
    a. Current portion (28.6% × 18.1%)   = 5.18%
    b. Fixed portion
       (see amortization table for the
       value of an 18.1% return for
       an average 10 year life. As
       interpolated above, this is
       12.5% × 71.4%)   = 8.93%
       Composite rate of return   14.11%

The true ROI is, thus, 14.1%, in between what it would be if all the assets were current, 18.1%, and the 12.5% if all the assets were fixed or wasting. The current portion of the result represents a return similar to drawing interest on a savings deposit. The fixed portion includes interest plus a return of a principal part of the wasting asset.

CONVERTING THE ROI FOR THE ENTIRE BUSINESS INTO A STOCK VALUE

Most companies utilize leverage, or debt financing, in addition to equity, as a part of their total capitalization. The Return, or Cash Flow, and the Investment, or net assets employed, must be adjusted to eliminate the effects of debt and to determine the portions of each, return and investment, which are left over for the stockholder. Using the previous set of facts, the balances attributable to the equity position are:

Cash Flow attributed to stockholders ($38,000 minus $3,000 after-tax cost) of interest on the long-term debt)	$ 35,000
Investment attributed to stockholders ($210,000 minus $70,000 of long-term debt)	140,000
Return on Investment attributed to stockholders (assuming 28.6% current and 71.4% fixed)	22.4%*

*This is recalculated based on a 25% cash flow ($35,000 ÷ $140,000 = 25% × 28.6% current portion = 7.15% current. Add to this the fixed portion determined from the amortization table, based on a 10 year average asset life with a 25% return. This interpolates to an ROI percent of 21.36 × 71.4% for the fixed portion, or 15.25%. Hence, 7.15% + 15.25% = 22.4%).

The simplified assumption has, of course, been made that the long-term debt was utilized proportionately between the current working capital needs of the business and its fixed asset needs. Therefore, the net investment after deducting the $70,000 of debt remains in the same 28.6% current and 71.4% fixed relationship. Normally, you would expect that long-term debt would primarily be associated with fixed or long-term assets. However, this is not always the case, and we may thus assume that the debt financing supplies permanent leverage, that it will be revolved and remain in the business for the long-term. Moreover, long-term investors do not necessarily look to the asset itself or the repossession of the asset to obtain repayment. They look to the generation of working capital to cover the fixed interest charges. Consequently, we may simply assume that only short-term liabilities should be netted against short-term current assets to fit our pre-defined working capital norm.

We may now translate these results into the actual worth of a share of stock. Our balance sheet indicates that 2,000 shares of common stock are outstanding. The Investment attributable to these 2,000 shares is $140,000 or $70 per share. Therefore, a stockholder who purchased a share of stock at $70 would be buying a 22.4% return on his investment. The stock, if publicly traded, must sell for a higher figure than $70. The amount that it would sell for is directly related to investors' expectations of the return on investment that they, as a whole, desire. If investors only expected an 11.2% return (½ of the 22.4% calculated ROI), then obviously the stock would sell for $140 per share, instead of $70. If normal investors' expectations were for, say, a 10% return, the stock should sell for $157 ($70 × 22.4% ÷ 10%). If an individual investor's own perception of Return on Investment were higher than 10%, then he would make a recalculation using the higher %, and this would result in his making an offer to buy the shares at a lower price in order to attain the higher ROI. Exhibit 21 which was used to calculate the ROI for an entire business is used, also, at the bottom of the form, to determine the worth of an individual stockholder's interest. The form shows 10% as the desired ROI, but this could be changed to any percentage that the company determines to be an acceptable profitability rate (see page 76 for a grading of rates.)

POST-INSTALLATION EVALUATION OF MAJOR CAPITAL APPROPRIATIONS

In many cases the capital investment program is used primarily as a tool for analyzing an investment before the investment is initiated. There is some evidence that much less progress has been made in the matter of making post-installation evaluations of capital appropriations, many of which involve very large investments. Management should be just as concerned with the progress and eventual conclusion of an investment as it is with a *preview* of what the results are *expected* to be. Obviously there is some need for a capital investment monitoring system, or post-completion audit.

PURPOSES OF POST-COMPLETION AUDITS

Post-installation evaluations, or performance reports, serve four major purposes:
1. To verify the resulting savings or profit.
2. To reveal reasons for project failure.
3. To check on soundness of various managers' proposals.
4. To aid in assessing future capital expenditure proposals.

The post-completion audit is usually the most reliable means of verifying the savings or added profit produced by a project. In some cases it may be pointed out that such projects are closely tied in with unit operating budgets that will reflect the expected benefits. In other cases, however, when results are not apparent, an audit is required to determine whether a project failed, or whether savings were realized as forecast but were offset by increased expenses elsewhere. Similarly, a post-audit may be the only means of determining whether an improvement in operating results stems from the new project or from improved savings elsewhere. Another possible value of the post-completion audit is in uncovering reasons for project failure. This would aid management in taking corrective measures, or if there seems to be no means of making the project profitable, of abandoning it with minimal additional loss.

Post audits also serve as a check on the soundness of capital expenditure proposals advanced by departmental or divisional managers. In addition, managers who know that they will be held to account for the results of their proposals might tend to make more effort to insure their reasonableness and accuracy. They also might manage them more carefully to avoid having to explain failures. However, managers should be informed that post-audits are made primarily to help them improve their abilities to manage capital investments. Otherwise, they may tend to become overcautious and to avoid proposing projects that are really needed rather than risk exposure to censure.

TIMING OF POST-AUDITS

This monitoring, or follow-up system, should not be activated after a long period of time, but should be effective almost as soon as the project commences. Any variation from the original plan or projection, whether it be in the amount of investment, the amount of payback, the timing of the payback, or any other pertinent factor should be determined immediately so management can be alerted. If actual developments after the investment is made reveal that there will be substantial deviation from the original justification circumstances, management should be notified immediately. Any unanticipated risks or reverses might possibly provide management with an option of either divesting itself of the investment, or at the least, reducing possible serious losses.

The shortest regular review period that is recommended is by quarters. Some companies may feel that annual reviews are adequate. At any rate, all reviews should be continued until management decides that follow-up is no longer necessary.

TYPES OF PROJECTS AUDITED

In general, post-completion auditing is restricted to capital projects that were proposed and approved on the basis of cost savings or added profits. Projects undertaken for the purpose of improving quality can also be audited to insure that the improvement in product quality was obtained.

It should not be necessary to audit all cost-savings or profit-oriented projects, but select only those that involve large capital outlays or have major significance to management. Since audits are often time-consuming and expensive, it is felt that they are not warranted in the case of relatively small projects.

PROBLEMS OF POST-AUDITS

Many companies will probably find that their regular accounting records are inadequate for post-audit purposes. For example, in auditing projects to increase the volume of existing product lines, the accounting system probably does not segregate incremental costs and income on the new investment from those arising from the previously existing facilities. One suggested means of overcoming this problem is to determine in advance which projects will be audited, and advise the accounting units concerned as to what records they should keep. Another solution is to maintain cost and income records by project until post-audits are completed.

RESPONSIBILITY FOR MAKING POST-AUDITS

Some companies may decide to assign responsibility for making post-completion audits to corporate headquarters finance and accounting staffs. Post-audits can also be carried out, however, by personnel of the plant or division that originated the projects, and may or may not be subject to verification by headquarters. Audit responsibility can be vested either in headquarters or local personnel, depending on the nature of the project involved and/or the amount of the expenditure.

FORM AND CONTENT OF POST-AUDITS

Post-completion audits will vary substantially in form and content, depending upon the nature and complexity of the projects involved. Many companies may not wish to use standard forms. Some will prefer to prepare each post-audit in the fashion that best lends itself to the project being audited. In some cases, the principal content, the explanation of variances from forecast results, can be best expressed in narrative form.

Nevertheless, for those companies who desire to employ standard post-audit forms we have included Exhibits 22 and 23 as examples of formal reports.

EVALUATION OF CAPITAL INVESTMENTS

1. Good sound capital expenditure decisions are a major factor in the successful growth of a company's earnings and competitive position. The "discounted cash flow" method for the economic evaluation of proposed major capital investments can reduce the risk and provide a priority rating procedure for investment opportunities.
2. The understanding and acceptance by management of the basic discounted cash flow concept can be greatly enhanced if the responsible staff people stress the importance of the necessary marketing, production, and engineering data without becoming unduly preoccupied with the fine points of the financial technicalities or calculations.

3. Top management approval for substantial capital spending proposals should be secured through the use of a formal appropriation request, as illustrated in Exhibit 19.

4. The "discounted cash flow" techniques may be used to determine the Return on Investment for an entire business, as well as for individual projects and may be converted into the value of a share of stock. This technique involves the concept of current, as well as wasting assets, and eliminates the type of debt financing from the determination of the return.

5. Capital spending projects involving large investments should be audited at regular intervals to insure the proper investment spending level and to verify the anticipated benefits or financial returns.

Date   July 15, 19xx

To: Comptroller's Dept.

Approval Date   October 1, 19xx

Appropriate No.   E-123

Completion Date   July 15, 19xx

Description: New HQ machine to manufacture product "D"

Period of Operation Covered

First Year*

*First year actual plus revised estimate of next 9 years.

	PROPOSED	ACTUAL	(OVER) UNDER
Investment	$ 14,000	$ 18,000	$ (4,000)
Annual Production - Additional Sales	$ -	$ -	$ -
Cost Savings - Additional Profit	$ 20,500	$ 23,500*	$ (3,000)
Return on Investment	19.7 %	17.0 %	2.7 %
Payback	4.5 Yrs.	4.9 Yrs.	(.4) Yrs.

Remarks - Explanation of Differences:

Capital investment portion cost $2,000 more than original estimate used in original profitability study and appropriation request. Most of the overage resulted from improved but more costly machine parts. Expense portion ran over estimate by $2,000 because of unforeseen building alterations at site of new machine. Net profit resulting from cost savings was better at the end of the first year, was better than original first year estimate and revised estimate was then determined for the balance of the expected economic life.

By _____

Exhibit 22

Post Installation Evaluation
Major Capital Appropriations

Appropriation No.   E-123

TIME SCHEDULE OF EXPENDITURES AND RECEIPTS
CASH OUTFLOW

ORIGINAL PROPOSAL

YEAR	ANNUAL PERIOD AT END	CAPITAL LAND	CAPITAL FACILITIES	EXPENSED ITEMS	WORKING FUNDS	TOTAL INVESTMENT
	-2nd					
	-1st					
	0		10,000	1,000	3,000	14,000
	1st					
	2nd					
	3rd					
	4th					
	5th					
	Total					

ACTUAL

YEAR	ANNUAL PERIOD AT END	CAPITAL LAND	CAPITAL FACILITIES	EXPENSED ITEMS	WORKING FUNDS	TOTAL INVESTMENT
	-2nd					
	-1st					
	0		12,000	3,000	3,000	18,000
	1st					
	2nd					
	3rd					
	4th					
	5th					
	Total					

Exhibit 23

Post Installation Evaluation
Major Capital Appropriations

CASH INFLOW

YEAR / ANNUAL PERIOD AT END	ORIGINAL PROPOSAL				ACTUAL			
	TOTAL DOLLAR REVENUE	OP. PROFIT AFTER .50 TAX	CASH FLOW BACK DEPRECIATION AND/OR DEPLETION	TOTAL	TOTAL DOLLAR REVENUE	OP PROFIT AFTER .50 TAX	CASH FLOW BACK DEPRECIATION AND/OR DEPLETION	TOTAL
-2nd								
-1st								
0		500		500		1,500		1,500
1st		1,182	1,818	3,000		1,218	2,182	3,400
2nd		1,364	1,636	3,000		1,437	1,963	3,400
3rd		1,545	1,455	3,000		1,654	1,746	3,400
4th		1,727	1,273	3,000		1,872	1,528	3,400
5th		1,909	1,091	3,000		2,091	1,309	3,400
6th		2,091	909	3,000		2,309	1,091	3,400
7th		2,273	727	3,000		2,528	872	3,400
8th		2,455	545	3,000		2,746	654	3,400
9th		2,636	364	3,000		2,963	437	3,400
10th		2,818	182	3,000		3,182	218	3,400
11th		-	-	-		-	-	-
12th		20,500	10,000	30,500		23,500	12,000	35,500
13th								
14th								
15th								

Exhibit 23 (con't)

CHAPTER 4

Statement of Changes in Financial Position: The Funds Statement as a Control and Planning Mechanism

The format presented allows for better control and planning because funds flows are sorted by responsibility.

In recent years the term "cash flow" has become widely used by corporation management people, security analysts, management specialists, accountants, and the investing public. The term "cash flow" now appears quite regularly in many company annual reports, and in some cases enjoys equal billing with net profit. Despite its current popularity as a measurement of corporate health and its utilization in appraising stock values, there is some controversy regarding its value and soundness in particular areas. A certain amount of criticism is justified because of the limitation inherent in the generally accepted method of calculating cash flow. The total of net earnings plus depreciation represents only a part of the cash flow. Actually it would be more correct to call it cash inflow, as it does not consider cash outlays such as capital expenditure, of which only a small percentage is charged to costs, thereby reducing the net earnings. We will call it "funds flow."

The cash inflow formula of net income plus depreciation is applicable and correct in appraising the profitability of capital appropriation requests as described in Chapter 3. It is also of value in making comparisons of performance between various companies, as demonstrated in Chapter 10. Where information about a company is limited to published financial information, such as their annual report, it is not likely that an accurate funds statement could be constructed. In this case, if the net earnings between two or more companies were about equal, the one with the largest depreciation charges should be in the better position to finance its own growth or increase its dividend yield. Perhaps the term "funds statement" should be adopted for internal financial analyses. At any rate, a thorough understanding of this key indicator will lead to its proper application in the various aspects of corporate finance. The traditional Statement of Changes should be revised, for internal analysis, so that it does not concentrate on working capital but, instead, paints a picture of the flow of all funds, including non-working capital items, through the business.

FUNDS FLOW DEFINED

The presence of cash on a balance sheet of any company is not always what it appears to be. This item merely records the number of dollars in the bank on the date that the balance sheet was made up. Actually, this cash represents physical things that are just as real, such as plant and equipment. In other words, cash is a tool used in the business. Every day dollars flow out of this balance and new dollars flow in. These dollars are constantly becoming such things as payroll, raw materials, finished inventory, etc., and are constantly replenished by the flow of money from the customers in exchange for finished inventory. (See Exhibit 24).

In its simplest form, cash flow measures the flow of cash through the corporate structure. It should indicate the total funds available to the company from a given period of operations for replacement and expansion of facilities, debt reduction, and dividend payments.

No generalization of conclusion can be drawn as to the significance of the "cash flow" without reference to the entire flow of funds as reflected in the complete statement of changes in financial position. Exhibit 25 illustrates the type of financial transactions and occurrences which provide or use funds. You will note that the source and use of funds flows from increases or decreases in all balance sheet items, both assets and liabilities, not just working capital items. The only factor not described as either an increase or decrease is the category "net profit." This could just as well be described as "increase in retained earnings," but "net profit" might be preferable for clarification and emphasis.

We believe that this chart is fairly representative of the situation in most companies in that the substantial sources of funds arise from net profit and depreciation. This, no doubt, leads to the popularity of defining cash flow, for many applications, as the total of

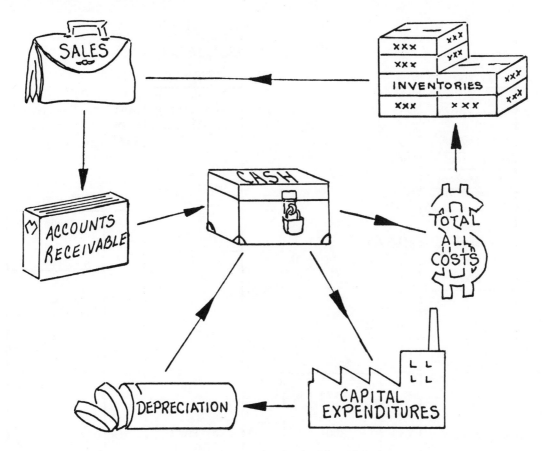

Exhibit 24

Diagram of Cash Flow

just these two factors. Net profit, obviously, is the most favorable source of cash income. Depreciation is perhaps the second most important source of cash income.

Depreciation money is actually cash-in-hand and represents an excess of income over operating costs and taxes. But it is not the same as earnings. The company has charged the money against current earnings to cover wear and tear and obsolescence on its physical property. The cash is in hand, to be sure, but it is not profit, because it is supposed to cover the physical and technological deterioration of capital equipment.

Depreciation, after all, is strictly a bookkeeping item. Thus, a company that reports a $1,000,000 deduction for depreciation still has the $1,000,000. It is, moreover, not subject to tax, since it is not legally income. But the company can use the money for many things: for modernization, for expansion, for mergers, for paying off debts, for working capital, for maintaining dividends during poor years, or it can be left in cash or short-term securities for use when needed.

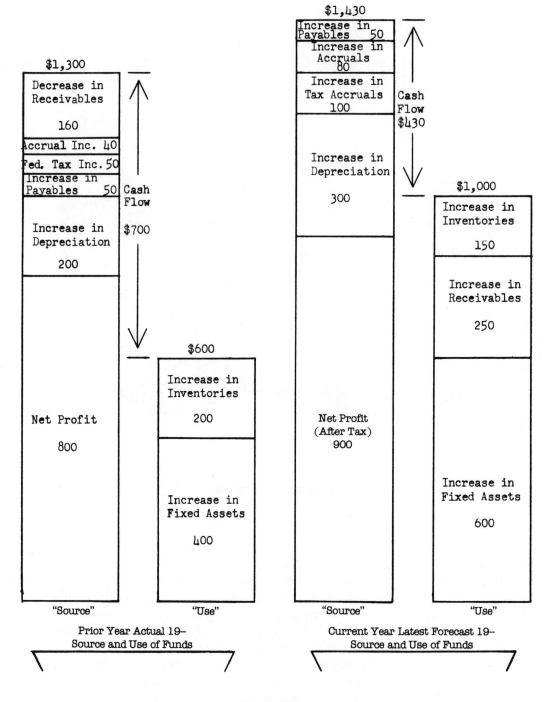

Exhibit 25

Illustration of Funds Flow

However, adding back depreciation provisions to show the total funds generated from operations can be misleading, unless the reader of financial statements keeps in mind that the renewal and replacement of productive facilities require substantial "cash outflow," which may well exceed the depreciation provisions, and is surely the case in an inflation economy. This is illustrated by the sizeable section for "increase in fixed assets" in the funds use bars in Exhibit 25.

CASH FORECASTING

The budgeting of cash translates business plans and operating forecasts into terms of funds needed at future time periods, both short and long-range. During those periods when excess cash is forecast, the excess portion can be anticipated for investment in short-term government securities, treasury certificates of indebtedness, commercial paper, etc. For those periods when a shortage of cash is forecast, arrangements can be made to procure cash through short-term loans, etc. It is apparent that not only is forecasting of cash requirements necessary to maintain sufficient operating capital, but also that skillful cash planning can generate a profit.

Actually, this is not a new concept, for many companies have always forecast probable future cash requirements based on historical cash receipts and disbursements at various levels of activity. However, cash forecasting is becoming more and more important as requirement for greater accuracy has resulted in the need for a more reliable procedure.

The cash forecast should be tied in with the profit plan referred to in Chapter 1 and the balance sheet budget covered in Chapter 2.

Exhibit 26 illustrates how these plans reveal their effect upon the cash position. It also provides the opportunity to make comparisons of these transactions with past periods.

The cash forecast is based on a complete budget program comprised of a series of individual forecasts covering every phase of operations. Each forecast is carefully prepared in detail by the individual responsible for the particular operation. For example, the sales manager of a division submits a forecast of sales showing the quantity of each product he expects to sell and the price he expects to receive. In a similar manner, executives in every part of a company contribute their forecasts to the budget program. This includes manufacturing costs and selling and administrative expenses leading to forecast net profit.

The individual forecasts thus obtained can be translated in terms of cash by the use of forms such as Exhibit 26, which clearly shows their relationship to each other. The resulting cash forecast then becomes the framework from which definite financial policies can be developed. In this illustration, the effect of changes in short-term debt is eliminated to permit a better analysis of the factors which resulted in cash changes.

Divisional cash forecasts can reveal which segments of a company are not producing sufficient cash to finance their own operations, and, conversely, which segments are providing operating cash capital in excess of individual needs.

DATE June 30, 19--

PARTICULARS	Actual 12 Mo. Prior Year 19--	Current Year 19-- Annual Plan	Actual 6 Mos Current Year 19--	Latest 10 Mo. Forecast Current
CASH BALANCE AT BEGINNING OF PERIOD	1900	2000	2000	2000
SECURITY BALANCE AT BEGINNING OF PERIOD	400	1000	1000	1000
FUNDS MADE AVAILABLE FROM OPERATIONS				
Net Profit (After taxes)	800	950	275	900
Increase in Depreciation Allowance	200	300	100	300
Increase in Deferred Income Taxes	—	—	—	—
TOTAL CASH FLOW FROM OPERATIONS	1000	1250	375	1200
Increase in Accounts Receivable	160	(200)	(400)	(250)
Increase in Inventories	(200)	(100)	(150)	(150)
Increase in Payables — excluding change in short-term debt	50	25	200	50
Increase in Accruals — payrolls, misc., taxes, etc.	40	30	20	80
Increase in Federal Tax Accruals	50	100	100	100
TOTAL FUNDS FROM OPERATIONS	1100	1105	145	1030
FUNDS USED TO SUPPORT OPERATIONS				
Increase in Fixed Assets — Replacements and Improvements	400	600	400	600
For Business Expansion	—	—	—	—
For Government Regulations Compliance	—	—	—	—
TOTAL SUPPORT FUNDS	400	600	400	600
NET FUNDS FROM OPERATIONS	700	505	(255)	430

Exhibit 26

Funds Statement Work Sheet

FUNDS MADE AVAILABLE FROM FINANCIAL SOURCES				
Decrease in Prepaid Expenses	—	—	—	—
Increase in Long-Term Debt	—	—	—	—
Increase in Capital Stock	—	—	—	—
TOTAL FUNDS FROM FINANCIAL SOURCES				
FUNDS INVESTED AND DISTRIBUTED				
Investments	—	—	—	—
Dividends	—	—	—	—
TOTAL FUNDS INVESTED AND DISTRIBUTED	—	—	—	—
INCREASE IN CASH, LESS CHANGE IN SHORT-TERM DEBT	700	505	(255)	430
CASH BALANCE AT END OF PERIOD	2000	2000	1900	2100
SECURITY BALANCE AT END OF PERIOD	1000	1505	845	1330

Exhibit 26 (con't)

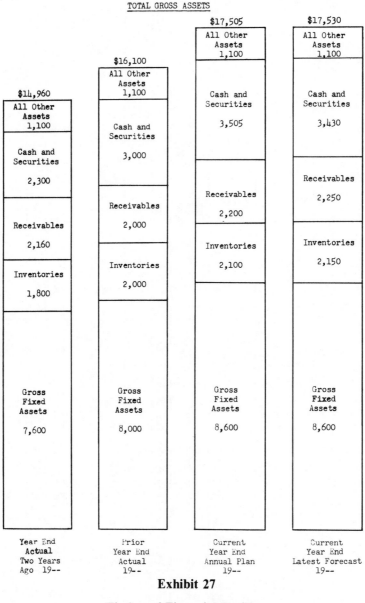

TOTAL GROSS ASSETS

Exhibit 27

Timing of Financial Position
Total Gross Assets

CASH MANAGEMENT

The optimum success of a business depends in large measure upon the skill of its management in foreseeing and preparing for future conditions and happenings. Thus, the funds statement, as a management aid, provides (1) the estimate of the amount of cash which a business will need, and (2) the amount of time that this need will exist. If the forecast internally-generated cash appears inadequate, short or long-term borrowing becomes necessary.

The format presented allows for better control and planning because funds flows are sorted by responsibility.

One way for a company to fail is to allow its cash balance to dwindle. These dollars are not "idle money." They are very fast moving, hard-working dollars, and in businesses subject to sudden change or seasonal fluctuation, the cash balance can mean the difference between success or failure to the corporation.

When a company is in a period of making heavy capital expenditures for expansion and growth, including acquisitions, the funds statement will indicate the type of financing necessary for the projects. It will also show when each new installation or addition will generate enough profit to make further financing unnecessary for a given period.

Skillful timing of capital investments and maximum utilization of accelerated depreciation provisions can build up annual depreciation charges at a faster percentage than the rate of capital expenditures. This will improve the ability of a corporation to provide for its financial needs from its own funds.

Funds flow does give a valuable measure of the speed with which a company is getting its fixed capital back in liquid form. It gives an indication of the company's ability to generate internally the money it needs for expansion and modernization. The company which is getting its fixed capital back fairly fast is far less likely to need outside borrowing or new issues of common stock than is a company whose cash flow is low in relation to the size of its business.

In most cases, management has better opportunity for control over the asset side of the balance sheet than the liability section. A high degree of vigilance over the various categories of assets should be rewarding. Exhibit 27 is a graphic illustration of how comparisons between various time intervals can be maintained and possible trends revealed.

Exhibit 1 in Chapter 1, Exhibits 2, 5 and 9 in Chapter 2 and Exhibits 25, 26 and 27 in Chapter 4 include sample figures. The same set of figures is used in all seven of these exhibits, to enable the reader to relate these exhibits to each other and to follow the transactions more easily by being able to identify the components of the financial model.

CASH ANALYSIS POINTERS

1. "Funds flow" is an important measurement of corporate well-being if properly employed.
2. Total funds flow, or source and use of funds, reflects changes in all balance sheet items, both assets and liabilities. It is not concerned only with working capital.
3 Cash forecasting translates business plans and operating budgets into terms of funds needed at future time periods, both short and long-range.
4. A cash forecast should be prepared from balance sheet budgets tied in with sales and profit budgets and captial expenditure plans, instead of historical cash balance levels in order to be really effective.
5. The Funds Statement should be constructed to highlight areas of responsibility, to permit better planning and control.

CHAPTER 5

Direct Versus Absorption Costing

It is management's decision which changes the characteristic of the costs involved, changing them from fixed to variable, period to direct costs, under different decision situations.

Financial analysis for decision-making leans heavily upon the cost accounting function in most companies. Whether the decision is to make or buy, lease or invest, drop a product or add a new one, the determination of its effect on the profit and loss statement must almost necessarily be obtained from cost accounting intelligence.

One of the most important influences on costs and profits is volume. The recognition of the relationship between cost, volume, and profit is utilized in the technique of "direct costing."

Direct costing is not a system which can be substituted for historical cost, standard cost, job cost, or process cost. However, it can certainly complement a job order, process, or standard cost method.

Accounting theory is not static and is occasionally subject to controversy. Much has been written and debated on the merits of direct costing versus absorption costing. Some advocates of the direct costing concept appear to be almost militant on the subject. Needless to say, less heat and more light will provide clearer answers.

SELECTION OF A COST ACCOUNTING METHOD

The evaluation of any cost accounting method must first consider the purpose for which it will be used and the relationships between the various uses. Whatever system is adopted, one single method of product and period costing should serve to determine past, present, and future costs. It should match costs to revenues for both internal and external reporting. The product cost system should provide a basis to determine selling prices, value inventories, measure performance, and provide management with data for decision-making and planning.

An important factor in any choice between various types of accounting practices is their acceptance by such rule-making bodies as the Financial Accounting Standards Board, the American Institute of Certified Public Accountants, the Securities and Exchange Commission, and the Internal Revenue Service.

To a great extent, the choice of a cost system depends upon the kind of business you are in and what management wants from your system. Either direct or absorption costing methods may be applied on an actual cost basis, but this chapter is confined largely to their use on the standard cost basis.

Consider a company in the business of constructing custom built complex machinery for a comparatively few large industrial customers. A large percentage of the total cost might be material which is obviously direct cost. Another large percentage of the total cost would probably be direct labor. In fact, practically all of the indirect labor could be easily allocated to the specific job. Selling, advertising, administrative, engineering, and research expenses might very well be a comparatively small part of the whole cost. It would probably be advantageous to employ not only a direct costing system, but even an actual job cost system. There would be a negligible amount of allocation of fixed costs. The only real estimating skill called on here would be in calculating a cost beforehand, to prepare a bid.

A quite different situation is found in a company engaged in the production and sale of an item sold to consumers through supermarkets. Here, it is possible that the packaging, selling, promotion, and advertising through newspapers, magazines, television, and radio would constitute the greater part of the total cost. Period costs, such as annual commitments in the promotion area, is one factor which might influence the choice of a cost system.

In view of the importance of the type of business in relation to the type of cost accounting, some of the controversy over the merits of the various systems becomes somewhat academic. Unfortunately, during the search for the one best system, decisions are sometimes deferred for years. In the meantime, a business could be dangerously handicapped. An imperfect system is better than none at all or an obviously unsuitable one.

UNDERSTANDING OF COMMON TERMINOLOGY

In attempting to appraise the relative merit of direct costing versus absorption costing, confusion can result from the various applications and interpretations of terms. We read of fixed costs, period costs, committed costs, indirect costs, and overhead costs.

Upon closer examination, we find that they all mean pretty much the same thing. Variable costs, direct costs, prime costs, and product costs have much in common, according to individual interpretation.

For purpose of clarity then, we will confine our terminology in this chapter to fixed expenses and variable costs. Quite simply, we can define fixed or period costs as expenses which remain relatively fixed regardless of production or sales volume and variable or direct costs as costs which vary according to the level of output or activity. Brief working definitions of key terms will serve as a basis of mutual understanding.

Fixed Costs

Fixed costs are indirect costs or period costs incurred merely by being in business, the amount of which is usually independent of the volume of production or sales for a determinable period of time, usually one year.

Fixed costs are incurred because of management's current or past decisions to maintain a facility with the potential to produce and sell a range of products in different volumes and markets.

Fixed costs are associated with facilities which are provided and kept in readiness without regard to the current actual volume of production and sales. Some of these facilities must be acquired and kept in a state of readiness more or less irrespective of the volume of orders on hand at any given time. Buildings, machines, and an organization comprising at least the key executive, technical, and supervisory personnel are examples of facilities which cannot be readily acquired or dispensed with in response to short period swings in volume. In addition, there are also fixed costs incurred because management has decided to make expenditures for a branch office in a territory, advertising, sales promotion, employee training, and research based on anticipated or potential sales or production volume. Thus, the significant characteristic of fixed costs is that their amount is related to the volume of business for which provision has been made, rather than to the currently prevailing volume. For this reason, the amount of the fixed costs is relatively independent of current volume changes.

Period Costs

Period costs are those fixed costs incurred for the establishment and maintenance of manufacturing and marketing capacity at a certain level, regardless of the sales and production volume actually experienced. Included are not only costs associated with plant, equipment, and manufacturing personnel, but also costs of maintaining a basic organization and expenditures for marketing, research, and administration which management has committed itself to make for a predetermined period of time.

The extent of this commitment is usually coordinated with either a normal volume level or an anticipated volume level. At any rate, period costs are those associated with time and the provision of the capacity to produce.

Period costs might be defined then as those costs which would be required to manage, maintain, and develop the business, whether or not specific products were actually made and sold. Under the direct costing theory, therefore, period costs would be charged against revenues of the period, rather than being deferred in inventory, since they are not directly related to the product.

It is important to understand, at this point, that certain costs may be considered direct costs for one purpose and period costs for another, depending on the analysis being performed. For example, rent for a factory would be a period cost at given production levels. However, rent expense for a salesman's office in a sales territory would be considered a direct cost, varying with the number of salesmen in the territory, and, hence, the volume in the territory. On the other hand, rent for a branch sales office, out of which all field salesmen operated, would clearly be a period cost related to maintaining a basic marketing organization in that territory. Judgments as to the classification of costs must obviously be made analytically, rather than subjectively.

Committed Costs

Committed costs is merely another term for period costs. It might be helpful to think of committed costs as a contract with some advertising medium for a period of time. For example, a contract with an industrial designer, management consultant, market research service, or office and warehouse leases could be categorized as committed expense.

Indirect Costs

Indirect costs are also called period costs, overhead costs, burden costs, and fixed costs. Specifically, they ususally refer to expense items such as supervisory wages and salaries, repairs to plant and equipment, plant protection, wage increments, or fringe benefits and the like.

Overhead Costs

Overhead costs are sometimes called burden costs and indirect costs. Specifically, these usually refer to telephone and telegraph, depreciation, property taxes, property insurance, heat and light, and the like.

Variable Costs

Variable costs are direct costs or product costs incurred because goods have been produced. They are associated with units of output (material, labor, and variable overhead) and are charged to the product. The term "variable cost" is often used as a synonym for direct cost.

Direct Costs

Direct costs are those costs which vary directly with volume (raw material, direct labor, and direct supplies) plus certain costs which vary closely with production and can be allocated to a product or group of products on a reasonably accurate basis. For incremental analysis, they are costs which would be eliminated if the cost center or product generating the costs were eliminated.

Prime Costs

Prime costs are usually used to describe direct labor and direct material only. Direct manufacturing overhead, such as wage increments or fringe benefits on direct labor would be treated as period expense when using this cost system.

Product Costs

Product costs are those associated with the units of output (material, labor, and variable overhead) and are charged to the product.

Under pure direct costing theory, product costs are compiled only in terms of costs which vary directly with production.

Semi-Variable Costs

The majority of cost categories contain both fixed and variable characteristics, although they usually predominate in one or the other. This has led to the classification of *semi-variable costs.*

When a cost is categorized as a variable or a fixed cost, it is a practical allocation only if it is kept in mind that most costs are in some part fixed and in some part variable with volume. It can be argued that there are few if any pure variable and pure fixed costs. Most variable expenses contain a non-related or fixed portion, and most fixed costs reveal a certain degree of variability which becomes apparent at subnormally low and abnormally high activity levels.

Because so many costs display characteristics of both direct and period costs, some accountants believe that the semi-variable category should not be employed at all. They feel that costs should either be handled as direct or indirect. It is true, of course, especially in the fixed cost category, that there are sizable gray areas. However, at any given time they are either black or white. A cost category may be changed or a cost can be avoided or recovered by a change in volume or product mix, but they can usually be considered as a committed cost at the time cost rates are determined. Too great a segment of costs relegated to this semi-variable status can result in lack of confidence and confusion in the cost accounting function.

Marginal Income

Marginal income is usually regarded as the net amount after deducting variable costs from sales income. This figure can be obtained for the total business, a manufacturing or sales division, a sales branch, a factory, a product line, or an individual product. This is sometimes called "contribution margin" or "profit contribution."

Gross Profit Margin

Gross profit margin usually represents the profit or loss resulting from total manufacturing cost, *both variable and fixed,* deducted from net sales. Stated another way, it is the contribution margin before the fixed selling and administrative expenses.

Standard Cost

The *standard cost* is made up of direct materials, direct labor, and allocated overhead. Direct materials are determined by the actual material in the finished product. Direct labor is determined by the number of units made by the budgeted crew at the budgeted speed. Fixed expense which has been determined from past experience plus future planning is added to the cost on the basis of budgeted speeds and efficiencies.

Fixed and Variable Costs

The successful application of either direct or absorption costing depends upon some practical separation of *fixed and variable costs.* Individual items of cost are often not inherently either fixed or variable in nature, but acquire fixed or variable characteristics as a result of decisions which management has made. Thus the decision to keep buildings, machines, and key personnel in a state of readiness, without regard to the volume of orders on hand at any given time, would result in fixed costs.

The important concept here which should not be overlooked is that it is management's decision which changes the characteristic of the costs involved, changing them from fixed to variable, period to direct costs, under different decision situations. Typical decisions under which direct costing concepts are used are product profitability, incremental analyses, and territory analysis, as well as the usual inventory valuation studies with which this chapter deals. For example, in studying product profitability, we would adopt a definition of direct costs which would assume the cost to be direct if the elimination of the product would eliminate the cost. Under this definition, branch rent expense would not be considered direct if many products were sold in the branch. If only one were sold, branch rent would be a direct cost. Incremental direct cost analysis, similarly, yields interesting results when compared to conventional costing. In making a decision as to whether or not to accept an order for Product X at a low price, and assuming that the available units of Product X could not be sold elsewhere (hence the sale is incremental), what would otherwise be direct costs could be ignored, as they would not be eliminated by losing this sale. Thus, for ordinary product profitability analysis, branch rent could be a direct cost, but for incremental analysis, it would be ignored entirely or classified as a period expense, below the contribution margin line.

The existence of semi-variable cost characteristics is recognized. There are numerous techniques available which attempt to separate individual cost categories into their fixed and variable components. Many of these are mathematical or statistical techniques which correlate these costs to production volume, and a separation is achieved by the method of least squares, scatter charts, and others.

For our purpose however, let us analyze the chart of accounts and classify each cost category as being either fixed or variable because they are predominantly either one or the other. Admittedly, this will not give us a 100% accurate separation. However, neither does any other method. Therefore, we are really talking about one method being more nearly accurate than another.

The following general and brief list of manufacturing costs, arbitrarily separated between fixed and variable, is intended to provide better understanding of the types of actual costs involved in the consideration of the direct and absorption concepts.

Fixed Expenses	*Variable Costs*
Salaries (all)	Direct manufacturing material
Plant watchmen and office janitors	Direct manufacturing labor
Retirement plan costs	Indirect hourly manufacturing labor
Stationery and office supplies	Shift foremen
Telephone and telegraph	Materials handling
Postage	Janitor service (mfg.)
Depreciation	Maintenance
Property taxes	Manufacturing supplies (used up
Property insurance	in the process)
Heating and light	Maintenance material
	Power cost (variable)

The costs which are regarded as variable are generally recognized to be the costs of activity of a business already set up to produce; those which are regarded as fixed are costs related to maintaining that capacity, physical and managerial.

Outstanding among variable costs are direct material, direct labor, and indirect hourly labor such as shift foremen and materials handling.

Major items of salaried labor are supervisory salaries and plant clerical staff, which are usually regarded as fixed expenses. Questions sometimes arise as to the dividing line on the manufacturing organization salary structure between variable indirect labor and fixed indirect labor. Perhaps fixed costs should cover wages and salaries of key personnel (managers, superintendents, and staff) plus wages and salaries of additional supervisory forces, including departmental foremen. In this case, variable labor cost would probably start with hourly supervision including shift foremen.

Depreciation, though admittedly a sunk cost, can be considered as a pure fixed cost only because it is not recoverable, even though actual wear and tear are the result of productive action.

Although many costs may actually be semi-variable, the practical problem of each company, if it is to make use of cost behavior information, is to have only fixed and variable costs. The starting point is a definition of costs applicable to the company.

Similary, in analyzing marketing costs, their classification as fixed or variable will depend on the decision being made—is the analysis incremental? Would the costs be eliminated if the product were eliminated? Are we studying product profitability and so classifying only incremental costs as variable? From a product line profitability standpoint, we want to define profit contribution as sales minus incremental costs.

Expenses would then be classified as fixed or variable as follows:

Fixed Expenses

General Expenses Relating to
All Products, to include:
Selling
General & Administrative
Manufacturing

Variable Costs

Sales Deductions:
Sales Allowances
Cash discounts
Commissions
Freight-out

Inventory Costs:
Direct material
Direct labor

Variable Overhead:

Any normal recurring
cost that varies with
volume but is not spec-
ifically identified with
one unit of product.

EXPLANATION OF DIRECT COSTING

There are numerous interpretations of what constitutes direct costing. They range from calling it an accounting technique to classifying it as a costing method or a concept of accounting. Apparently direct costing is many things to many people. A simple definition is that direct costing is a concept of accounting which recognizes the fundamental characteristics of costs as segregated between:

1. Direct costs, or product costs incurred because goods have been produced and sold. These are called variable costs and are used to value inventory, cost of production, and cost of sales.

2. Indirect costs, or period costs incurred to maintain a potential to produce and sell a range of products in different markets and quantities, the amount of which is independent of the volume of output. These are called fixed expenses and are excluded from the product unit cost.

One of the major purposes of direct costing is to recognize and clarify the concept of "contribution theory." In simple terms, each sales dollar might be considered as being comprised of two parts: (1) a reimbursement of total variable costs, and (2) that which contributes to the recovery of fixed expense and the production of profits. In analyzing expense contribution and profit margin, therefore, we recognize that no profit can be realized until all fixed expenses are recovered. We further recognize then, that profit margin does not accrue on an individual unit basis, but must be related to volume and thus to the total performance of the total entity. For example, it seems incongruous to consider profits as relating specifically to individual product items. The sale of one small order of one product item to one customer would not of itself produce a profit to the company, even though the particular individual item's selling price would be adequately higher than the total standard cost of the specific item. The variable cost of the individual item might be more than recovered, but the contribution margin of one item would hardly make a dent in the total entity fixed expense.

Total profit, then, cannot be entirely determined by the margin between selling price and full unit costs, fixed and variable. The difference between the aggregate value of sales and the aggregate variable cost of the products sold provides the gross contribution margin from which to recover the fixed expenses and produce the profits of the entity. After all fixed expenses have been recovered, additional sales of product units results in an increase in net profit by an amount roughly equal to the difference between the selling price and the unit's variable cost.

Volume has an important influence on costs and profits. Direct costing is a plan for providing management with more information about cost-volume-profit relationships and for presenting this information in a form more readily understandable by management at all levels. This might be accomplished by the introduction of a group of related techniques which includes the flexible budget, breakeven chart, and marginal income analysis. While most of the same facts can be obtained by statistical analyses prepared to supplement accounting reports in conventional form, direct costing is designed to provide the desired results with a minimum of additional analyses.

Exhibit 28 is a graphic illustration of the effect of sales volume on the absorption of fixed expenses. This breakeven chart relates sales and costs over a time period, in this case one month, to the percent of capacity operated. It shows that during an average or normal month's sales of $230M, the variable manufacturing cost will be $150M, the fixed manufacturing cost will be $30M, and the fixed selling and administrative expense $20M, or a total of all costs of $200M. This will result in a profit of $30M for the month and shows that with this standard sales and costs relation, the profit will not begin until after the production capacity reaches 63% of total. A breakeven point is that exact level of operations at which there is neither profit nor loss. Exhibit 28 could be described as a graphic variable income statement. For purposes of illustration, the assumption is made here that costs move in a straight line as volume changes. In actual correlation analyses you would probably find that the cost-sales relative positions would be in curving lines or steps. When additional volume is obtained by adding another shift, sometimes a complete set of supervisors, clerks, etc., must be added. When such costs are charted against volume, their movements appear as a series of steps rather than a continuous line. Fixed expenses would probably behave similar to a flexible budget, which is often merely a series of fixed budgets at different levels of activity. However, within the range of volume for which provision is made, period costs usually should not be increased in total by added production, nor decreased by reduced production. At any rate, an income statement can be analyzed to determine net sales and total costs and expenses expressed in percent of facility capacity at different levels of operations. Starting at zero, the daily sales can be plotted cumulatively, and a straight line drawn as close as possible to the plotted sales points. This straight line could be either drawn to fit by eye, or the method of least squares could be used if desired. The lines for fixed expenses and variable costs could be determined by their actual percentage relation to net sales. You will note that in this particular exhibit, the point of breakeven happens to be 63% activity. At any rate, budget standards and standard costs would probably be established based on historical activity combined with current forecasts.

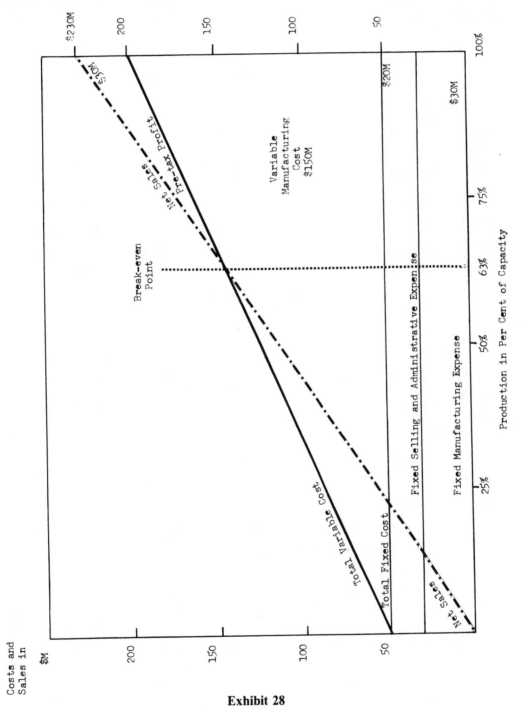

Exhibit 28

Simple Break-Even Chart

Under the direct costing system, most of the fixed expenses would not be included in inventory and so accounted for on the balance sheet. By definition, they are incurred to put the business in the position of being ready to produce. Theoretically, they are not incurred to manufacture a specific quantity of a specific product decided on for a specific

ABSORPTION COST METHOD

	Jan.	Feb.	Mar.	Total Quarter
Sales in Units	200,000	250,000	150,000	600,000
Sales in Dollars (@ 1.15 ea.)	$230,000	$287,500	$172,500	$690,000
*Mfg. Cost of Sales (@ .90 ea.)	$180,000	$225,000	$135,000	$540,000
Gross Profit Margin	$ 50,000	$ 62,500	$ 37,500	$150,000
Fixed Sell. & Adm. Expense	$ 20,000	$ 20,000	$ 20,000	$ 60,000
Net Pre-tax Profit	$ 30,000	$ 42,500	$ 17,500	$ 90,000
% Profit to Sales	13.0%	14.8%	10.1%	13.0%

FIXED COST METHOD

	Jan.	Feb.	Mar.	Total Quarter
Sales in Units	200,000	250,000	150,000	600,000
Sales in Dollars (@ 1.15 ea.)	$230,000	$287,500	$172,500	$690,000
Variable Mfg. Cost (@ .75 ea.)	$150,000	$187,500	$112,500	$450,000
Fixed Mfg. Cost	$ 30,000	$ 30,000	$ 30,000	$ 90,000
Total Mfg. Cost	$180,000	$217,500	$142,500	$540,000
Gross Profit Margin	$ 50,000	$ 70,000	$ 30,000	$150,000
Fixed Sell. & Adm. Expense	$ 20,000	$ 20,000	$ 20,000	$ 60,000
Net Pre-tax Profit	$ 30,000	$ 50,000	$ 10,000	$ 90,000
% Profit to Sales	13.0%	17.4%	5.8%	13.0%

Effect of Sales Volume on Fixed Cost Absorption

	Jan.	Feb.	Mar.	Total Quarter
% Fixed Mfg. Cost to Sales	13.0%	10.4%	17.4%	13.0%
% Fixed Sell. & Adm. Expense to Sales	8.7%	7.0%	11.6%	8.7%
% Total Fixed Cost to Sales	21.7%	17.4%	29.0%	21.7%

*Variable portion @ .75 ea.
Fixed portion allocated @ .15 ea. based on normal volume of 200,000 pcs./mo.

Exhibit 29

**Comparison of Absorption vs. Direct Costing
as Affected by Changes in Sales Volume**

period. Therefore, they would be reincurred each period, regardless of the level of production. Variable costs are the current costs of production, and are incurred only as production occurs.

Fixed factory overhead expenses are excluded from product costs and are charged to revenue in the period in which they are incurred.

Only direct material, direct labor, and other variable factory costs are charged to product, and hence to inventory and cost of sales.

Exhibit 29 is a tabular example of how costs and profits vary with sales volume. It shows the effect on the profit and loss statement of standard versus actual and also shows how the profits can be overstated or understated by absorption costing versus direct costing. One of the arguments for this type of presentation is that it is easier to understand than the conventional statement with its volume variance concept.

The model of an income and expense statement (Exhibit 29) showing the absorption cost method is incorrect as applied to a business entity, as it does not include the manufacturing variance. The income and expense statement correctly prepared under the absorption cost method is illustrated in Exhibit 30. The omission of the manufacturing variance factor in Exhibit 29 was intentional. Firstly, it more clearly reveals the basic difference between the two methods; secondly, the manufacturing variance can readily be assigned to the total factory, but cannot be, without great difficulty, relegated to product lines or units.

Exhibit 29 covers the first three months of the year and the total for the first quarter. The month of January is based on the same sales volume as shown on the breakeven chart, Exhibit 28. For this month, the gross margin contribution and the profit is the same for both the absorption and the fixed cost method. The month of February shows an increase in sales volume of 50,000 units over January, which results in a $7,500 overabsorption of fixed expense, and an understatement of gross profit. The month of March shows a decrease in sales of 50,000 units from January, which results in a $7,500 underabsorption of fixed expense and an overstatement of gross profit. With January at standard volume, February at 50,000 units higher, and March 50,000 units lower, the total quarter would again show the same results under both systems, just as in January. Under the conventional method of preparing an income statement for a total business entity, the $7,500 would in both cases be identified as the manufacturing variation from standard. In Exhibit 30, the month of March is used as the example.

ADVANTAGES OF DIRECT COSTING

The direct costing system has considerable merit in the areas of flexible budgets, marginal income analysis, profit contribution by product category, and better relation between cost and revenue during the time period in which related costs and revenues are experienced.

The prime advantage claimed for direct costing is the clarity in which the cost-volume-price relationships can be expressed in the formal accounting statements. Such statements would show that sales minus variable cost of sales equals "marginal contribution," or the amount available for fixed expenses and profit. The sale of a unit of product is considered not to contain a profit in itself but to contribute toward profit, after overhead costs are paid. Fluctuations in inventory, under this concept, would not affect reported profits, which must necessarily move in the same direction as sales if standards are met and variances are constant.

Direct costing should improve cost control by making the application of responsiblity accounting and flexible budgets more clear-cut.

When fixed manufacturing expenses, such as executive salaries, depreciation, and insurance are allocated to productive cost centers, responsibility for the control of these expenditures can be diluted. In a large multi-plant manufacturing company using absorption standard costs and flexible budgets, let us assume that there is a large staff of engineers and expeditors at headquarters. These costs would be distributed to each plant and finally to each productive cost center in order to get them into the unit standard product cost for inventory valuation. When monthly statements are reviewed, each plant manager might dispute the size of this charge, and the controller would probably have to defend the expense and the basis for the allocation. This situation could possibly create just enough of a diversion to take the pressure off the plant managers in other matters closer to their responsibility.

Conversely, when a company introduces a direct standard cost system, it should no longer be necessary to allocate these fixed expenses to the plants and productive centers. They would be shown as the direct responsibility of the headquarters executive in charge of manufacturing. This might lead to a staff reduction or some degree of decentralization which might result in overall saving to the company. Responsibility accounting with direct costs should provide for more effective action at the point where the expense is incurred. Naturally, the assignment of responsibility for all costs may require judgment to be exercised in classifying costs as fixed or variable. While the classification process may, on occasion, be inexact, the clarity of the analysis and the insights obtained more than compensate for the inexactitude.

Another area where direct costing might improve the lines of responsibility is in the analysis of variance from profit plan due to sales volume, price, and product mix. This variance can easily result in a balancing figure, which is no one's responsibility although it is possible that it may result in the largest variance on the report.

With direct costing this problem is minimized, because there should be no manufacturing volume variance. The sales performance can be analyzed each month in terms of variance due to sales volume, prices, product mix, and control of expenses.

DISADVANTAGES OF DIRECT COSTING

Costs which are considered independent of production activity are classified as fixed expenses and are accounted for when they are incurred. In the attempt to establish a case for direct costing, it has been contended that these fixed expenses are not costs of production, but expenses of maintaining a facility to do business. Here, one could ask if the term "direct costing" might not be a misnomer. If variability of the cost determines its classification, we have not necessarily included all costs which are directly applicable to manufacturing a product, such as the salary of the supervisor of the department making the product, and many other "fixed" expenses which would be discontinued quickly if production were to cease even for a short time.

This objection is overcome by direct cost proponents by classifying costs as direct or period based on the analysis being performed or the decision being made. Thus, in the preceding analysis, were a product line profitability study being made, the supervisor's salary would be variable if only one product were made in the department, and semi-variable or fixed if more than one were being manufactured. The decision as to whether the supervisor's salary would be semi-variable would depend on whether an additional supervisor would have to be added or eliminated as volume varied. These are possibly capricious judgments and, at best, subjective. They make direct cost analyses subject to dispute in critical management overviews.

It is much simpler to analyze sales performance and margin contribution under direct costing. However, this simplicity has its pitfalls. Direct costing tends, in fact, to oversimplify the complex cost relationships which actually exist. Many costs do not vary with production as much as they do with order size, number of customers, and inventory policy. Fixed costs are seldom 100% fixed. The longer the time period involved, the more variable they become. In the direct or variable costing application of contribution analysis to the pricing function, the limitations of the method must be recognized. Marginal business accepted at a lower price, based on an incomplete contribution analysis, may require enough additional variable expense for supervision, overtime premium, and other items that it would make no contribution to the original fixed expenses and result in a reduction of profit.

In actual practice, the classification of period costs as time-dependent rather than production-dependent might not be considered entirely realistic. Without the start of production, these costs would never have been committed in the first place. The cessation of production would result in their speedy elimination. Therefore, in actual origin even period costs are a function of production more than of time. Should a facility be reduced to zero volume, the only remaining period or fixed costs would probably be insurance, taxes, and plant protection. Under direct costing only direct material, direct labor, and other variable factory costs are charged to product and hence to inventory. Conversely, most of the fixed expenses would not be included in inventory, and thus would not be accounted for on the balance sheet. In the case of highly mechanized operations, there may be such a large amount of fixed expenses that the practice of carrying inventory at only variable costs could possibly vitiate the conventional concept of inventory valuation.

ABSORPTION COSTING IN A NUTSHELL

Under full absorption costing, all manufacturing expenses are considered to be costs of production. Therefore, the product costs which are compiled include all variable costs plus an applicable portion of fixed expenses. Inventories and costs of sales are charged on this full cost basis. Standard full absorption costs would include fixed expenses in product costs at a predetermined rate, based on a predetermined "standard" or "normal" production volume (or level) of activity. It is recognized that most fixed expenses do not vary proportionately with the rate of activity. The unit cost, therefore, is influenced by the volume chosen as a base for allocation purposes. Selection of this volume base is very important, but to some degree it must be a subjective decision.

With this method, there is necessarily a manufacturing variance item on the income statement, for over or under-absorbed fixed expense which results mainly from volume variations. When production is at a higher level than normal, it will create over-absorbed fixed expenses which appear as a variance from standard (manufactured gain). Conversely, with lower than normal production, failure to absorb fixed costs will also show up in the manufacturing variance figure (manufacturing loss). Since inventory is valued at the more consistent standard costs, the manufacturing variance actually results as a period charge.

Cost of Production Statement March 19xx

Direct Materials Used	$50,000	
Indirect Materials Used	4,000	
Direct Labor	40,000	
Indirect Labor	5,000	
Fuel, Power & Water	10,000	
Depreciation, Taxes & Insurance	11,000	
Total Actual Cost of Production	$120,000	
Standard Cost Value of Production	112,500	
Manufacturing Variance from Standard	(7,500)	(a)

Cost of Sales Statement March 19xx

Standard Cost Value of Goods Sold	$120,000	
Packaging Materials Used	7,000	
Shipping and Delivery Costs	8,000	
Total Normal Delivered Cost	$135,000	(b)
Manufacturing Variance from Standard	7,500	(a)
Total Actual Cost of Sales	$142,500	(c)

Income & Expense Statement March 19xx

Total Gross Sales	$175,000	
Less Discounts & Allowances	2,500	
Net Sales	$172,500	
Standard Cost of Value of Goods Sold (Delivered)	$135,000	(b)
Manufacturing Variance from Standard	7,500	(a)
Total Actual Cost of Sales	$142,500	(c)
Gross Profit on Sales	30,000	
Selling Expense	$ 9,000	
General Administrative	5,000	
Research and Engineering	6,000	
Total Actual Operating Expenses	$ 20,000	
Net Profit Before Tax	$ 10,000	
Provisions for Federal Tax	5,000	
Net Profit	$ 5,000	

Exhibit 30

APPLICATION OF FULL ABSORPTION COSTING
USING A CONVENTIONAL STANDARD COST SYSTEM

A standard cost is the normal or expected manufacturing cost of a product unit as determined by past experience and expected performance.

In developing the standard cost for a product item, the amount of direct materials needed for the completed unit is determined by actually measuring the amount of the direct material in the complete item.

To the direct materials is added the direct labor applied to making the item. Direct labor used in the standard is determined by the rate of pay for each job, the necessary crew, and the speed at which each operation should be performed.

In addition to the direct material and direct labor a certain proportion of the fixed expense or overhead of the factory is charged to each item. Fixed or indirect expenses usually consist of supervision, light, power, repairs, supplies, depreciation, taxes, and insurance. These expenses will have been accumulated in separate accounts and then spread back to each department in the factory. A rate per hour of operation for each machine or each line can then be determined. In some departments, where machine hours do not govern production, fixed expense might be calculated on the basis of a percentage of the direct labor. When the overhead fixed expense per hour is established, it can be applied to the product item by using the budgeted or normal production per hour.

Each of the total number of individual product units manufactured during the month should then be multiplied by its standard cost to obtain the total cost the factory should have incurred during the month. This total standard cost, compared with the actual costs and expenses which the factory *did* incur, will give the manufacturing variation from normal which the factory incurred from the month's operations.

Exhibit 30 is a simple example of three major financial statements which illustrate the mechanics of the manufacturing variance in profit and loss calculation. In the *Cost of Production Statement,* the total actual cost for the month is greater than the standard or normal value of the production. This resulted in a manufacturing loss. The volume of sales of product units for this month was lower than the sales volume orginally estimated and used as the basis for the spread of fixed expenses. The unabsorbed fixed expenses, therefore, appear as a manufacturing loss. The total actual cost of production represents the actual costs for the period. The standard cost value is obtained by extending the product units manufactured by their individual standard costs from production reports.

In the *Cost of Sales Statement*, the total normal delivered cost is arrived at by adding the actual cost of shipping to the standard cost value of the ware sold. The manufacturing loss, as determined in the *Cost of Production Statement,* is added to the total normal delivered cost to obtain the total actual cost of sales for the month. The standard cost value of sales is obtained by extending the product units sold by their individual standard costs from the office copy of customer invoices or ware out of inventory reports. The manufacturing variance used in the *Cost of Sales Statement* can be taken from the cost of production calculation, because the normal value of production, sales, and inventory is based on the same consistent standard cost. The manufacturing gain or loss, therefore, results as a period charge, and the same figure is used in both statements.

On the *Income and Expense Statement*, the total cost of sales (taken from the *Cost of Sales Statement*) is deducted from the total net sales to obtain the gross profit margin. The gross profit margin was enough to absorb the total selling and administrative expenses and provide a net profit.

The code letters *a, b,* and *c* are shown opposite those figures which are related in the three statements.

The standard cost is also used to determine whether or not a product or product line is profitable to make. If the standard cost is compared with the selling price, it is possible to determine to some extent whether or not the gross margin is large enough to absorb the selling and administrative expense which is estimated to be applicable against the particular item. This operating expense is usually very difficult to allocate to specific product items, and in many cases is distributed to individual standard costs on an overall percentage basis. (Total operating expense as a per cent of total manufacturing cost for one year experience.)

Standard costs are used to value the inventories of products on hand. Among other things, they determine the amount of property taxes and insurance. Furthermore, as a valuation of inventories they affect the determination of the value of the company assets. This not only is reflected in the net worth of the company, but is also reflected in the profit or loss and cash position reported for any period.

ADVANTAGES OF ABSORPTION COSTING

At the present time, absorption costing, more than direct costing, seems to be the more acceptable and conventional system. This is especially true in the areas of inventory valuation for balance sheet purposes and property taxes, pricing decisions, and tax accounting, but not for profitability evaluations of products and product lines.

Advocates of absorption costing consider fixed expenses as contributing to production to the limit of the utilized capacity to produce. Fixed expenses relating to idle capacity result in a volume gain or loss which they feel is important to measure. Backers of this system believe that if fixed expenses are not absorbed in the product unit cost, it is difficult to show net profits by products or customer and ware classes. Without these net profit figures, it is difficult to make full appraisal of operating results for management decisions.

DISADVANTAGES OF ABSORPTION COSTING

In the application of absorption costing theory, one of the most difficult problems is in allocating fixed manufacturing costs to production units. Because many fixed manufacturing costs cannot always readily be related to specific units of production, allocation relies on assumptions which cannot possibly be completely accurate. In addition, since many fixed manufacturing expenses do not vary with production, it is necessary to establish a level of activity upon which to base the allocations. The resulting product cost and gross margin figures are correct only for the standard volume and consequently must be considered in forecasting costs and profits at other volumes.

Fixed expenses allocated on the basis of a predetermined volume result in under or over-absorption of costs. This has created the problem of accounting for and analyzing such over and under-absorbed balances. Although most simple breakeven charts and schedules show this manufacturing variance as changes in volume, in actuality there are other contributing factors, such as gains or losses in standard efficiencies and budgets.

"Pure" absorption costing usually does not provide variable versus fixed cost information or marginal contribution data. The lack of this information could result in a decision not to make and sell a product because the price is lower than total cost, although a more complete analysis might indicate that the product would make a satisfactory marginal contribution.

CONCLUSIONS

From a practical point of view, all costs incurred by a business are intended to produce sales and profits. In strict theory, therefore, all costs attach to the product or service that provides the sales and profits from which costs are recoverable. And, in any long-run analysis, *all* costs are variable.

The separation of fixed and variable costs has been stressed as the principal characteristic of direct costing. Many of the examples contrasting direct costing with absorption costing which have appeared in articles and texts imply that costs are not separated into fixed and variable elements under absorption costing. This is not the case in many companies which employ the standard full absorption costing system. There is nothing inherent in the absorption costing method which prohibits the separation of costs according to cost behavior. Furthermore, a substantial number of companies feel that this separation is necessary for adequate product costing purposes under absorption costing.

It is true that many companies more conventionally charge some or all fixed manufacturing costs to product without separating costs into fixed and variable elements. Because the most effective methods of absorption costing have not always been followed, this does not necessarily justify the replacement of an inadequate absorption costing system by a direct costing system. It might be better to improve the present system and introduce direct costing principles into it.

A combination of these two systems, which permits consideration of both of these two basic cost functions—related to each other but placed in their proper perspective— would lead to better decisions in both the pricing and selling areas. Moreover, the coding of expenses into fixed and variable categories, even if not introduced formally into the accounting system, would allow these expenses to be retrieved for off-line direct cost analysis.

There are many management problems which relate to the cost accounting function. Let us consider a well-managed and progressive company which has just built a new factory. The new plant is not only more modern and efficient than their existing older plant, but also its manufacturing operations are highly automated. Plant "A", the old plant, and plant "B", the new plant, both make essentially the same products, although within their product mix there is a considerable variation in profit margin between various product items. Under the direct costing method, it appears that the variable cost per unit of any given product is much lower in the new plant than the old. Conversely, the fixed costs per period are much higher in the new plant than in the old. Obviously, the substitution of automatic machinery and its accompanying high indirect costs for direct labor and its comparatively low direct costs is the reason for this loss of relative cost comparison for the same product between the two plants.

If the individual product costs contain only the variable or prime costs, an analysis by the pricing department, the sales department, and management might infer that it would be more profitable to schedule all production in the new plant. They might even feel that selling prices could be reduced because of this lower prime cost and resultant higher margin contribution.

Under absorption costing, the total cost of an individual product in the new plant might be higher than the same product in the old plant. Using this method it might appear that it would be more profitable to schedule all production in the old plant. It can even lead to decisions to attempt price increases or discontinuance of product lines. In practice, however, it might be best to obtain more sales for the new plant and let the increased volume take care of the higher period costs accruing from the automated and more efficient facilities.

When determining product unit cost, there is no apparent conflict between absorption costing and direct costing insofar as direct labor, direct material, and all variable manufacturing expenses are concerned. It is the disposition of fixed manufacturing expenses that is primarily in dispute.

Keep in mind that fixed manufacturing expenses in most companies account for a comparatively large part of the total cost of production. This kind of expense is growing because of increasing automation. In future years it is possible that fixed manufacturing expenses will exceed the variable cost as presently defined. With some industries this is probably already the case. The time is not distant when machines will perform a good deal of the manual work presently performed by workers. Because of the ever-increasing proportion of so-called fixed cost to the total cost, a thoughtful appraisal of the "pure" direct costing theory is indicated.

There is considerable controversy as to the real differences between direct costing and absorption costing systems. It might be more rewarding to concentrate on the identification, separation, understanding, and control of the various cost elements—such as fixed versus variable—and to seek a realistic compromise or combination of the two methods which would satisfy the needs and objectives of your own company.

RECOMMENDATIONS

The examination of both systems reveals that there are distinct disadvantages to the exclusive use of either "pure" direct costing or "pure" absorption costing. There are indications that, in practical application, many companies have found it necessary to supplement pure direct costing by allocating fixed expenses. Other companies using absorption costing have had to make additional analyses of their period costs.

ITEM NO. 123A SIZE 2 × 4

DESCRIPTION PRODUCT A B C D

STANDARD QUANTITY 10,000

FIGURED BY C.J.B.

DATE 3-5-XX

Dept. No.	Operation	Std. pcs. per hour	Dir. lbr. cost per hour	Prepar- ation and job change cost per Std. run	Prepar- ation and job change cost per C pcs.	Dir. lbr. cost per C pcs.	Dir. matl. cost per C pcs.	Variable machine & overhead cost per hr.	Variable machine & overhead cost per C pcs.	Standard spoilage cost per %	Standard spoilage cost per C pcs.	Total direct cost per C pcs.	Fixed machine & overhead cost per hr.	Fixed machine & overhead cost per C pcs.	Accum. total mfg. cost per C pcs.
	Material						3.00					3.00		.25	3.25
A	#1	1000	8.00	100	1.00	.80		15	1.50	5	.17	3.47	5	.50	7.22
B	#2	500	5.25	36	.36	1.05		13	2.60	10	.80	4.81	5	1.00	13.03
C	#3	750	3.50	16	.16	.47		11	1.47	2	.27	2.37	5	.66	16.06
D	#4 Pack	750	1.50			.20	2.00	7	.93	3	.50	3.63	5	.67	20.36
	Total direct cost by cost band				1.52	2.52	5.00		6.50		1.74	17.28		3.08	20.36
	TOTAL FULL MANUFACTURING COST														20.36
	Fixed selling and promotion expense @ 15% of manufacturing cost														3.05
	Fixed general administrative expense @ 10% of manufacturing cost														2.04
	TOTAL STANDARD COST PER C PCS.														25.45

Exhibit 31

The choice should not be between a "right" and "wrong" cost accounting plan. Management should not have to choose between them, to live with the disadvantages of one in order to secure the advantages of the other. Direct and absorption costing are not really incompatible, but are complementary to each other. It may be more practical to combine direct and absorption costing into one total system.

Exhibit 31 is a rough example of how a standard cost card for a product unit could be prepared with separate cost bands organized to satisfy both direct costing and full absorption requirements.

Exhibit 31 is only one example of how standard costs can be computed. Naturally, the actual design and makeup of such a cost card should reflect your own company policy and corporate attitude.

This type of standard cost calculation would permit the costing of inventories, cost of production, and cost of sales by total direct cost only, total full manufacturing cost and/or total all cost including selling and administrative expense.

Inventories could be costed at the full manufacturing cost. Cost of production could be costed at the direct or variable cost only and the actual fixed costs charged on a period basis, thus eliminating the manufacturing variance. The separation of the basic cost categories (Exhibit 31) should be valuable to the pricing and selling functions, since the overhead and profit contribution can readily be determined.

COST CONTROL CONCEPTS

1. Financial analysis for decison making relies heavily upon cost accounting intelligence in most companies, particularly when dealing with specific products, product lines, facilities, or any other segment of the total entity.

2. Because of the influence of manufacturing or sales volume upon costs and profits, the type of cost accounting system employed is of prime importance.

3. There are many methods, concepts, and variations of cost accounting systems. The major differences seem to fall into one of two categories, direct costing versus full absorption costing. In either case it is necessary to categorize and separate cost functions between "fixed" expenses and "variable" costs.

4. It is believed that this problem could be resolved by combining the two techniques in such a manner as to obtain the advantages of both. Exhibit 31 suggests how this could be accomplished.

CHAPTER 6

Distribution Cost and Profitability Review by Products

It is necessary to review product lines for possible addition or discontinuance on the basis of profit potential and margin contributions.

There is considerable evidence that a substantial proportion of the consumer's dollar goes to pay for the cost of marketing goods. Some type of distribution cost analysis and product profitability study should be employed to stabilize and control marketing cost per unit.

Such analysis might be carried out in special studies by marketing analysts, operations research teams, or controllers' staff groups. However, it probably would be much more effective if it could be incorporated in the regular cost accounting procedure.

Analyses of distribution costs and product profitability might lead to improved profits through raising selling prices or dropping unprofitable business. Conversely, the profit picture might be improved by lowering selling prices on high profit business when it results in greater volume and strengthened competitive position. In either case, appropriate analyses will assist management in establishing policies and initiating appropriate actions.

The direct cost concepts introduced in the previous chapter are used in these analyses.

125

DEFINITION OF DISTRIBUTION COSTS

In general, we might say that there are two basic kinds of costs: the cost to make the product, or the manufacturing cost, and the cost to get it into the customer's hands, or the distribution cost. Costs such as salesmen's salaries, commissions, bonuses, travel and entertainment expense, sales conventions, branch sales office expense, delivery expense, supplementary warehouses, sales promotion, and advertising are clean-cut examples of dsitribution cost. In the factory cost area, some controversy might be encountered. Such functions as job change cost, production scheduling, order processing, billing, price estimating, warehousing, and shipping are considered as distribution costs by some authorities. In most companies which employ standard full absorption cost methods, these costs are presently handled as plant overhead and distributed to the variable or direct costs on a percentage or other spread basis. In other companies, they may be included with other fixed factory costs on a period basis.

Distribution cost might reasonably be separated into two broad categories:

1. Costs incurred in obtaining a sales order.
2. Costs incurred because a sales order is received.

Although both categories deal pretty much with fixed costs, there is a degree of variability in many cases. In addition, many distribution costs are incremental, particularly in the first category.

DISTRIBUTION COST REDUCTION

An obvious method of improving profits in the distribution cost area might appear to be the reduction of selling costs. There seems to be a typical sales phenomenon in most large companies particularly, that somewhere between 70% and 85% of the total product volume is apparently being sold to between 15% and 25% of the customers. When this is the case, it might imply that 50% to 75% of the accounts being called on are too small to warrant a salesman's time and expense. Perhaps the further implication might be that the sales force should be cut in half. By taking this kind of cost reduction approach without proper analysis, a company might be commencing a program to economize itself right out of business. Mere cost-cutting is not the only way to improve profitability. Rather, it might be well to make comprehensive distribution analyses and market research studies to help the sales organization be more effective. Higher sales volume, more selective selling, better utilization of salesmen's time and effort, reconstruction of sales territories, use of manufacturer representatives and outside distributors in low productive geographical areas, and many other approaches might do much more to enhance profits and stimulate growth.

Because the characteristics of those distribution costs, which include channels of distribution, territories and salesmen, products, and physical distribution are usually quite different between different industries and even different companies in the same industry, this chapter will emphasize the problems inherent in small volume orders as they affect many manufacturing companies. Small customers and small orders so often turn out to be the single biggest problem and affect all the other distribution functions.

The small order problem is of particular significance in either or both of the following two types of manufacturing plants:

1. Plants which manufacture highly diversified types of products and product lines.
2. Plants which manufacture a line of products which are made to individual customer's designs and specifications.

In either case, there will be items ordered in small quantities which cannot be carried in stock, and hence must be manufactured in small runs.

THE SMALL ORDER PROBLEM

In analyzing the profitability or unprofitability of customers, product lines, products, sales territories, salesmen, factories, divisions, geographic areas, et cetera, it seems that small volume customers and small orders invariably cause more of a problem of higher distribution and manufacturing costs than the selling price, or even the overhead absorption contribution, can recover. This is mainly because so much of the "overhead" expense is actually related to the number of orders and customers rather than to the sales dollar volume. It is not uncommon to find numerous invoices where the paperwork cost alone of processing the order and invoice was greater than the sales value of the billing. In most cases, it takes just as much clerical time and forms to process a $5 order as a $5,000 order. It also takes just as long and costs just as much to change dies or set up a line of machines to run a five-piece job as a 5,000-piece job. The small order penalty in the cost per unit is obvious.

It is an accepted fact that small orders and small volume customers are an obvious cause of high distribution costs in many manufacturing companies. It is an equally accepted fact that small order losses cannot be entirely eliminated either by raising prices or dropping unprofitable customers. The important thing is that management be informed of which types of products and which sizes of customers and orders are unprofitable. Further, management should be informed as to what elements of cost are involved, to what degree, and what remedial action, if any, could be taken. The identification of order size to customers and products is of major importance in such an analysis. The experience of many companies which have attacked the small order problem successfully is evidence that numerous approaches are open and that the problem is not unsolvable.

ANALYZING SMALL ORDER COSTS

A common sense approach should be employed in making this type of analysis, and the technique or procedure followed should be as simple as possible, at least for the first general survey. After the initial study, use of statistical formulas to determine economic lot size might be indicated. Also, the separation between manufacturing costs and distribution costs should be undertaken and special analyses readily obtained.

For the first step, it is suggested that a simple tabulation be made of orders or invoices by "size of order" category. A sample of what this might look like is depicted in Exhibit 32.

From Exhibit 32 the following information is immediately noted:

November, 19XX

Size of Order	No. of Orders	% of Total Orders	Sales Value	% of Total Sales	Avg. Sales Value/Order
Under $10	477	17.2	$ 2,599	.3	5.45
$10 to $25	462	16.8	8,607	1.0	18.63
$25 to $50	558	20.3	21,059	2.4	37.74
$50 to $100	388	14.1	29,798	3.4	76.80
$100 to $200	151	5.5	23,450	2.7	155.30
$200 to $500	156	5.7	50,039	5.7	320.76
$500 to $1,000	209	7.6	163,559	18.7	782.58
Over $1,000	352	12.8	576,588	65.8	1,638.03
	2,753	100.0	$ 875,699	100.0	$ 318.09

Exhibit 32

Sales Analysis
Order Size vs. Sales Volume

1. 84.5% of the total sales volume is accounted for by only 20.4% of the number of orders.
2. Conversely, 34.0% of the total number of orders only accounts for 1.3% of the total sales volume.
3. The average sales value of 17.2% of the orders is only $5.45 each.
4. The average sales value of 12.8% of the orders is $1,638.03.

The next step might be to determine the total cost per month of those distribution costs, which could be considered in direct ratio to the number of orders handled. This would include the marginal or direct costs of warehouse and shipping cost, job change cost, order processing department, scheduling department, billing department, price estimating department, etc. This total cost figure could then be divided by the total number of orders processed per month. For illustration, let us say that this cost totals $40,000 per month, which divided by 2,753 orders averages $14.53 per order for the factory portion of distribution cost alone. It is readily apparent, then, that those orders in the "order size" category which average $5.45 are obviously unprofitable.

A similar type of analysis as shown in Exhibit 32 can be made for number of customers versus annual sales volume, broken down by sales volume categories. Exhibit 33 illustrates what this might look like.

Here we see that 20% of the customers contribute 75% of the sales volume. In most companies, it will be found that the small orders as shown in Exhibit 32 will be identified with the small volume customers.

In this case, it might be determined what the total cost per month is of those distribution costs which relate to customers. This would include the marginal or escapable portion of branch office expense, salesmen's remuneration, travel and entertainment expense, and all other direct sales solicitation expense. In this situation, however, rather than determine an average cost per customer, it might be more accurate to allocate the actual sales solicitation expense to the specific customers. This could be based on analysis of salesmen's "call" reports, or at least, salesmen's estimates.

At this point, if there is evidence that a small order problem exists, the analyses as illustrated in Exhibits 32 and 33 might be expanded to include a breakdown of sales by product line. If we have a profit and loss statement by product line, the three types of data might then be correlated so that the direction of further analysis can be determined.

12 Months 19XX

Annual Sales Volume Category	No. of Customers	Sales Volume	Avg. Sales per Customer	% Customers to Total	% Volume to Total
Under $4,000	310	$ 353,324	$ 1,140	79.7	24.8
$4,000 to $5,000	16	69,392	4,337	4.1	4.8
$5,000 to $7,500	24	149,431	6,226	6.2	10.4
$7,500 to $10,000	11	98,898	8,991	2.8	6.9
$10,000 to $15,000	13	156,036	12,003	3.3	10.9
$15,000 to $25,000	9	177,036	19,671	2.3	12.4
$25,000 to $50,000	5	194,028	38,806	1.3	13.5
Over $50,000	1	232,779	232,779	.3	16.3
	389	$1,430,924	$ 3,678	100.0	100.0

Exhibit 33

Sales Analysis
Number of Customers vs. Annual Volume

DISTRIBUTION EXPENSE APPLIED TO STANDARD COSTS

The analyses as depicted in Exhibits 32 and 33 have pointed out that a large proportion of the number of customers and orders bring in only a minor portion of the total sales volume. This in itself would not necessarily mean that this portion of the business is automatically unprofitable. However, distribution costs generally are related to the *number* of customers and orders rather than to the actual dollar sales. In many companies, job change cost and other factory distribution expense are handled as fixed or

Article No. _____ Size _____ Order Quantity 10,000   Date Figured _____
Description _____ Starting Quantity 12,300   Figured By _____

Dept. No.	Operation	Standard Production Per Hour	Job Change Cost Hours	Job Change Cost $ Amt	Job Change Cost Per C Pcs.	Direct Labor Cost Hour	Direct Labor Cost Per C Pcs.	Mach & O.H. Cost Hour	Mach & O.H. Per C Pcs.	Distr. Portion Of Factory O.H. Factory Order	Distr. Portion Of Factory O.H. C Pcs.	Material Cost Per C Pcs.	Standard Spoilage %	Standard Spoilage Cost Per C Pcs.	Accum. Total Cost Per C Pcs.
—	Material									25.00	.25	3.00			3.25
A	#1	1,000	5	100	1.00	8.00	.80	20	2.00				5	.17	7.22
B	#2	500	2	36	.36	5.25	1.05	18	3.60				10	.80	13.03
C	#3	750	1	16	.16	3.50	.47	16	2.13				2	.27	16.06
D	#4 Pack	750				1.50	.20	12	1.60			2.00	3	.50	20.36
	Total Manufacturing Cost				1.52	—	2.52	—	9.33	—	.25	5.00	—	1.74	20.36

	% Mfg. Cost	Cost/CPcs.
General Selling Expense	15%	3.05
General Administrative Overhead	10%	2.04
Total Standard Cost per 100 Pcs.		25.45
Suggested Selling Price per 100 Pcs.		32.00

Exhibit 34

Article No. _____ Size _____ Order Quantity 500   Date Figured _____

Description _____ Starting Quantity 615   Figured By _____

Dept. No.	Operation	Standard Production Per Hour	Job Change Cost Hours	Job Change Cost $ Amt.	Job Change Cost Per C Pcs.	Direct Labor Cost Hour	Direct Labor Cost Per C Pcs.	Mach & O.H. Cost Hour	Mach & O.H. Cost Per C Pcs.	Distr. Portion Of Factory O.H. Factory Order	Distr. Portion Of Factory O.H. C Pcs.	Material Cost Per C Pcs.	Standard Spoilage %	Standard Spoilage Cost Per C Pcs.	Accum. Total Cost Per C Pcs.
—	Material									25.00	5.00	3.00			8.00
A	#1	1,000	5	100	20.00	8.00	.80	20	2.00				5	.42	31.22
B	#2	500	2	36	7.20	5.25	1.05	18	3.60				10	3.47	46.54
C	#3	750	1	15	3.20	3.50	.47	16	2.13				2	.95	53.29
D	#4 Pack	750				1.50	.20	12	1.60			2.00	3	1.65	58.74
Total Manufacturing Cost					30.40	—	2.52	—	9.33	—	5.00	5.00	—	6.49	58.74

	%Mfg Cost	Cost/C Pcs.
General Selling Expense	15%	8.81
General Administrative Overhead	10%	5.87
Total Standard Cost per 100 Pcs.		73.42
Suggested Selling Price per 100 Pcs.		92.00

Exhibit 35

overhead cost, and allocated to the direct or variable costs on the basis of direct labor dollars, direct labor hours, machine operating hours, etc. This results in the standard cost of small orders being understated and the cost of large orders overstated. Exhibit 34 and 35 graphically illustrate this point. These exhibits are a facsimile of a standard cost card or price estimating form and are exactly the same except that one shows an order quantity of 10,000 items and the other 500. You will note that in both cases the direct labor cost, the machine and overhead cost, and the material cost are exactly the same per unit or 100 pieces. The job change cost, the factory distribution cost and the spoilage cost are much higher *per C pieces* for the small quantity order than the large quantity order. Thus, the method of calculating these standard costs shows that the small order manufacturing cost is almost three times as much as the same item with a substantial order quantity. This method reflects the *actual cost* experience in the plant. However, if the job change cost and the factory distribution expense are included with the balance of the machine and overhead cost and prorated on the basis of pieces produced per hour, the *same* total manufacturing cost per unit figure would apply regardless of the order or run size.

Extending this disproportionate spreading of distribution costs to include customers, territories, and products could conceivably result in sales effort being concentrated on unprofitable customers, and perhaps being priced out of the more desirable business because the standard costs are overstated, thus negating the possibility of lowering selling prices to meet competition and increase volume.

The type of standard cost or cost estimate, as illustrated in Exhibits 34 and 35, should help support the Robinson-Patman Act requirements in establishing realistic quantity price differentials. Actually, if the selling prices applied to small orders are adequate to recover the cost penalties inherent in the small order, there is no reason why this type of business should not be as desirable as larger orders. Some large companies who will negotiate over a few cents differential per unit on items they purchase by the carload, *expect* to pay a premium on a small order of a non-catalog item. If they are not asked to pay a premium on a small special order, they may regard with suspicion the prices on large volume orders on the premise that small order cost penalties are probably being recovered in the selling prices of the large volume and more desirable business. Again, regardless of the circumstances, the cost accountant should be in a position to advise his management exactly what the facts are.

In the manufacturing cost determination, as demonstrated in Exhibits 34 and 35, the full absorption costing method was employed. In these examples, the direct materials, direct fabricating labor, and direct selecting and packing labor is included complete with factory overhead allocation. The full absorption product cost method was used here in order to show the full influence of the small order to the total business and the importance of recognizing this total situation in establishing pricing policies and sales direction. It also points up the fact that the type of cost accounting system can have considerable effect upon pricing and selling decisions relating not only to size of orders but to type of product. Although costs are usually recorded in any case by category such as material, labor, depreciation, taxes, etc., we are concerned here with individual product costs.

You will note, however, that the sample form provides a separation of the manufacturing cost areas which lends itself to the direct costing concept and profit margin contribution analysis. For example, the variable costs would be direct labor, job change cost, material, and spoilage. The machine and overhead cost and the distribution cost portion of the factory overhead could be considered either variable, semi-variable, or fixed, depending upon the cost accounting system of the company concerned.

The type of cost accounting system employed by any company will surely have an effect on management decisions in many areas of a business. The concept of direct costing versus absorption costing, in particular, appears to permit more incisive decision making. Chapter 5 deals exclusively with this matter in enough detail to provide adequate practical knowledge of the subject.

SELLING EXPENSE

This classification covers all other distribution costs not incurred under the manufacturing plant roof. It includes general selling expense, branch sales office, salesmen, advertising, etc. Here again, it has been common practice in many companies to find the relationship of total manufacturing cost to total selling expense for the whole company and apply it as a flat percentage to the individual product cost estimate, regardless of size of order, customer, product line, territory, etc. This practice could very well result in certain profitable sales divisions, manufacturing divisions, product lines, etc., actually subsidizing other unprofitable sections of the business, all without management being aware of the facts.

In Exhibits 34 and 35, the general selling and administrative expenses shown at the bottom of the form are operating expenses which are not incurred at the factory and would be considered as fixed, period, or committed costs in most companies.

In this particular example, the selling and administrative expenses are allocated to the product cost on a percentage of total product manufacturing cost. In actual practice, many companies do allocate these operating expenses by percentages based upon total operating expenses to total manufacturing costs by company, division, plant, product line and product at a predetermined or historical level of activity. Of course, there are numerous other ways of allocating fixed operating expenses and period costs, including the philosophy of not allocating them at all, but, rather, showing them below the contribution margin line in direct cost studies.

In this area of selling and administrative expense it might be much more feasible, and even quite satisfactory, to spread or allocate these operating expenses to individual item standard cost cards on this general percentage basis. However, this is usually a very substantial segment of a company's total cost, and probably should be analyzed in considerable depth at least annually as a special study.

Marketing research is usually specific-product oriented, and thus can be charged to a product line or group. Advertising and sales promotion, aside from total corporate image projection, are usually related to creation of demand, and it should be possible to allocate these costs also to product lines and groups.

The order-getting function usually consists of the actual costs incurred in getting an order and servicing the customer. These costs include salesmen's salaries and commissions, travel and entertainment expense, and costs of maintaining branch offices. These costs can often be related to specific customers based on salesmen's call reports or estimates of time spent. In many cases, costs identified with specific customers can be further related to products and product groups.

A typical market analysis is seen at Exhibit 36. The marketing index can usually be obtained from industry sources and serves to quantify the amount of sales which can be expected from one territory compared to every other territory in the country. Typical indexes are Sales Management magazine's BPI (Buying Power Index) or Hearst Publication's, The General Market Buying Power Index, or the NOPA Index of the National Office Products Association. Most of these indexes are weighted to reflect the market's share of national income, retail sales, factory payrolls, business offices, or other pertinent information. A company can construct its own index, based on market research, industry statistics, and judgment. On Exhibit 36, our company's sales are plotted against the index and an Index of Performance is obtained by dividing "our sales at 100%" by the "market at 100%". Market performance is, thereby, reduced to an integer for easy reference and comparative purposes to the norm of 100. In this exhibit, because the 5 boroughs and Long Island both are at 91, a further analysis should be done within the territory.

This could take the form of Exhibit 37 which compares earned commissions to sales potential and actual profits in the territory. The territory forecast column is for the entire U.S. and is based on the company's budget or operating plan. The 5.5% forecast, in this example, is an expression that the company expects the four salesmen in the 5 boroughs to meet the "marketing index" for that area. In practice, of course, the forecast could vary from the index. The column "sales per 1% of forecast" is found by dividing "actual sales" by the "U.S. territory forecast." This shows that only salesman B was above the forecast standard of $727, but A and C were well below it. Despite this, A received a 6% commission rate, higher than all the other salesmen, and his "commission earned," as a percent of all commissions earned, was 30%, the second highest. Furthermore, when compared to the "profit contribution," it is seen that his commission percent exceeded his 25% profit contribution. He is the only salesman showing that condition. The "profit contribution %" is obtained from a direct cost study of sales in that territory. In this example, it is assumed that the profit contribution is in the same percentage as actual sales to total sales. Salesman C, on the other hand, earned only a 4% commission versus the 5% standard, and while he was below the forecast sales average, he earned only 10% of total commissions paid, and his sales contributed 12.5% of total profits. Salesman B, of course, is ahead on all points, earning 4.7% commission against the 5% norm, showing $1,071 sales per 1% of forecast against the average of $727, and an earned commission of 35% against a 37.5% profit contribution.

These studies indicate that several salesmen are not performing up to others and that the commission structure is not fairly rewarding sales performance. Further studies are indicated to compare commissions and profit contribution to other salesmen in other territories. It is possible that closer attention to distribution cost control could result in decreased costs and increased profits for industry and at the same time reduce the ultimate cost of goods to the consumer.

SPECIALIZATION IN SMALL VOLUME BUSINESS

In most cases, high volume business or long runs in a factory permit high efficiencies, good volume, high overhead absorption, etc. However, high volume business has the keenest price competition. The company that deliberately decides to compete in the small order type of market can be at least as successful as the company that pursues the high volume market and turns it back on the small customer. The philosophy here is that on small runs and small orders, selling prices can usually be set high enough to at least cover all costs and overhead and still include a reasonable profit. This is usually possible because of the small size of the order. In large volume business, however, where perhaps the product is made, sold and shipped in carload lots, the price per unit becomes extremely important. Another way to look at it is that a company which deals in small orders and small customers may have to take care of 300 customers; if they lose five customers they still have two hundred and ninety-five customers left. However, where a company pretty much goes after the high volume market, perhaps only two or three customers may keep their facilities occupied. Here the loss of only one customer would bring disaster. I know of one company manufacturing specialty items which has about three hundred small customers and which produces a high quality product with machinery geared for this type of business. Time after time this company has turned down orders from large customers because it did not want to become captive to a handful of large companies, but prefers to have many small customers, thus greatly reducing the risk of not keeping its facilities fully utilized.

ANALYSIS OF THE MARKET

NYC Area	Marketing Index	Market at 100%	Our Sales $000	Our Sales at 100%	Index of Performance
5 Boroughs	5.50	44.0%	$ 4,000	40.0%	91
Long Island	2.75	22.0	2,000	20.0	91
Lower Connecticut	.75	6.0	700	7.0	117
Near New Jersey	2.25	18.0	2,000	20.0	111
Westchester County	1.25	10.0	1,300	13.0	130
TOTAL	12.50	100.0%	$10,000	100.0%	

Exhibit 36

ANALYSIS OF SALES COMMISSION TO SALES POTENTIAL AND PROFIT CONTRIBUTION

5 Boroughs Salesman	Actual Sales $000	Commission Paid $000	Commission Paid %	U.S. Territory Forecast %	Sales per 1% of forecast $000	Commission Earned %	Profit Contribution %
A	$1,000	$ 60	6.0	1.7	$ 588	30.0	25.0
B	1,500	70	4.7	1.4	1,071	35.0	37.5
C	500	20	4.0	1.0	500	10.0	12.5
D	1,000	50	5.0	1.4	714	25.0	25.0
TOTAL	$4,000	$200	5.0	5.5%	$ 727	100.0%	100.0%
TOTAL U.S.	$72,700			100.0%			

Exhibit 37

PRODUCT ANALYSIS

Some of the most important and difficult decisions that management is called upon to make concern the review of product lines for addition, deletion, or price adjustment, with regard to the diversion of capital into more productive channels.

This type of decision making requires the development of financial analyses procedures which obtain the determination of costs versus selling prices in terms of individual products. It should also obtain determination of profits by customer, by sales territory, by class of customer, by salesman, and by quantity bracket.

Many companies which show a total net profit on their conventional profit and loss statement can actually be harboring loss operations which they do not know exist. Sometimes profits in one area will offset losses in another, and vice versa. With appropriate financial analysis, management can act to capitalize on product strength, focus on profitable distribution channels or customers, and increase total operational efficiency.

QUALITY OF SALES MIX

Most published financial statements look at all the products of a business in total, and not one at a time. However, the product breakdown by group and by individual item is normally a most important and revealing analysis. It is also important to analyze customers, markets, distribution channels, and manufacturing facilities as to their current and expected contributions to profit. The marginal income or profit contribution by product reveals the favorable or unfavorable sales mixture factor and should play an important part in the analysis of customers and markets. It is possible to increase total sales and yet experience a reduction in profits because of a drop in the quality of the "sales mix." Obviously, it is important to know which products and product groups make the principal profit contributions and the relative volume of each group.

Exhibit 1 (in Chapter 1) is a monthly key report, encompassing a broad scope of information covering a total company's operations. It is suggested that this format can also be followed for major product divisions and individual plants. However, this format is not practical for analysis of products and product lines. Therefore, it is suggested that this key report be augmented by supporting detail data by product, in whatever depth is desired or feasible.

TABULATION OF DATA

Exhibits 38, 39, 40, and 41 are simplified examples of the type of information which could be prepared to assist decision making in this area. In most companies of substantial size and scope, computers would be required to produce this data in adequate accuracy, detail, and speed. Information such as sales value, standard cost, item number, item description, factory code, customer code, branch sales, and region code would be collected on punch cards or magnetic tape from each individual invoice office copy. This stored input information could be programmed so that monthly and year-to-date reports could be produced, with the information arranged for various appropriate analyses.

SALES AND COST ANALYSIS

Exhibit 38 depicts a form of sales and inventory value analysis suggested as back-up information for the key management report, illustrated by Exhibit 1. Exhibit 38 provides sales, inventory value of sales, and percent to sales by month and year-to-date. It accumulates and lists these categories by individual product items, subtotals by product line classifications, and adds down to total company. For this illustration, the inventory value of sales is the standard cost value of sales. This standard cost figure could be direct costs or total plant absorption costs, depending upon the preferences or circumstances of the company concerned. In these examples we have arbitrarily used full absorption costs, and will further assume that this standard cost figure is half direct and half variable. For convenience, a very small population of product items and product groups are used in these examples, and there is considerable exaggeration in the ratios.

This report shows that for year-to-date, product group "B" accounts for about 60% of the sales volume, and the cost ratio is 18% higher than product group "A." For the month of June, the two product groups are evenly divided in sales volume, which should result in better total profit for June than for year-to-date. Within both product groups, it is easy to see which products are the high cost items. Further analysis of the high cost ratio to sales items could provide direction in cost reduction effort, or , in some cases, possible sales price increases.

Month	June, 19xx					Year to Date 19xx		
Sales	Inventory Value	% to Sales	Product Item No.	Product Description		Sales	Inventory Value	% to Sales
$ 190,000	$152,000	80%	A-1			$1,000,000	$ 800,000	80%
10,000	7,500	75	A-2			99,000	74,250	75
200,000	110,000	55	A-3			700,000	385,000	55
—	—	—	A-4			1,000	400	40
100,000	35,000	35	A-5			700,000	245,000	35
$ 500,000	$304,500	61%	Group A	Subtotal		$2,500,000	$1,504,650	60%
$ 200,000	$170,000	85%	B-1			$ 900,000	$ 774,000	86%
50,000	40,000	80	B-2			500,000	400,000	80
150,000	126,000	84	B-3			1,300,000	1,091,350	84
100,000	60,000	60	B-4			800,000	480,000	60
$ 500,000	$396,000	79%	Group B	Subtotal		$3,500,000	$2,745,350	78%
$1,000,000	$600,000	60%	Company	Total		$6,000,000	$4,250,000	71%

Exhibit 38

Sales and Cost Analysis
By Product and Product Group

PROFIT CONTRIBUTION ANALYSIS

Exhibit 39 is similar to Exhibit 38, except it shows gross profit and is confined to year-to-date figures only. This could be by month (also similar to Exhibit 38), but, for illustrative purposes, year-to-date alone should serve the purpose. Technically, this information should be more valuable on a cumulative basis, particularly as favorable or unfavorable trends become apparent. This exhibit shows the percent of gross profit margin to sales and the percent contribution each item and product group makes in relation to the total. Gross profit margin represents the sales less the inventory or standard cost value of sales, as covered in Exhibit 38.

In Exhibit 39 we also show the two product groups as being manufactured in two different factories. For example, product "A" is manufactured in the South Bend plant. For the first six months of the year it accounted for 42% of the total sales. The gross profit for the product group and the plant was 40% of sales. The profit contribution was 57% of the total, and the biggest contributor in group "A" was product item A-5, which was 26% of the total and 46% of the product group. Product item A-4 shows a gross profit margin of 60%, which is the second highest in the line. However, the volume of this item is so small that its margin contribution to the plant and the company is practically nil. The gross profit margin for item A-1 is only 20%, but it contributes 20% of the total gross margin to the plant and product group.

PROFIT ANALYSIS BY PRODUCT AND PLANT

Exhibit 40 extends beyond sales and standard cost value of sales and allocates manufacturing variance, other cost of sales, research and development, and selling and administrative expenses to product line and plant. This permits the determination of net pre-tax profit by product, product group, and manufacturing facility. There is an assumption here that the company is able to spread these overhead costs back to the products. It is more likely that a company would be able to allocate these expenses only to product groups, departments, and plants. It is possible that in many companies such allocations could not be made in any satisfactory or equitable manner at all. For purpose of this illustration, however, we will assume that it can be done. The sales and standard cost values might be obtained direct from office copies of invoices. Manufacturing variance is assumed to be spread by each plant by analyzing and comparing actual volume, efficiency, and budget performance against standard factors. All other cost of sales could be distributed by sales volume percentage if not practicable to identify and allocate specifically by products or product groups. Research and development effort could possibly be identified by project or some other manner, and definitely allocated to specific products or product groups. In this exhibit, selling and administrative expenses were prorated to the products on the basis of sales volume percent to total. A good distribution cost control system could be used for this purpose if available.

PROFIT ANALYSIS BY PRODUCT AND SALES BRANCH

Exhibit 41 is the same as Exhibit 40, except that we have added profit after tax and percent to sales and grouped the sales by sales branch instead of product group and

Year to Date as of *June, 19xx*

Factory	Product Item No.	Product Description	Sales	% to Total Sales	Gross Profit	% to Sales	Total Contribution	Group Contribution
South Bend	A-1		$1,000,000	16%	$ 200,000	20%	12%	20%
"	A-2		99,000	2	24,750	25	1	3
"	A-3		700,000	12	315,000	45	18	31
"	A-4		1,000	—	600	60	—	—
"	A-5		700,000	12	455,000	65	26	46
"	Group A		$2,500,000	42%	995,350	40%	57%	100%
St. Louis	B-1		$ 900,000	15	$ 126,000	14%	7%	17%
"	B-2		500,000	8	100,000	20	6	13
"	B-3		1,300,000	22	208,650	16	12	28
"	B-4		800,000	13	320,000	40	18	42
"	Group B		$3,500,000	58%	$ 754,650	22%	43%	100%
Total Company			$6,000,000	100%	$1,750,000	29%	100%	—

Exhibit 39

**Gross Profit Analysis
by Product and Product Group**

Year to Date as of *June, 19xx*

Factory	Product Item No.	Product Descr.	Sales	Standard Cost	Mfg. Variance	All Other Cost of Sales	R&D	S&A	Pre-Tax Profit
South Bend	A-1		$1,000,000	$ 800,000	$ 10,900	$ 48,000	$100,000	$ 72,000	$(30,900)
"	A-2		99,000	74,250	39,000	6,000	—	9,000	(29,250)
"	A-3		700,000	385,000	20,000	36,000	—	54,000	205,000
"	A-4		1,000	400	100	—	—	—	500
"	A-5		700,000	245,000	30,000	36,000	50,000	54,000	285,000
"	Group A	Subtotal	$2,500,000	$1,504,650	$100,000	$126,000	$150,000	$189,000	$430,350
St. Louis	B-1		$ 900,000	$ 774,000	$ 25,000	$ 45,000	—	$ 67,500	$ (11,500)
"	B-2		500,000	400,000	20,000	24,000	—	36,000	20,000
"	B-3		1,300,000	1,091,350	35,000	66,000	—	99,000	8,650
"	B-4		800,000	480,000	70,000	39,000	50,000	58,500	102,500
"	Group B	Subtotal	$3,500,000	$2,745,350	$150,000	$174,000	$ 50,000	$261,000	$ 119,650
Total Company			$6,000,000	$4,250,000	$250,000	$300,000	$200,000	$450,000	$ 550,000

Exhibit 40

**Profit Analysis
by Product and Plant**

factory. For reason of brevity, we have grouped standard cost, manufacturing variance, and other cost of sales into one heading, "Total Manufacturing Cost." Research and development and selling and administrative expenses are grouped to form "Total Operating Expense." The arbitrary tax figure of 50% was used for purpose of simplification and because it is subject to change in future years from the current figures.

This is an informative and revealing report, but it is also a risky one in the area of decision making for expanding or dropping specific products. Many factors must be considered in addition to the purely statistical indicators. For example, the single largest net profit producer in ratio to sales is product item A-4 at 25%. However, the volume of this item is so small that it has practically no effect on the company's total performance. The next three highest profit performances are items A-3 at 14.6%, A-5 at 20.4%, and B-4 at 6.4%. These three items represent a total sales of $2,200,000, and net profit of $296,250 or 13.5%, three times as good as the total of all products. It appears from the figures that the company would improve its total profit picture by dropping all products except these three. At sales of $2,200,000 and related standard cost of $1,110,000, see Exhibit 40, the gross profit margin for these three items would be $1,090,000. However, the total volume variance for the company could jump from $250,000 resulting from the current total volume to as high as $1,820,000 (see Exhibit 40). This figure is based on the premise that the standard cost is 50% fixed and 50% variable. Under this hypothesis, the total fixed cost would be $2,125,000, and the three items in question would have absorbed only $555,000 of this total (50% of $1,110,000, the total standard cost of the 3 items). This $2,125,000, less $555,000 plus $250,000 would be the new volume loss of $1,820,000. Even if "all other cost of sales" and "research and development" applicable to the balance of the products are incremental, it would be unlikely that the "selling and administrative expense" could be reduced proportionately. It should be obvious that in the "two plant, two sales branch" company illustrated here, these three top profit producers need the support of the less profitable items in order to absorb overhead.

Sales Branch	Product Item No.	Product Description	Sales	Total Mfg. Cost	Total Operating Expense	Pre-Tax Profit	Net Profit	% to Sales
Chicago	A-1		$1,000,000	$ 858,900	$172,000	$(30,900)	$(15,450)	(1.5%)
"	A-3		700,000	441,000	54,000	205,000	102,500	14.6
"	A-5		700,000	311,000	104,000	285,000	142,500	20.4
"	B-1		900,000	844,000	67,500	(11,500)	(5,750)	(.6)
"	B-3		1,300,000	1,192,350	99,000	8,650	4,325	.3
"		Subtotal	$4,600,000	$3,647,250	$496,500	$456,250	$228,125	5.0%
Atlanta	A-2		$ 99,000	$ 119,250	$ 9,000	$(29,250)	$(14,625)	(14.8%)
"	A-4		1,000	500	—	500	250	25.0
"	B-2		500,000	444,000	36,000	20,000	10,000	2.0
"	B-4		800,000	589,000	108,500	102,500	51,250	6.4
"		Subtotal	$1,400,000	$1,152,750	$153,500	$ 93,750	$ 46,875	3.3%
Company		Total	$6,000,000	$4,800,000	$650,000	$550,000	$275,000	4.6%

Exhibit 41

**Profit Analysis
by Product and Sales Branch**

An analysis of item A-1 reveals that $100,000 of the total operating expense of $172,000 is research and development cost. If or when this cost is directed to other projects, the net profit would be $34,550 instead of a net loss of $15,450. This would represent a net improvement of 5% ratio to sales just by the conclusion of the development project cost. Additional profit improvement could be anticipated as accruing from the successful result of the development effort in process or product improvement.

We can expand this analysis with a report similar to that in Exhibit 42. Referring to the data in Exhibit 37 for the NYC area, we can extract the variable or direct cost information from our records and calculate the ROI for the territory. This report assumes the same 50% variable manufacturing costs from Exhibit 41, the $200 of commission expenses from Exhibit 37, together with the sales data from that exhibit, and lists the other specific variable expenses which our direct cost system has generated. Fixed or period costs are ignored, as we are examining contribution margins only.

Territorial Return on Investment

		NYC Area
Sales		$4,000
Less:	Standard Variable Manufacturing Costs	2,000
Standard Manufacturing Contribution		2,000
Less:	Specific Variable Territory Expenses:	
	Salesmen's Commissions	200
	Travel & Entertainment	75
	Branch Office Expenses	50
	Bad Debt Provision	40
	Prizes and Shows	50
	Freight out	50
		465
Territorial Contribution		1,535
Territorial Investment:		
	Accounts Receivable	1,300
	Inventory	1,300
		$2,600
Contribution as a % of Sales		38.3%
Turnover (Sales ÷ Investment)		1.54
Territorial Return on Investment		59.0%

Exhibit 42

You can see that Exhibit 42 can be prepared for each of the four salesmen in the NYC area, and a similar report could be prepared for each territory in the company. These reports could, then, be summarized for all territories in the company, in the format of Exhibit 43. This form extracts the key information for the territory from Exhibit 42 and ties-in to the company figures in Exhibit 1 of Chapter 1, using the average 6 month figures.

Territory Marketing Targets

Territory	Sales	Earnings	Investment	ROI
NYC Area	$4,000	$1,535	$ 2,600	59.0%
Other Area	1,000	282	837	33.7
Other Area	1,000	283	838	33.7
Total Company	$6,000	$2,100	$ 4,275	49.1%
All Other Expenses		1,825		
Net Income		$ 275		
All Other Assets			12,173	
Total Company Assets Employed			$16,448	
Total Company Return on Assets (annualized)				3.3%

Exhibit 43

An examination of the foregoing schedule will highlight those marketing areas which have an inadequate ROI. Any of the three factors, sales, earnings, or investment could be changed to increase the return, and further review of detailed Exhibits 32 through 38 should focus on the problem and permit remedial action.

Product line profitability studies are a useful source of input for the preparation of SEC line of business reporting required in the Form 10-K.

REMEDIAL ACTION PROGRAMS

Management attention should be directed to the profitability and volume of individual products and product groups in addition to major incremental units, especially when unfavorable "product mix" trends appear. It could be that competition may be shifting their emphasis from low margin items to high margin items in your industry through profit-oriented rather than just volume-oriented sales effort. Your company could very possibly maintain its industry position in sales volume and find their profits deteriorating. The hypothesis that if enough volume is obtained then profits will follow is only partly true. The remedies for this situation will naturally vary from company to company. There may be some cost reduction possibilities attainable in certain low margin products, both in manufacturing and distribution. I know of one company which manufactured a low margin item that amounted to a high enough volume to seriously lower the margin of the total product group. Although the sales department was instructed not to "push" this item, more and more orders were being received. Investigation revealed that competition had obviously experienced the same low margin difficulty, and most of them had discontinued the line altogether. This company decided to follow suit, but instead of officially dropping the line, they decided to raise the selling price to a figure adequate to produce a reasonable profit, but much higher than the current and historical quotations. They felt that this would produce the same result as dropping the line, as their customers would certainly not accept such a price increase. To their suprise, there was not even a tapering off of their orders. Apparently, the line had just been underpriced. The net result was the retaining of the volume with a substantial increase in profitability.

CORPORATE SURGERY

There are cases in some product lines where a company has cut costs just as much as possible and where competition precludes price increases. This can easily happen when the total supply of a commodity far exceeds the total demand. One multi-plant, multi-product company acquired a facility to manufacture a certain product as part of their diversification program. Over the years, this particular product and plant became an increasing drain on the profit return of the total company. They successively tried to cut costs by buying the latest automatic machinery, reducing capacity, and laying off workers. Results were still unsatisfactory. They finally had to close down the plant and get out of this particular business. This is a drastic move and is usually done only after all other conceivable remedies and alternatives have been exhausted.

Sometimes product items can be pruned from within product groups and produce very good results. One company which manufactures an extremely comprehensive group of products eliminated 25% of their catalog items. Some of the differences between items were of no real consequence functionally, but over the years had gathered little innovations and improvements without dropping any of the original items. Many customers had merely continued to reorder the old familiar numbers from old purchase and stores records. Better sales effort, customer education, and product standardization resulted in substantial cost reduction with no loss of sales.

MAXIMIZING PROFIT THROUGH PRODUCT DISCRIMINATION

In order to intelligently plan for profit improvement and maximum utilization of facilities, *it is necessary to review product lines for possible addition or discontinuance on the basis of profit potential and margin contributions.*

A volume item should not be discontinued because of a low profit margin unless and until another and higher contributing product can be secured to replace it. Otherwise, the overhead it absorbs would probably have to be spread over a lesser volume of the remaining products and result in a lower total net profit.

It would be equally undesirable to purchase additional equipment to continue manufacturing low margin products. It might be better not only to cut down the line, but also to retire older equipment which may be operating at a low capacity utilization with no chance of obtaining additional or higher profit business. This kind of product discrimination could even help avoid building an additional plant, which might add substantially to a company's fixed costs but produce very little additional values and revenues.

The type of financial analysis by product recommended in this chapter is designed to aid decision making but not to substitute for managerial judgment. Products which may be serving shrinking markets may be revealed by these analyses, but remedies must be found through market research, engineering research, and development resources. In some instances, selling effort can be directed to concentrate more on future important products and opportunities and less on costly attempts to revive sales of products which may have been the backbone of the company a decade ago but are now facing obsolescence. It may also be found that good solid bread and butter items in the current product lines are not exploited to obtain maximum sales and market position. In allocating the resources of a company, first priority should be accorded those areas, products, and opportunities of a company which are judged to offer the greatest potential for present and future profit and growth.

PRODUCT PROFITABILITY POINTERS

1. Distribution or marketing related costs are sometimes neglected in the area of cost reduction because of fear of reduction of sales volume. In actuality, they often prove to be one of the most fertile opportunities for profit improvement programs.

2. Small orders and small volume customers are a major problem for many companies. Losses can possibly be converted to gains by proper cost analyses which could lead to improved operating procedures, marketing practices, and pricing policies.

3. Accurate analyses of the profitability of specific products, product lines, manufacturing facilities, and marketing organizations can lead to the investment of corporate resources into those areas which produce the highest return.

4. Periodic analyses should be made to determine the relative profit contribution from the different products, customers, markets, distribution channels, and manufacturing facilities.

5. When profit deterioration areas are revealed, prompt remedial action should be taken. Such action might take the form of closing down a plant, dropping unprofitable items when possible, raising selling prices when justified, obtaining new and more modern equipment if needed, withdrawal from shrinking markets due to geographic location, and redirection of selling and promotion effort when indicated.

CHAPTER 7

Financial Analysis
for Cost Reduction

It is doubtful that there is any area of any business which does not provide some opportunity for cash reduction and profit improvement.

Cost reduction is probably one of the most important and widely used methods for obtaining profit improvement. There are cases when a company introduces a new or outstandingly superior product sufficiently ahead of the competition that it can price its product on what it is worth to the customer rather than on the cost of production or a competitor's price. In most industries, however, selling prices are pretty much established in the market place, and the profit represents the spread of the margin between the selling price and the cost. When this is the case, cost control determines profit position to a substantial degree.

Many companies have recognized the relationship between cost reduction and profit improvement and maintain such a program on a continuing basis, whether times are good or bad, to keep cost levels as low as practicable, consistent with product quality and good customer service. An effective cost reduction program enables a company not only to maintain its position, but also to increase sales and improve profits, even under highly competitive conditions.

The term cost reduction sometimes has a distasteful connotation if it brings to mind visions of arbitrary payroll cuts, impossibly tight budgets, use of cheap materials, and cutting corners on quality and service. Cost reduction as an end in itself can do much more harm than good. An organization can be adversely affected by irresponsible cost reduction. For example, the elimination or reduction of an effective staff, a dynamic sales force, or a sound advertising program can seriously hamper a company's normal growth. A better technique is to call these efforts Profit Improvement Programs (PIP).

The right kind of cost reduction can be rewarding, but the wrong kind of cost reduction can be damaging. A sound and well-planned cost control program, in which all employees are informed and motivated to participate, can result in a stronger company and better job security for everyone.

THE COST REDUCTION CONCEPT

Far too often a cost reduction program is triggered by a bad year, diminishing sales volume, deteriorating profits, loss of one or more big customers, or other adverse developments. At this point, remedies are already late and the cost-cutting effort usually becomes a crash program. Even if the trouble spots are found and corrected, this sporadic cost reduction approach often results in return to the same poor situation after the emergency has passed.

Cost reduction should be a continuing function, punctuated by a periodic tightening of existing controls. If cost reduction can help stave off losses or improve profits when business is bad, logically it can make profits even better when business is good. Excess or unnecessary cost of any kind is a form of waste and benefits no one. Cost improvement does not always mean lower costs per se. Costs should be equated with revenue. For example, more production with the same labor force might be more desirable than the same production with a reduced labor force.

PARTICIPATION IN COST REDUCTION PROGRAMS

Decision making in regard to cost improvement cannot possibly be isolated to the top management echelon. Cost control must be a team effort. All levels of management and all segments of the working force should be integrated into the program. Cost reductions in one area should not pop up as cost increases in another. Even though there is evidence that certain areas of the business contain more excess costs than others, it might be wiser not to single them out. Special effort in just a few areas can result in resentment and resistance. Company wide cost control on a continuing basis should afford a better chance for lasting improvement. Also, a company wide program can better be designed to encourage and promote the broadest participation.

In the operation of a company, various decisions are constantly made at all levels of the organization. Many of these every-day decisions affect income or cost to some degree. In this sense, practically every decision might be considered a financial decision. If this is true, a department foreman will, for all practical purposes, be making financial decisions with respect to this particular job. In most cases, top management decides when capital expenditures are to be made in order to obtain cost reductions. However, operating decisions made from day to day involving little or no additional investment can also result in substantial cost savings. This type of cost reduction is often decided by judgment instead of analysis of accounting data. There are no doubt many circumstances where the direct observations of production men prove to be the best approach to cost reduction. Even in this case, however, the accounting record of operations should be a valuable supplement. In addition, accounting people can help by assisting in the actual analyses of contemplated or proposed cost reduction measures.

Manufacturing performance can only be measured in top management reports by total company, by division, by plant, and perhaps by departments within a plant. For manufacturing control in detail, however, top management must rely on plant managers, production superintendents, department foremen, and crew leaders. For financial control in detail, the company comptroller must rely on plant chief accountants, budget supervisors, department heads, and accounting clerks. In addition, there are industrial engineers, quality control people, personnel departments, and similar functions depending upon the nature, size, and complexity of the business. These various groups must work closely together and integrate their functions to provide maximum effectiveness.

COST REDUCTION OPPORTUNITIES

It is doubtful that there is any area of any business which does not provide some opportunity for cost reduction and profit improvement. In evaluating various cost cutting proposals, it might be well to establish some general guidelines and policies. Getting the most for the money being spent can often be more rewarding than merely spending less money. It has been said that sometimes the "cheapest" is the "dearest." The following examples are offered in support of this hypothesis:

1. A company has a budget of $200,000 annually for research and development. This could represent salaries for 20 laboratory assistants at $10,000 each per year, or 4 top-notch scientists at $50,000 each per year. Either one of these two extremes would no doubt be unlikely. Yet the proper balance of scientists, engineers, technicians, etc., is very important, both functionally and economically. Obviously, it would be costly to permit a situation where a physicist with a doctor's degree would perform routine work which could just as competently be performed by a laboratory assistant. Conversely, it might be even more costly to assign an extremely complex problem in solid state physics to a neophyte mechanical engineer. Proper evaluation of a research and development operation should be concerned not only with the total amount spent, but how it is being spent, how the spending is related to the degree of technical sophistication, and what results are being obtained.

2. A company purchases a piece of expensive and complex industrial equipment. They then tie up a group of their own engineers to install the equipment and get it running smoothly. Many large equipment producers furnish engineering services at little or no additional cost, and it is possible that the purchasing company would not have had to divert their own engineering people for this purpose. Cost savings can sometimes be obtained by using vendor services to the full.

3. A company follows a policy of quantity buying in many goods and commodities to obtain quantity discounts. Judicious quantity buying can certainly contribute to cost reduction. Indiscriminate quantity buying can increase costs if it results in inordinately high carrying costs of inventories, obsolescence risks, excess warehouse costs, and enough capital tied up to adversely affect cash position.

In any business enterprise, costs are incurred to accomplish many things. Unless there is a profit, however, other objectives, no matter how lofty, become pretty much academic.

Most products have distinct differences in characteristics. These have a direct effect on costs, making some products more costly to handle than others. High value products tie up more capital than others. Large products take up more storage space, and some others require special handling. Different products call for different types of advertising and promotion campaigns. Many times, costs are knowingly raised instead of reduced. For instance, if a business decides to open up a new sales territory, its profit and loss statement for the new territory will normally show losses during the early periods. The decision-maker accepts such excess costs in a current period as an investment in future sales and accompanying profits.

In commencing a cost reduction program, it might be strategic to prepare an initial list of cost improvement areas, at least until some momentum has been attained. The following suggestions are quite general and are intended to spark specific ideas and programs:

Short-Term Programs

1. Audit payments of vendors' invoices to assure that they are paid in time to obtain cash discounts when entitled.

2. Review shipping and warehousing operations to insure systematic storage, lowest possible freight rates, shipping full loads whenever possible, and advantageous location of warehouses.

3. Check labor situation for possible excessive overtime, part time, idle time, and absenteeism. Insure proper balance of workloads. Consider employee training programs.

Long-Term Programs

1. Exploit value engineering techniques. "Value engineering" might be defined as precise cost accounting plus applied industrial engineering. It is a scientific method of obtaining equal or better performance and value from a specific product or product component at a lower cost. This is done through step by step scrutiny and testing of every part and every operation in the manufacture of a product.

2. Study plant layout for possible improvement in work flow. Evaluate performance and condition of present equipment for replacement, if necessary, with newer and more efficient machines. Improve quality control procedures and reduce spoilage when possible.

3. Utilize the best possible accounting methods and procedures. Obtain the most appropriate data processing equipment. Provide management at all levels with the most useful information reports possible for decision making.

Specific programs

The following list will serve as a checklist of more specific cost reduction programs. The list will vary depending on the individual company. The best programs are probably neither continuous nor cost-cutting explosions, but a compromise between the two. Cost controls need to be maintained on a continuing basis, but there is slippage in every system, and a periodic tightening of controls will always produce savings. These areas should be reviewed as part of the profit improvement (PIP) effort:

1. *Advertising and promotion*—may be discontinued with no deleterious effects for brief periods of time. Promotional work in the securities and investor relation area may also be curtailed.

2. *Branch offices*—or decentralized independent operations may be discontinued if they are direct loss operations. These are sometimes maintained for marketing purposes, to hold a national posture, or provide a network of offices, which may be unnecessary in a short-run period.

3. *Cafeteria operations*—are usually provided for employees at a loss. These can be closed, sandwich machines substituted, or the operation of the cafeteria may be contracted out to an independent service on a fixed-fee basis, thereby eliminating the loss. Problems such as food shortages and employee turnover are eliminated.

4. *Centralized purchasing*—may be employed where the company has many locations. A low limit, say $100, could be established and only items under that limit may be purchased in the local office. This procedure submits the over $100 purchase order to closer centralized (and less involved) scrutiny. Quantities and even need can be independently evaluated. There may be a personnel savings—a central office can do the same job with fewer people than many independent offices.

5. *Collections*—of accounts receivable may usually be decentralized without adding people. Most such work is done on the phone, at a significant saving in the telephone cost, if done through the local office. Collection staff need not be added since regular order takers may be trained to check credit lists or aged trial balances and to obtain collections, on the same phone call in which the order is placed.

6. *Commissions*—for salesmen, may be restructured, raising them, and eliminating base salary or guaranteed draw. This will tend to shake out the unproductive salesmen more quickly and to compensate the big producers more highly. Unit selling cost per man will be reduced.

7. *Compensation policy*—should be reviewed with regard to having quotas or bonus programs for salesmen and their managers. These programs work better

in an expanding economy, but then, so do any programs. Quotas and bonuses can be eliminated at all levels and, instead, profit sharing can be substituted to give salesmen and managers a share in profits which equals last year's bonus (if the same level of profits is at least achieved), and also gives them 50% of the increase in net income (or any desired percentage), before such profit sharing. This type of program, if properly structured, should eliminate bonuses and extra commissions during periods when the company's profits are declining, due to disparities in product mix sales.

8. *Contests*—for salesmen or classes of customers may be eliminated with no short-run effect. Or, national contests (at high cost) may be eliminated in favor of less expensive local contests.

9. *Demonstration materials*—and free give-aways used by salesmen may be eliminated, or more carefully doled out by supervisors. Total amounts should be budgeted at lower levels.

10. *District offices*—and zone or outlying staff offices may be closed and operated out of other local sales offices. Some managers try to become empire builders, creating their own sphere of control—separate staff and offices which often duplicate other corporate functions.

11. *Freight charges*—may be raised to more than offset the increase in freight costs. In many cases, freight and delivery charges are intended to be borne by the customer but they are not, due to creeping increases in freight costs which are accepted at lower levels and not called to management's attention. Freight companies do not send out formal notices of rate increases—they just happen.

12. *Inventory controls*—are a continuous and on-going program. Costs are controlled and profits improved by good inventory taking and good inventory management. However, some immediate steps can be taken if there are inventory losses. A watchman can be hired for sensitive areas during working hours and alarm systems connected to detective services installed for night hours. One watchman can watch a vast inventory area using in-house television monitoring. If necessary, undercover men can be used to staff working crews to protect against mysterious disappearances of inventory. An immediate warehouse security system should be installed to prevent mysterious disappearance. Establish an immediate perpetual inventory control, a manual procedure, wherein the inventory clerk reports not to the warehouse manager, but to the accounting manager. He should control the location and picking of each order and spot-check and cycle-count inventories.

13. *Legal costs*—may be reduced by negotiating issues instead of litigating them. Settle, don't sue, in the short-run to keep costs down. Hold off new issues until a later time—patent infringement suits and anti-trust issues. Institute a legal liaison procedure and policy.

14. Study the size of the product line. Reduce it by eliminating loss items and leaders which may not be necessary in the near term.

15. *Mail and messenger service*—may be curtailed with no loss in revenues. Mail once a day instead of picking up several times in the morning and afternoon. Eliminate messengers, limousines, and special delivery services.

16. *Office machines*—should be examined for effective utilization. Word processing units (automatic editing typewriters) can save 25% of a secretary's time. Photo copy machines can replace carbon paper and duplicate typing at less cost. Dictating machines, even inexpensive portable tape recorders, can save the substantial time spent by an author and secretary in personal dictation.

17. *Office temporaries*—should not be authorized and should be eliminated in interim periods of cost reduction. Regular staff will handle the work if it needs to be done.

18. *Order handling*—can be streamlined to eliminate main office edits and reviews. Just give the order a cursory check and process it. Put teeth in this by penalizing salesmen for errors they make on the order. This can save personnel.

19. *Office services*—may be curtailed in central locations. Eliminate private secretaries in favor of a secretarial and typing pool.

Helpful Hint: This saves having to hire a new secretary every time a new managerial job is created. You simply don't have secretaries, using the pool instead.

Failing this extreme, double-up or quadruple-up on the use of secretaries, several managers sharing. Share by location of office, rather than division or type of work.

Other office service areas—clean and maintain premises twice weekly, instead of daily; have individual department heads do their own interviewing for new hires, by-passing personnel; examine dial 9 or centrex telephone systems to save on phone operators.

20. *Payroll costs*—may be reduced by simplifying payroll systems (see Zero Balance Accounts and Imprest and Color-coded Accounts in Chapter 2). Reduce payroll taxes by considering payments as consulting fees instead of payroll. Also, determine that portion of a salesman's pay and earnings which is attributable to travel expenses, and therefore not subject to withholding or payroll taxes as wages. Consider your cost of handling payroll check writing and record keeping. Perhaps an outside payroll service will be more economical. This should be reviewed periodically, as the cost effectiveness will change with the type and amount of payrolls and number of people.

Other payroll saving steps: Freeze wages over a limit, say $15,000 per year; grant wage increases under that limit only once each year, whether from merit, annual, or promotion, and then subject to a percentage limit, say a range of 5% to 10%; Reduce salaries of key managers and officers by 10% to 20% if over $30,000 per year.

Helpful Hint: Partially offset payroll reductions with company paid insurance benefits. Under Sec. 79 of the IRC company paid term insurance in amounts over

$50,000 a year is taxable to the employee, but at substantially lower than regular income tax rates. This may be tied to insurance with a cash surrender value which will exceed the employee's income tax. The company, thus, will obtain a tax deductible expense, in full, and the employee will pay less tax. This makes it possible to reduce his salary and offset it, partially, with an insurance benefit increase.

Helpful Hint: Avoid personnel recruitment costs on hiring new or replacement employees by advancing agency fees and then recovering this from the employee over a six-month period, through payroll deductions. Caution—some states do not permit such deductions unless they are an employee loan being repaid.

Freeze new hires; require two approvals on any replacements; review each individual job with the supervisor and determine the necessity for that job (there is probably 10% to 20% inefficiency built into every organization that does not practice continuing cost control); eliminate all overtime.

21. *Petty cash*—may be reduced in outlying offices by scheduling prompt central payments. The reduced fund results in reduced expenditures.

22. *Postage*—can be budgeted at 80% of the previous run rate. Discontinue the use of air mail or special delivery. Batch mail to repetitive locations; mail only once a day; defer direct mail programs.

23. *Price increases*—should be effected, selectively, to pass on appropriate cost increases to customers. This requires good product pricing control to avoid cost increases creeping through without pricing actions.

24. *Relocations*—of company personnel from one location to another should be avoided. Relocation policy includes personnel benefits such as air fare to search for a home, home closing costs, fixing up costs, costs and losses of moving from the old home, and interim hotel expenses. These far exceed the cost of hiring someone new in the immediate location. The benefit of the experienced employee in the relocated job is a short-lived one (in six months the new employee is experienced) and may be considerably offset by hiring someone experienced in the same industry.

25. *Reports*—which no one wants are often generated. Request managers to review the distribution, frequency, and discontinuance of reports. With such a study, many reports may be eliminated.

Reporting Hint: Discontinue distribution of some reports which you suspect are not needed. See whether you get any complaints after two successive periods of non-distribution. If not, write the recipients and "tell them" you have discontinued the report due to lack of need. Always give an alternate source of the information, perhaps in another format.

26. *Second source*—should be considered from suppliers. This may result in lower prices or reduced quantity ordering requirements. If quantities are large enough, purchases can be made from two sources, with the original vendor reducing his price to meet the second source. Alternatively, single sourcing may result in savings when two sources are being used to divide up insufficient quantities.

27. *Service support functions*—may be discontinued. This may include goodwill ambassadors, institutional showrooms, public relations personnel and services, or customer relations people who follow-up after the salesmen. All will result in short-run savings, but the cost of discontinuing these services and then restarting them may obviate their discontinuance.

28. *Severance policy*—should be defined, in writing, for terminated employees, particularly at times of layoffs. Superiors tend to soften the blow with extra severance pay.

Helpful Hint: Many companies pay one week of severance for each year of service, with a minimum of one week and a maximum of two months. Severance is a company option, not an employee right, and its grant should depend on the employee's cooperation and attitude.

29. *Shipping and distribution costs*—should be studied by qualified in-house people or outside professionals, every several years or when the company changes its distribution methods. Outside consulting firms will perform the initial analysis and teach future analyses to company personnel so that distribution costs may be monitored internally. Methods of shipping, routing, and warehousing are studied, together with effective space utilization for various types of inventories. In short, the logistics of shipping and distribution are studied. The result may be a shifting of inventories, storage in different locations, shipping in carload lots or containers, drop shipping from vendors to customers, storage in bonded warehouses, shifting to consignment sales—but whatever the change, it will be cost effective.

30. *Staff functions*—much like service support functions, may be reviewed and reduced or eliminated. These would include levels of administrative or marketing management which are not direct to the operation. For example, four salesmen may have a team leader; four team leaders may report to a sales manager; two sales managers may report to a general manager. All levels between salesman and general manager could be eliminated for limited periods without reducing sales effectiveness. Many headquarters functions such as staff assistants, liaison managers, administrative assistants, secretaries, assistant supervisors, product managers, assistants to, are performing functions which could be reduced or discontinued without affecting the profit objective in the near term, and many of them are probably doing work which their superiors should be doing, or could be doing in tight times.

31. *Sundry expenses*—are a catch-all category in any business used to record those expenses which are not able to be classified in the chart of accounts as it presently exists. Sundry expenses are hard to analyze and control when they are improperly recorded this way. Eliminate the caption. When an item arises that does not fit the chart of accounts, add a caption to the chart which does fit. Provide for numbering expansion in the chart of accounts.

32. *Telephone and Telex expenses*—are one of the most fruitful areas for cost control. Telex messages should be typed in advance and sent, using tapes, at

maximum speeds. Telexes may be eliminated by using telephone (WATS lines), facsimile devices, or magnetic tape transmission over dial-up phone lines to central switching terminals. The efficacy of these systems depends on the volume of transmissions and the need for speed and accuracy.

Magnetic tape transmissions off word-processing equipment may offer side benefits of being able to store correspondence on tape, rather than in traditional files.

Special self-dial systems may be used in place of operator assisted telephone service. These are dial 7 or 9 systems and Centrex systems which completely by-pass the operator. Long-distance calls are blocked out on these systems. Calling long distance by using a central in-house operator only keeps better control. Use a long-distance log and have the employee's supervisor initial every call; budget long-distance calls at 80% of prior levels; charge department heads 25¢ on each dollar in excess of the budgeted levels (do it as a contest to get cooperation, with the winner getting all contributions from the losers); eliminate inter-branch phone calls; when calls must be made, direct dial to save 30% of the cost of the call if operator assisted; require messages to be written, not phoned, to outlying offices; use the telex in lieu of the phone; remove instruments from every desk— keep only one or two in a department; eliminate private wires and telephone numbers unless they fit in to the phone system being used. Managers and executives abuse private numbers more than anyone; use WATS lines if you have many short calls in specific covered areas; require supervisors to personally sign every telex message before it is sent.

The phone company is a regulated utility. It makes a guaranteed profit. You don't!

33. *Training expenses*—may be curtailed or eliminated for brief periods, both in the selling and administrative areas. As a substitute, use on-the-job training. Have new salesmen trail experienced ones. Have administrative, technical, and service personnel instructed in one step at a time, on-line, before proceeding to the next. Eliminate the costly travel and hotel expenses of central training courses; substitute cassette tape training programs augmented with on-location in-house television or film projectors; design programmed learning courses, consisting of successive question and answer steps.

Helpful Hint: Develop a competent salary level and benefits program to eliminate most employee turnover. This will keep training costs down for new employees and permit them to be trained on-the-job.

34. *Travel expenses*—require special control. Employees often like to travel, create trips, and end up visiting friends and family, and as a side benefit, making a profit on their per diem expenses.

Try These Steps: Budget travel at 80% of previous levels; require a Travel Authorization Form from all employees who do not customarily travel as a part of their jobs; require two levels of approval on employees who do customarily travel, one of which must be the division manager; do not permit approvers to delegate approving authority to secretaries or subordinates; discontinue all credit cards; do not pay meal expenses unless the travel is overnight; specify by title only those who are permitted to entertain; do not authorize or reimburse company employees who entertain other company employees—thus, eliminate working lunches or dinners; use a uniform Statement of Reimbursable Expenses form which sets out some of the rules and limitations, and back these up with a written travel procedure.

35. *Typing*—of reports, interoffice memos and schedules can be reduced substantially to take the load off the typing pool. Require interoffice memos to be hand written; reports are not typed unless for external or Board submission; all schedules are to be hand written. Save the time to prepare, type, and proofread, when a single preparation will achieve the same result.

Answer correspondence by replying directly on the same letter, photocopying it, and returning the original, or use snap-out carbon type speed memos. The degree of clarity and formality obtained on typewritten letters for unimportant purposes is unnecessary and costly.

ORGANIZING FOR COST REDUCTION PROGRAMS

Cost control starts with the accurate measurement of costs. The ability to retrieve data and to present it in meaningful reports, on a timely basis, is dependent on the company having a viable organizational structure and a functioning budgeting system.

The organizational structure establishes a framework within which operations are conducted. The framework includes organizational charts, position descriptions, procedures and policies as described in the chapter titled "Organizing for Financial Management." The budgeting system is described in the chapter "Financial Analysis Through Budgeting." This deals with creating a Profit Plan and presenting it in the form of a Budget which is then communicated throughout the organization. Monitoring the budget requires comparing actual results to plan. The company is divided into Profit Centers using the responsibility accounting concept. One manager is responsible for the costs and profits generated by each box on the organizational chart, and an intercompany transfer price is used which makes all profit centers competitive to each other and to outside competitors.

Exhibit 44 is an example of how a budget for the coming year might be prepared for a branch sales office. It consists of expenses for which the branch sales manager is responsible and can control. The salary expense is the single largest cost category and represents the total salaries of his salesmen, office staff, and himself. In this budget you will note that he starts out the coming year with a total monthly salary expense of $7,000. In April it goes up by $100, and in July it increases another $300. This could be salary increases in both cases, or the second increase might represent the hiring of an additional stenographer or file clerk. The actual detail salary by individual would probably be known only to the branch sales manager, the division sales manager, the payroll department, and possibly the company budget director. By lumping the salary amounts into one total, they can be kept confidential. Travel expense and car expense could be handled in the same manner, with only total figures appearing on the published budget. This type of planned budget

YEAR 19xx

DALLAS SALES BRANCH	JAN	FEB	MAR	APR	MAY	JUNE	JULY	AUG	SEPT	OCT	NOV	DEC	TOTAL
Salaries	7000	7000	7000	7100	7100	7100	7400	7400	7400	7400	7400	7400	86,700
Travel & Entertainment	2000	2000	2000	2000	2000	2000	2000	2000	2000	2000	2000	2000	24,000
Telephone & Telegraph	100	100	100	100	100	100	100	100	100	100	100	100	1,200
Postage	30	30	30	30	30	30	30	30	30	30	30	30	360
Office Supplies	20	20	20	20	20	20	20	20	20	20	20	20	240
Meeting Expense	100			100			100			100			400
Dues & Subscriptions						50						100	150
Sample Expense	50	50	50	50	50	50	50	50	50	50	50	50	600
Leased Auto Expense	1000	1000	1000	1000	1000	1000	1000	1000	1000	1000	1000	1000	12,000
Office Rent	300	300	300	300	300	300	300	300	300	300	300	300	3,600
TOTAL	10,600	10,500	10,500	10,700	10,600	10,650	1,000	10,900	10,900	11,000	10,900	11,000	129,250

Exhibit 44

Operating Budget Detail

Dallas Sales Branch   *June 30, 19xx*

	Month		Expense Classification	Year To Date		
Budget	Actual	Better (Worse)		Budget	Actual	Better (Worse)
$ 7,100	$ 7,000	$100	Salaries	$42,300	$42,000	$ 300
2,000	2,050	(50)	Travel & Entertainment	12,000	14,000	(2,000)
100	80	20	Telephone & Telegraph	600	550	50
30	25	5	Postage	180	170	10
20	25	(5)	Office Supplies	120	115	5
—	100	(100)	Meeting Expense	200	350	(150)
50	75	(25)	Dues & Subscriptions	50	75	(25)
50	40	10	Sample Expense	300	250	50
1,000	800	200	Leased Auto Expense	6,000	5,500	500
300	300	—	Office Rent	1,800	1,800	—
$10,650	$10,495	$155	TOTAL	$63,550	$64,810	$(1,260)

Exhibit 45

Budget Statement

would probably be originally prepared by the branch manager based on forecast sales volume for his territory. It might then be amended and approved by the division or product sales manager, and progress higher up into the management echelon for further approval by general sales manager, general manager, budget director, treasurer, comptroller, and possibly even president, depending upon individual company policies and procedures. At any rate, the permissible spending rate or financial yardstick will have been established, and deviation from this level will probably have to be explained during the coming year.

Exhibit 45 is an example of how a budget statement for this same branch office might look by the end of June. This report compares actual cost and budgeted cost for current month and year to date. You will note that salaries are under budget by $100 for June and $300 for year to date. Apparently the $100 increase originally budgeted for April 1st did not go through. Travel and entertainment is $50 higher than budget for June and $2,000 higher for the first six months total. Perhaps there is a good reason for this. The division sales manager will surely want to know what it is.

PROFIT IMPROVEMENT POINTERS

1. Cost control is often the only key to maximizing profit, especially in industries and businesses where the prices of goods and services are determined in the marketplace.

2. Cost reduction and profit improvement programs should be practiced on a continuing basis in both good and bad times in every company, with periodic belt-tightening, in order to maintain competitive strength and even survivial.

3. Good accounting records and management reports will reveal areas and opportunities for cost reduction.

4. Cost control programs should be designed for the broadest possible participation together with specific responsibility designation within profit centers.

5. Reasonable operating budgets, intelligently designed, operating within a structured organizational framework, are a requirement in a cost control program.

CHAPTER 8

Successful Management of Cost of Capital and Debt

The cost of debt is not simply the interest rate paid for funds, nor even the after-tax rate, but rather is based on the expected costs or outflows and the discount rate that makes these outflows exactly equal to the net proceeds of the loan.

Financial management requires the provision of the capital required to operate the business. The need for capital may be short-term, usually less than a year, or long-term, anything longer than one year. Some companies define a medium term as one to three years, usually by stable companies that utilize long-range planning techniques of five years or longer. Capital planning alternatives should be considered in the light of their cost, advantages and disadvantages, and accounting considerations.

Short-term capital alternatives will not be considered here. These usually consist of banking arrangements, financial arrangements with vendors, accounts payable terms and controls, near-term investments, and a variety of short-term borrowing arrangements which are usually revolving in nature. These may include commercial receivables financing and factoring, commercial paper, letters of credit, link financing (borrowing money based on the letter of credit of a customer or a supplier), inventory reductions, sale of treasury stock, and the working down of bank balances. Short-term capital alternatives are usually operational expedients, not involving financial decision making, or the cost of the alternatives is clear from the quoted rate.

This chapter will consider the following long-term capital and debt alternatives:

1. Equity
2. Bank debt
3. Straight debt
4. Debt with equity
5. Installment loans and leases
6. Acquisitions

EQUITY

Equity heads the list. You may not ordinarily think of it as long-term debt, but it really is the ultimate and longest-term debt, and usually the lowest cost. Unlike other debt, stockholders give up the right to repayment of a fixed amount of principal and interest in favor of the right to share in the company's fortunes, whatever they may be. If the company succeeds, their share in that success will be much greater than the lender's fixed interest. If it fails and is liquidated, the stockholder's fate is much worse since he stands behind, or junior to the lender's principal and interest before he can be paid whatever remains of the company's assets, if anything.

Stream of Earnings Analysis

The cost of equity, viewed from a cash flow standpoint, is the least expensive cost of any capital available. This cost includes the underwriting spread, legal, accounting, and printing costs, as well as the cost of future cash dividends. In a growth company, or one which stresses the price of its publicly traded shares, dividends may never be paid and equity is veritably the cheapest capital, its issuance costs being minimal. Conceptually, however, all earnings belong to the stockholders, and the cost of equity is equal to the minimum rate of return that the company must earn on these equity funds to avoid any fall in the market price of the company's stock. Expressed as a formula, the cost of equity capital is:

$$\frac{Ea}{P}$$

in which Ea is expected earnings per share and P is the current stock price. The concept is that the value of any share to its owner is a claim on a stream of company earnings, rather than a claim upon cash flows from the company in the form of dividends. Using this claim on earnings concept, we may compute the cost of raising capital in this example:

A company decides to raise $1 million of new equity at a time when its stock is selling for $12 per share; it has 1 million shares outstanding, and it earns $1 per share after taxes (its price/earnings ratio is therefore 12). The new shares will probably have to sell at a more attractive price than the current $12, say $10 and, so, 100,000 new shares must be issued to raise the required $1 million.

There will now be 1,100,000 shares outstanding, and if earnings remain the same at $1 million, the earnings per share will fall from $1 to $0.91 ($1,000,000 ÷ 1,100,000), and the price of the stock will fall from $12 to $10.92 (p/e of 12 × $.91). The cost of this equity may then be said to be 8.3% ($0.91 ÷ $10.92) (using the formula Ea/P).

In the foregoing calculation, note that we have used the old reported earnings of $1 million, but our formula calls for EA or anticipated earnings. One must assume that the company has no need to raise $1 million of additional equity unless it has a productive use for that capital, one which will produce additional earnings for the company. The effect on earnings per share of these new earnings will offset the fall in earnings per share that results from selling the additional shares. If the earnings on the new capital are high enough, they will fully offset the effects of the dilution caused by selling the new stock, and each shareholder's share in the company will be unaffected. Therefore, EA, or expected earnings, may be assumed to be those earnings which will cause zero dilution in the price of shares held by existing shareholders. Using this assumption, the cost of equity may then be determined to be:

Earnings per share continue at $1 or $1,100,000; the price of the stock remains at 12 times earnings (p/e ratio) or $12, and the cost of this equity may then be said to be the same 8.3% as before ($1 ÷ $12). Obviously, the price per share has increased in proportion to the earnings per share, and the cost of equity remains constant. The cost of this capital would rise only in the event that earnings continued at $1 million and an earnings per share of $0.909 would result ($1,000,000 ÷ 1,100,000). The capital cost would then be 9.1%, assuming a stock price of $10 per share, based on the current market price at which the new shares were sold.

The price/earnings ratio expected, then, is the determinant of the cost of capital, based on the expected stream of earnings. Examining this further, you may determine this to be the least costly alternative, depending on the p/e ratio, especially when related to the cost of other debt. If long-term institutional debt is available at 7%, it would be preferred to an 8.3% cost of equity. On the other hand, if the p/e ratio were 20, the cost of equity would be 5% ($1 per share ÷ $20 per share), and this would appear to be the most desirable alternative.

Cash Flow from Dividends Analysis

Another approach, as inferred in the foregoing, for dividend paying companies or those which are expected to become dividend paying is to cost the equity based upon the cash flows expected from dividends, using this formula:

$$V = \frac{Do}{k-g}$$

in which

  V   is the present or market value of the stock
  Do   is the current annual divident (say $.40)
  k   is the investor's required rate of return
  g   is the rate of earnings growth, which is less than k, say 6%

Then, using the facts in the example above,

$$k = \frac{Do}{V} + g = \frac{\$.40}{\$12} + 6\% = 3.3\% + 6\% = 9.3\%$$

This is compared to the 8.3% in the example above. Either approach to the cost of equity may be used, depending on whether or not dividends are expected.

Cost of Retained Earnings Analysis

A subset of equity is retained earnings, after tax profits which have been plowed back into the company rather than distributed to shareholders through cash dividends. The cost of these funds is the same as externally raised equity, except that earnings paid out in dividends are subject to double taxation. The company pays a tax on the pre-dividend income, and the individual pays a tax on the dividend. Retained earnings, however, avoid this double tax. Thus, the cost of retained earnings (which may be considered to be internal equity, compared to raising external equity) is the cost of raising external equity times the reciprocal of the average tax rate of the company's stockholders. For example, if the cost of raising equity were 8.3% as in previous examples and average stockholders were in a 30% tax bracket, then the cost of retained earnings is:

$$8.3\% \times (1.0 - .30) = 8.3\% \times .70 = 5.8\%$$

This method may not be used for single proprietorships, partnerships, nor corporations that elect to be taxed as partnerships, as they are not subject to the double tax. It also has limited use for very large corporations with many stockholders in that the average tax bracket is difficult to estimate for all shareholders.

BANK DEBT

Demand loans, short-term bank borrowings, are the most common form of bank debt. Banks generally initiate their borrowing relationships with short-term debt. As confidence is built, banks will participate in longer-term relationships, usually two-or three-year revolving credits. By revolving credit, we mean those loans which have a debt ceiling in dollars, funds being lent on a formula, for example total dollar value of receivables and inventory. The loan fluctuates up or down based on the formula and subject to the lending limit, and the overall agreement may run for a year, or two, or three. It is a term loan, by any definition, despite the revolving nature of the collateral, since the company's borrowings will tend to remain the same from year to year. At any rate, given constant collateral conditions, the loan will remain approximately the same, being reduced only by profits which are turned back into the operations.

Even short-term bank debt may be considered long-term under certain conditions. Demand notes may not be called and 30- or 60-day notes are continually revolved. If the loan is outstanding more than a year or is contemplated to be, then it is term in nature. Many banks lend short-term for 11 months, with a requirement that the loan be paid off for 30 days and then renewed. The payoff may be from corporate working capital or another bank. Cash may be generated internally, by reducing inventory or slowing accounts payable, in anticipation of the payoff. Or, a line of credit may be established, but not used, with another bank or two being used for the paydown. In this event, the short-term debt is extended beyond a year, almost indefinitely, and the loan may be characterized as long-term for all practical purposes. Your accountants will, of course, continue to classify it as short-term.

Short-term debt of this nature is usually available only when a good credit rating is presented. The debt carries a favorable interest rate and may not be secured. The revolving credit, on the other hand, is secured, and contrary to most long-term debt, carries a higher rate than short-term borrowings. The revolving credit also is subject to specific operating constraints, which may be onerous to the management but which, generally, bankers will consider to be prudent restrictions necessary to protect their secured interest. These include requirements to maintain net worth and working capital at pre-determined levels, debt to equity limitations, and limits on capital spending. The cost of this type of long-term bank debt is simply the interest rate, expressed as the formula:

$$k = 1/P$$

where k is the rate of return, 1 is the annual interest cost, and P is the total value of the debt—in short, the simple interest rate. This cost, and this formula, may be considered to be valid where the company maintains a stable amount of debt; as one bank loan is paid off it is replaced with another. If the debt is one-time, that is, not replaced, its true cost is not the simple interest rate, but such cost must consider the expected outflows and the discount rate which makes these outflows just equal to the net proceeds obtained from the lending source. In short, the outstanding loan balances must be discounted to a present value basis.

From an accounting standpoint, revolving loans may usually be treated as long-term liabilities if they have a maturity of more than one year and the borrower has the right and a clear intention to renew or revolve the loan.

STRAIGHT DEBT

Straight Debt refers to long-term borrowing in the form of bonds, notes, or debentures, without options, warrants, stock, or other equity features attached to it. Straight debt is available from private individuals, funds, institutions, or insurance companies. It may be new debt or a refunding of an older bond issue. The debt is, in essence, an interest-bearing IOU. The IOU contains stipulations as to the principal sum to be repaid, dates of repayment, specific claims or liens against assets, and protective covenants. The latter are a normal feature since the bond is a long-term investment with risk presumed to increase as the time-span of the investment increases.

The cost of debt is not simply the interest rate paid for funds, nor even the after-tax rate, but rather is based on the expected costs or outflows and the discount rate that makes these outflows exactly equal to the net proceeds of the loan. This is a discounted cash flow concept or return on investment concept as described in Chapter 3 and expressed by this formula:

$$Po = \frac{C1}{(1+k)^1} + \frac{C2}{(1+k)^2} + \ldots + \frac{Cn}{(1+k)^n}$$

where:

Po = net proceeds in year o
C1 = total cost in year 1 and so on
k   = the discount rate: the pre-tax cost of the debt funds

For example:

Assume a $1 million bond issue, for 20 years, with a sinking fund of $50,000 per year, a 7% interest rate, and an annual cost of mailing, administering and handling the bonds of $30,000 (total cost of the bonds is $70,000 interest + $30,000 handling, or $100,000), then the cost of the bonds will be the discount rate, k, determined from the above equation, or:

$$\$1,000,000 = \frac{\$100,000}{(1 + k)^1} + \frac{\$100,000}{(1 + k)^2} + \cdots \frac{\$100,000}{(1 + k)^{20}}$$

which is 7.5%.

This type of discounted cash flow calculation is readily available from many time-sharing computer services at a small monthly cost of as low as $80. Such calculations are also available on electronic calculators, hand models, like the Hewlett-Packard HP 80 selling at about $200. The calculation can be done in minutes with these aids.

On the other hand, if it is assumed that the company has perpetual debt, or revolves its debt by paying off one issue and replacing it with another, or does not use sinking funds, or pays off a final balloon amount with another issue's proceeds, then the cost of debt is simply the interest rate using the formula $k = 1/P$ as set out on page 163, which is a pre-tax expression. This may be translated to an after-tax amount by:

Taxable Income

$0 - $25,000	$= k \times (1 - 0.17)$
$25,001 to $50,000	$= k \times (1 - 0.20)$
$50,001 to $75,000	$= k \times (1 - 0.30)$
$75,001 to $100,000	$= k \times (1 - 0.40)$
Over $100,000	$= k \times (1 - 0.46)$

The above rates assume bonds sold at par. If they are sold at a premium or discount, then P, the total value of the debt must be adjusted by the average of the bond's current sale price and its maturity value, and 1, the annual interest cost must be adjusted by adding or subtracting the effect of the difference between the proceeds of the debt and the amount of principal that will eventually have to be refunded.

DEBT WITH EQUITY

Subordinated Debentures are unsecured debt, ranking ahead of preferred and common stock, but behind all other secured and unsecured debt. As such, they are higher risk to the lender and usually give him a greater rate of return. These may be issued when existing bond indenture agreements prohibit the issuance of additional debt having an equal claim against the corporation's earnings and assets. Several stages of subordination may be used, resulting in layers of subordinated debt with titles like "second subordinated debentures" and "third subordinated debentures." Successive subordination usually results in higher interest rates. These rates may be reduced by combining the subordinated debenture with a convertible feature.

Income Bonds are also near equity, ranking ahead of preferred and common stock. Their interest payment, however, depends on earnings. There is no legal obligation for interest payments unless earnings are adequate enough to permit such payments. These bonds are appropriate for companies with large fixed capital investments and large fluctuation in earnings, or for emerging companies with the expectation of low earnings in the early years. Railroads, hotels and motels have used Income Bonds for these reasons. The interest on such bonds, like the dividend on preferred stocks, may be cumulative or not. Because of the added flexibility these bonds give to the corporation, they usually carry a higher interest rate than all other bonds. Many corporations have used Income bonds to retire preferred stocks, since the interest paid on the bond is tax deductible but the preferred dividend is not.

Neither Income Bonds nor Subordinated Debentures create or eventually result in the lender having equity in the corporation. There are two types of debt that do give this result:

1. *Convertible Bonds*—are the debt equivalent of preferred stock, differing from preferred in that before conversion they have the characteristics of debt. The conversion feature sets out circumstances when, at the option of the holder, the bonds may be converted into common shares. Convertibility is expressed as a price (say $20 a share, meaning a $1000 bond may be converted into 50 shares), or as a ratio (say 50 common shares per $1000 of face value of the bond issue). The conversion price may vary over the life of the security, specifying a higher conversion price or a declining conversion ratio, reflecting the expectation of a higher common stock price over the years as corporate earnings increase. The value of a convertible bond may be based only on its interest rate and the current rates of interest in the capital market, this value giving the bond's value on a yield basis. This value usually provides a downside floor on the value of the bond. It also has an alternative value based on its conversion price, say convertible into 50 shares with a market value of $15 equals $750. The two values are not the same and the bond will tend to sell for close to the higher of the two. If the bond sells on a conversion basis and the price of the common stock falls, the bond price will fall, too, but not below its yield basis. In the absence of a call provision, the bond probably will not be converted as its value will rise whenever the common stock rises. Thus, the lender enjoys all the capital appreciation on the common, without converting and without even losing the convertible's limited downside risk. In this case, the bondholder would convert only if the dividend yield on the common were to be greater than the interest yield on the bond—an unlikely circumstance. When the company calls the bond for conversion, the holder's decision is based on the comparison of the current call price and the market value of the stock, plus taxes and transaction costs. The corporation will consider the use of convertible bonds when:

a. Increased debt is desirable, but difficult or expensive. It may be difficult due to existing indenture restrictions in previous bond issues or simply because interest rates are too high. The equity feature and the possibility of capital appreciation because of the convertibility make a lower interest rate possible.

b. The corporation desires to sell common stock, but the price of the common is too low or market conditions do not permit the sale of straight equity. The company is willing to pay the interest cost on the bond, temporarily, as it believes all the bonds will eventually be converted into common. The use of a call feature may force such conversion. The effective cost of this type of equity is reduced, prior to conversion, as the interest paid is tax deductible.

The conversion price must be set carefully if the company desires to attain its objectives of converting its bonds into common stock at the appropriate time. This requires a sensitivity to the technical aspects of the bonds as well as the capital and money markets which is usually best fulfilled by a competent investment banker. A miscalculation will mean:

a. If the conversion price is too high, the conversion value of the bond may never reach its call price and the issue will be uncallable. The company is then saddled with continuing debt.

b. If the conversion price is set too low, the corporation will not achieve its objective of selling its common stock significantly above the current depressed market price. The cost of this type of equity may be too high.

2. *Debt with Warrants or Options*—is a bond issue with an option to buy common stock in the corporation at a stated price. The bond may be any of several types, and the warrant may be for a fixed period of time, or indefinite. They may also be at a single stated price or varying on an increasing scale, based on the expectation of the company for higher prices. They usually are exercisable at 10% to 25% above the present market value price of the stock. The warrants may be detachable from the bond and, therefore, separately tradable, or may be permanently attached and not separable from the bond. This should not be confused with a convertible security which gives the right to change or exchange the bond for stock under certain conditons. The warrant, on the other hand, gives a right to buy, not exchange.

Debt with warrants offers certain advantages:

a. The investor has greater flexibility than with convertibles as the warrants may sometimes be detached and traded separately.

b. The exercise of the warrant produces additional cash for the company; the conversion of convertible debt does not. As with conversion, exercise of the warrants presupposes a rise in the stock price above the warrant price.

c. The use of warrants may permit a company to issue bonds when it would not otherwise be considered strong enough to do so.

d. The use of warrants may offset the higher rate the corporation might have to pay without the warrants in view of a weak financial position.

Debt with warrants, however, has the following disadvantages:

a. Stock price may have a ceiling while there are outstanding warrants. As the stock price tends to rise above the warrant price, warrant holders will exercise. The resultant exercise dilutes total holdings and tends to depress the price of the stock. Hence, a market value of the stock tends to be established at a level slightly above the exercise price, not higher, until all the warrants are exercised.

b. It is more costly to issue new stock while there are outstanding warrants since the market price of the stock is depressed due to the warrants.

ACCOUNTING FOR CONVERTIBLE DEBT AND DEBT WITH STOCK PURCHASE WARRANTS

Accounting Principles Board (APB) Opinion No. 14 sets forth the accounting principles and rules for dealing with convertible debt and warrants.

No portion of the proceeds from the issuance of convertible debt securities should be accounted for as attributable to the conversion feature. This is a different position from that originally taken under paragraphs 8 and 9 of Opinion No. 10, since suspended, which advocated that the conversion feature be given accounting recognition. Since Opinion 10, experience has indicated that the debt and conversion option are inseparable and so Opinion 14 and its new requirements better reflect both the theoretical situation and the practical considerations. Expressed simply, this means that since there is no discount set up on the issuance of the convertible, there is no loss in profits in later years through amortization of this discount as a charge to earnings.

The Board also reaffirmed in this opinion its previous position regarding debt issued with detachable stock purchase warrants. The proceeds should be allocated to the debt and to the warrants based on their respective values at the time of issuance or shortly thereafter. The value attributable to the warrants is to be accounted for as paid-in-capital, with the resulting discount, or reduced premium, treated as debt discount. Once again, any debt discount must be amortized as a charge against future earnings and will serve to reduce earnings per share.

However, when warrants are not detachable from the debt, and the debt security must be surrendered in order to exercise the warrant, the two securities are taken together and are the equivalent of convertible debt; hence there is no attribution to the warrant. If there is a choice and market conditions and interest rates permit it, the warrants should be attachable to avoid a future reduction in earnings per share due to amortization of debt discount.

It is not always possible to clearly identify every type of debt security, as to its broad classification. There are many types of debt with varying conversion features, stock purchase warrants, or a combination of such features. In such case, proper accounting dictates looking to the substance of the transaction. For example, if convertible debt is issued at a substantial premium, there is a strong presumption that such premium represents paid-in-capital and that a portion of the proceeds should be accounted for as being attributable to the conversion feature.

INSTALLMENT LOANS AND LEASES

Installment loans are those obligations payable over a period of years, usually one to five, on a periodic basis, usually monthly or quarterly. While such loans may require payments during the current twelve-month period, they are included in the discussion in this chapter on the cost of debt, since the major part of such loans is given long-term classification on the balance sheet.

As used in this context, installment loans include equipment lease financing and any other type of capital equipment purchasing which includes a payment schedule with installments.

The most common type of installment financing is equipment leasing. It offers these decided advantages:

1. Leasing is available to companies of any size, and particularly to smaller companies that are not large enough to float bond issues and to newer companies that have not established a track record which would enable them to sell bonds.

2. The lease liability need not necessarily be shown on the balance sheet. When it is not, the corporation's debt capacity is increased. Present accounting principles require that the lease be capitalized if it is, in fact, an installment purchase. Leases, however, are so varied in their terms, nature, and purchase options that they can readily be constructed so as to preclude capitalization and balance sheet presentation.

3. Lease payments are fully tax deductible. If the lease period is shorter than the useful life of the equipment, this will supply greater tax deductions than would depreciation if the asset were purchased outright with proceeds from a bond issue.

4. 100% financing of the equipment, usually with little or no down payment, is available on terms tailored to the user.

5. Most loan indenture agreements and restrictive covenants do not prohibit debt created through leasing, or if they do, a ceiling is set to permit significant amounts of such leasing.

6. Debt financing through the use of leasing does not contain restrictive covenants. There are no limitations on debt to equity, working capital, or dividends.

7. There is no tax problem at audit time over lease payment deductions, as there well might be over useful life and the amount of depreciation claimed.

8. The lease may be structured to provide higher book income in the early years than under outright ownership. The early years' rental payments are generally less than the combined interest expense and depreciation under ownership.

9. State and city franchise and income taxes may be reduced as the property factor, one of three, is reduced.

There may be some disadvantages to leasing, including:

1. Residual rights to the property may be lost at the end of the lease period. In a pure lease, the lessee may have renewal rights or the right to purchase, but these rights require the payment of additional sums.

2. Rentals under the lease may exceed comparable debt service. The lessor probably had to borrow the financed amount and tacked on a profit, structuring his required lease payments to meet this total. If the corporation borrowed its own funds for the purchase, it could avoid the profit factor.

3. There is a loss of operating flexibility and less protection against obsolescence. If a new and better piece of equipment were to become available, it might not be possible to sell or exchange the old equipment. This can be avoided if the lessor will allow a trade-up to newer equipment and will execute a new lease.

4. The lease payment is based on a fixed interest rate. If the cost of money declines, and with it interest rates, the lessee continues to pay the same amount. If, on the other hand, the asset had been purchased outright and financed, the debt could probably be refinanced at a lower rate in a declining money market.

5. There may be a loss of tax benefits which would accrue due to using accelerated depreciation and high interest deductions on the debt in the early years. This would produce a short-term cash advantage if the equipment were bought instead of leased.

LEVERAGE LEASING

The Leverage Lease is a comparatively recent financial vehicle for companies involved in making significant capital investments. These leases are those in which the funds for the purchase of the leased property are provided in part by one or more third parties (loan participants) in addition to the financing institution or the company (the owner or equity participant). The owner participant typically invests 20% of the purchase price of the equipment, and the loan participant invests 80% on a non-recourse basis, meaning he can look only to his note receivable for repayment, not to the equipment itself. Under these leases, a major portion of the lease payments may be typically assigned to the third party as a repayment for this investment, together with interest thereon. Where the lessee is not an owner participant, the loan participants generally have no right to recover against the owner participant. The loan participant must look, then, only to the lessee and his first lien on the property. The owner participant's return on his investment usually includes some portion of the lease payments, in addition to the income tax benefits (depreciation and flow-through of investment tax credits) during the lease period, as well as the proceeds from the sale or re-lease of the property during or at the end of the lease period. This type of lease produces high cash flow in the early years, with the total investment usually being returned to the owner participant within two years.

Structuring a leverage lease is a complicated process, requiring familiarity with the tax and accounting requirements of such leases. The Return on Investment on these leases can typically be 20% after taxes, when considering proceeds from the sale or re-rental of the residual values. Tax considerations may be reviewed in Code Sec. 167(m); Reg. Para. 1.167 (a) - 11 (The Class Life Asset Depreciation Range (ADR) System), and Revenue Procedures 75-21, 75-28 and 76-30 (guidelines which will be used for advance ruling purposes in determining whether or not certain transactions purporting to be leases of property are, in fact, leases for Federal Income Tax purposes). These tax guidelines require:

1. A minimum "at risk" investment of 20% of the cost of the property with no arrangements for the return of the investment after the property is placed in service.

2. The residual value of the property must be at least 20% at the end of the lease term.

3. The lease term must include all renewal or extension periods, unless they are at the lessee's option at fair market value.

4. The lessee may not have any contractual right to purchase the property at less than fair market value, nor may the lessor abandon the property to the lessee.

5. The lessee may not pay any part of the cost of the property, nor of improvements, nor may he lend funds to the lessor, or guarantee any indebtedness related to this property.

6. The property must provide a profit exclusive of the tax benefits. This guideline is met if the sum of the rentals to be received during the lease term, plus the residual value, exceeds the sum of all payments to the senior lendors plus the equity investment including any direct costs.

7. No rental payment may be 10% higher or lower than the amount calculated by dividing the total rent payable over the lease term by the number of years in the term.

8. The only feasible use for the property may not be to continue to lease it to the lessee. It must be usable by another unrelated party; otherwise it can be considered a sale rather than a lease.

The guideline for accounting for leases is found in the Statement of Financial Accounting Standards No. 13 of the Financial Accounting Standards Board, dated November 1976, titled "Accounting for Leases." Present income tax laws make the tax benefits of leveraged leases more attractive to corporations than to individuals, as the latter are subject to the "at risk" limitations—that is, they can only utilize the tax benefits to the extent of the funds they have at risk, in this case 20%. These limitations do not apply to corporations.

SALE AND LEASE BACK

A form of leasing is the sale and lease back and, in nature, it is similar to a mortgage bond. It is, however, often accomplished quickly, with little cost, and without any elaborate bond indenture.

Owned property, like land, buildings, or equipment, may be sold to an independent finance company at a high percentage of its appraised value, say 80% (subject to negotiation and often contingent on the credit of the owner), and the resultant cash received may be more than original cost if the property has appreciated in value, either as a result of inflation or economic utility. The property may then be leased back, usually for terms of three to eight years.

This is an excellent device to use in inflationary times. The property will usually have appreciated far over its cost, providing windfall cash on the sale. If the property has a long future life or is not expected to be replaced, then the debt incurred on the sale may be paid over future years of the lease with inflated dollars.

Such leases are as varied as the parties desire to have them. Factors receiving particular attention in negotiation are the term of the lease, the rate, and the residual value or renewal option at the end. The rate will be determined by the utilization either party may have of the investment tax credit and depreciation. Sales and lease backs may be structured as leveraged leases and, on occasion, may even be structured as straight debt.

When structured as straight debt, a tax-oriented corporation is usually formed to purchase the equipment. The equipment is sold for 8% to 10% cash, the balance due on two notes. One of the notes is amortizing, the other is a non-recourse balloon note. The "at-risk" rules do not apply to corporations. Hence, tax benefits for the amount of the non-recourse note will be available to a corporate lender. The amount of the monthly rental is set at a level exactly sufficient to pay for the interest and amortization on both notes. At the end of the lease back period, usually five years on this type of program, the balloon note is canceled, and since it is non-recourse, the equipment reverts to the company. The company may account for this as a straight long-term loan, at an interest rate substantially below bank prime, not even accounting for the sale and lease back for financial accounting purposes. For tax purposes, the company will pay a capital gain on the sale and will lose the depreciation advantages of owning its equipment. It may also have an investment tax credit and depreciation recapture. These tax disadvantages will be offset by higher monthly rental which is a tax deductible charge. The entire transaction can be structured with no unfavorable tax aspects.

The lenders, on the other hand, receive the full tax benefits and cash flow advantages of the tax-sheltered corporation, including depreciation, investment tax credit, and other benefits depending on the structure of the transaction.

MAKE OR BUY DECISIONS

The management problem of vertical integration seems to be a continuous and persevering one. One reason is that product quality and specifications, purchasing situations, and manufacturing conditions rarely remain static for any long period of time. There are numerous management tools available and appropriate with which to evaluate the desirability of producing your own raw materials, components, and fittings, or purchasing them from outside suppliers. The technique of value analysis should certainly find application here. A good solid cost accounting study, plus the company's cash position, might be an adequate basis for decision. The overriding consideration is the objective of obtaining the best quality materials at the lower cost, at the proper times, and in adequate quantities.

LEASE AND LEASE BACK VERSUS OWNERSHIP

Capital investment in plant and equipment is an important factor in the rate of long-term growth of both an individual company and the total economy of the country. A firm's capital expenditure program is a key part of its long-range financial plan and current and long-term operating plans. Under certain conditions or circumstances, however, it may be more expedient to lease a facility or to rent certain equipment than to make a capital investment with its accompanying reduction of cash funds. This type of transaction could range from the leasing of salesmen's automobiles to the sale and lease back of a factory building or warehouse. A company with limited funds or liquidity may have much better opportunities of obtaining profit-producing leverage through expansion or acquisitions than by investing in its own buildings, autos, trucks, etc.

An outright lease is a simple transaction whereby a company pays rent to a landlord for the use of a building or facility for manufacturing or warehousing operations. A sale and lease back arrangement is primarily used as a means of obtaining capital or cash funds. In this case, a company sells its factory and/or warehouse building to an insurance company, for example, under a contract to occupy the property and pay a specified rent for a long-term period. It is not unusual for the total amount of rent contracted for by the terms and length of the lease to more than cover the initial selling price plus interest.

The advantage or disadvantage of leasing versus owning can be measured on an economic basis by the discounted cash flow method described in Chapter 3. In the event that cash in-flows cannot be related to an investment (say the purchase of a piece of furniture or non-revenue producing equipment), then the decision to purchase or to lease should be related to the company's overall return on investment (as computed in Chapter 3). If the effective rate of the lease, for example, is 12%, compared to an overall ROI of 20%, the decision should be made to lease. The company can make more on the leverage, that is by using the lessor's money and receiving a greater return on the funds used in its own business. This assumes, of course, that the company's capacity is underutilized and that the funds can be invested in areas where they are needed. This decision would then be subject to previously described considerations—indentured restrictions in debt agreements, the need for off-balance sheet financing, and the terms and conditions of the lease agreement. It would probably be difficult to justify leasing rather than owning on a strictly economic basis, especially in the case of accelerated depreciation, investment credit, and other possible tax benefits accruing to ownership, except in the case of specially structured situations, like the Captive Finance Subsidiary or the Leveraged

Lease. Usually, however, resorting to leasing rather than owning is initiated because of cash position, expediency, or convenience, not because there might be economic advantages.

THE CAPTIVE FINANCE SUBSIDIARY

Companies that manufacture equipment which qualifies for investment tax credits may find it advisable to establish a wholly-owned finance subsidiary. The parent will sell the equipment to the sub., taking full accounting sale treatment. The finance sub. will then lease the equipment to the ultimate user, with these advantages:

1. The finance subsidiary can support a debt to equity ratio greater than the parent's.
   a. Finance subs. do not report traditional balance sheets showing current assets and liabilities. Instead, all assets and liabilities are lumped in a group, without the current classification.
   b. Banks and institutions will traditionally lend from 2 to 1, to 4 to 1, on debt to equity, since the sub's. assets are always accounts receivable (leases receivable) and are usually secured by the equipment underlying the lease.

2. The customer receives terms of payment in accordance with the lease, from one to five years. This is a great marketing device which the parent would not ordinarily supply.

3. The finance subsidiary usually has an independent name, which facilitates its collection activities against slow-paying lessees.

4. The parent treats the sale to the sub. as a sale, taking in to income the full profit on the sale. This usually requires that the parent's salesman has negotiated a full-pay-out lease with a third-party customer, using the subsidiary's lease document.

5. The finance subsidiary need not be consolidated with the parent, avoiding the necessity of picking up the long-term lease receivable and the short-term bank borrowings used to finance such receivables. If consolidated, this would kill the parent's current ratio and hurt its own credit capability. The authority for non-consolidation is found in Accounting Research Bulletin (ARB) No. 51, which exempts finance companies and insurance companies from the normal consolidation rules.

6. The finance subsidiary may utilize finance lease accounting, for financial accounting purposes, which would permit it to reflect higher earnings in the early years.
   a. Sum-of-the-digits accounting methods are proper, to match income in the early years to the higher debt balances.
   b. The sub. may reflect acquisition costs of new leases by front-loading income with a portion of the unearned interest income.

7. The finance subsidiary may utilize operating lease accounting for tax purposes, reflecting less income and taxes in the early years. It may also reflect income on a cash basis, eliminating unpaid lease receivables (past-dues) from its determination of income.

8. The subsidiary may file a consolidated tax return with its parent, despite not consolidating for financial accounting purposes. This will permit the consolidated group to use the tax losses of the subsidiary which usually result in the early years and the investment tax credit may be utilized, it otherwise being lost to the parent. This is a tremendous benefit.

The captive finance subsidiary, then, if properly structured, offers immediate cash flow, tax advantages, and permanent investment tax credit benefits while providing long-term financing to the company's customers. The use of a subsidiary permits the company to obtain bank financing and long-term institutional money more readily than through the parent. A word of caution, however. Such a subsidiary is "capital intensive" requiring increasing amounts of borrowings each year to continue to finance the installment sales to the parent's customers. This requires a constant and inexorable fund-raising effort on the part of the subsidiary, year in and year out. This is difficult to accomplish in tight money times and requires careful long-range planning to provide advance funds to weather the tight money times. A way out of this eventuality is participation on a 50-50 partnership basis with an independent finance company, preferably a public company, which is in the business of raising funds in the public markets on a continuing basis. The benefits of a limited partnership would be obtaining a stepped-up basis for depreciation and investment tax credits. In any event, the wholly-owned finance subsidiary could be set up for as short a period as three or four years to obtain the significant advantages offered, and then discontinued if tight money markets persist.

The American Management Association offers several excellent seminars on leasing and the benefits of establishing a captive finance subsidiary. Since it is so highly specialized a field, the responsiblity for the project should be placed in the hands of the Treasurer or Controller who should personally supervise the project and be prepared to devote most of his time to establishing the project to include:

1. Formation of the corporation and qualification in required states
2. Design of the lease, guarantees, and other legal documents
3. Establishing the format for tax and financial accounting
4. Creating the marketing plan and promotional literature
5. Setting appropriate and competitive rates
6. Structuring the debt and equity aspects
7. Preparing short-and long-term operating and cash projections
8. Establishing the short-and long-term lending relationships

ACQUISITIONS

Acquisitions are usually thought of as being made to increase earnings, to diversify products, to vertically integrate, to acquire assets, and sometimes, even for the sake of creating excitement in a company's stock. Rarely are they considered as an alternative to the issuance of long-term debt, but this effect often results and, indeed, when it does, there is a cost to this debt. Long-term debt may be acquired through acquisitions if:

1. The acquired company is in the business of obtaining long-term debt on a continuing basis. Examples are a fixed asset company, say steel or rail, which makes major investments in fixed assets through such borrowings, or a finance company which is capital intensive and constantly raising funds to operate. The acquirer may use these relationships to obtain direct debt or debt funnelled through the subsidiary.

2. The acquired company may manufacture a product which is marketed or used in manufacturing by the parent. If such a product has been long-term financed by the subsidiary, the parent has, in effect, obtained long-term financing for its product, due to the intercompany eliminations in consolidation.

3. The parent, by issuing stock at the cost of equity previously described in the Equity section, has obtained all of the assets and liabilities, including the long-term liabilities of the acquired company.

Acquisitions may be treated as Purchases or Poolings of Interest, for accounting purposes, in accord with APB Opinion No. 16. In a pooling, an acquiring company takes the assets of a merged company onto its own books at their original cost. This has sometimes allowed a company to issue stock at a worth much more than the original cost of the acquired assets and then to sell the assets at present value and take the difference as a profit. It has also been possible to include the profit of an acquired company in an annual report, even though the pooling occured at the end of the fiscal year reported on. Opinion No. 16 requires that either the pooling or purchase method be used, not a combination; pooling may be used only if companies combine through an exchange of common stock, subject to certain restrictions. All other business combinations must be accounted for as purchases. In purchase accounting, any difference between the price paid and the value of tangible and identifiable intangible assets acquired, as good will, must be systematically written off against future earnings for a period not to exceed 40 years. Moreover, under Opinion No. 16, it is not possible to include the profits of an acquired company in net income reported to stockholders if the pooling took place after the end of the year reported on.

COSTING CAPITAL AND DEBT

1. Capital, including Equity and Retained Earnings, and debt have a cost which may be measured as a percentage, using proven mathematical formulas.

2. The features and limitations of existing debt, together with the market price of its shares, will determine whether the corporation should utilize convertible debt.

3. Leasing offers advantages which are often non-economic, but necessary due to cash position, expediency, accounting and tax considerations. Under specially structured situations, such as with leverage leases and with captive finance subsidiaries, substantial return on investment may provide economic advantages.

CHAPTER 9

Computer Utilization: Prime Tool for Modern Financial Decision Making

The surest route to disaster in distributed processing is a helter-skelter melange of terminals, each programmed by a local group, with improper interfaces to the central data processing department.

The computer is, perhaps, the least understood of the tools available to financial managers, but it may be viewed as nothing more than that—a financial tool. We understand the techniques of accounting, manufacturing, operations research, and value engineering, but the mystique of the computer often eludes us. This may be due to the fact that the computer has been with us, in commercial use, for only twenty-five years, whereas accounting, production, and engineering arts have been practiced for thousands of years. The jargon of the computer is unfamiliar. Words like byte and baud threaten our respect for our own knowledge. Immense computer-related decision making requirements constantly test our mettle—do we lease or buy the monster?; are operations to be centralized or decentralized?; how do we charge user departments, if at all?; do we use outside computer services or in-house?; shall our reporting system be manual or computer based? The answers to all of these questions depend on a thorough understanding of the computer, its capabilities and limitations. The solutions are found through increased knowledge and education. The financial manager who avoids this understanding out of fear or insecurity will completely avoid making the necessary computer-related decisions. He will be missing out on using one of the best financial decision making tools available to him.

WHAT IS IT AND HOW DOES IT WORK

Understanding starts with education. Colleges offer night school courses in computer orientation, systems and procedures, or data processing analysis. These courses take from eight to thirteen weeks, two to three hours a night, one or two nights a week, and provide a sound basis for future decisions. They are also offered by state professional accounting societies and the American Management Assn. The content includes the mechanics, language, and operation of the computer. An overview is presented below.

Any data processing problem requires recording, storage, processing, and output. The recording is called input, in computer language. Input devices read cards, tape, or scan documents (Optical Character Reading - OCR) and store the data. The computer storage or memory is the brain of the machine and all arithmetic numbers must be in it, in storage, before they can be processed. Since the memory must be large and fast, able to send hundreds of thousands of numbers to the arithmetic processing section of the machine, the cost of an adequate memory is often prohibitive. As a result, auxiliary systems may be used to store away that part of the data which is not currently being used. This side memory "talks" only to the main memory. Main memories are magnetic cores, drums, disks, chips, and microprocessors. Auxiliary storage is mostly magnetic tape, disks, and smaller drums. The processing of data is done by the central processing unit (CPU). In addition to the four arithmetic functions, the CPU shifts numbers, has registers which temporarily store numbers, and helps make decisions. In addition, there is a fifth section which like a calculator, performs control functions, that is, sending electric signals to the computer based on information it receives from memory. The output section, obviously, records the processing results on cards, printed paper, or on tapes for further storage or processing. Think of it as analogous to you, an individual with memory, operating a desk calculator. The keyboard is your input; your memory holds the data and the instructions as to the type of arithmetic function to be performed. You key in a number; it is temporarily stored in a register. You key in a second number, hit the multiply key, and see the output result on another register. The computer, then, may be simply thought of as a high speed calculator with a prodigious memory.

Planning the logic of a problem, including the flow charting, is called programming. This includes storing instructions in memory as to when certain arithmetic functions are to be performed—in certain situations, multiply, in others, subtract. The control section of the computer decodes these instructions and signals the machine to so perform. The process of planning and charting the program and coding the instructions, is called a computer routine. The following exhibit demonstrates the relationship between the main computer functions previously described. The dotted lines represent electrical signals from the electronic control section of the computer to the other segments, giving instructions on how to perform.

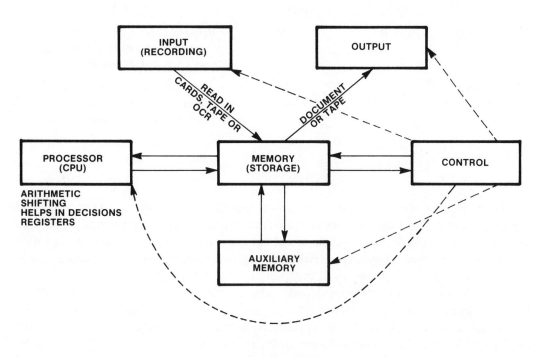

Exhibit 46

The Functional Relationships of a Programmed Computer

This "system" of devices and electronics "reads" words from the input device (punched cards, paper or magnetic tape, or optical character read documents), and transfers the words to memory. A "word" is a number or group of characters, say letters and numbers, that the computer sees as one unit. Computer memories are measured in terms of words, such as a 4,000 word memory (called a 4k memory). A word could be eleven "characters," with a character being a combination of numbers, letters, or symbols (like *, #, or &), each symbol having a specific meaning. The eleven characters of the word constitute an "instruction format" which is placed in memory. These characters, in general, specify the type of arithmetic to be performed, (add, subtract, multiply, divide), the address or location in memory (at which a word is to be found which is to enter a calculation, or where in memory the result of the calculation is to be stored).

Looking at an actual example, if a payroll calculation were being done, year to date pay of $10,000 from the previous payroll would already have been read in to the computer and been stored at location 1000; this week's pay of $1,200 is read in and stored at location 1001; and the resulting new year to date pay, $11,200, is to be stored at location 1002. Moreover, the "instructions" to perform these operations are part of the "routine" from a previously planned program, and they are to be found stored at 4000, 4001, and 4002. The computer coder or programmer would write this routine as:

Instruction Location	Operation	Data Location	Description
4000	B	1000	Bring year to date payroll from location 1000 to the register to await calculation
4001	A	1001	Add the current week's pay found at location 1001 to the number in the register
4002	S	1002	Store the resulting new year to date pay at location 1002.

The computer operator might start this routine by reading in a card showing 4000, meaning that memory location 4000 contains the instruction to be performed at this time. The control section would send out electrical signals to memory to bring instruction 4000, the previous year to date pay, to the arithmetic register. Card number 4001 is then read in, and the "routine" is continued until completed.

How does the control section decode each number? The computer word of eleven characters specifies each character in binary, rather than decimal digits. A binary digit is often called a "bit." Each number is represented by a 0 or 1, rather than by 0 through 9 in the decimal system. The system is sometimes referred to as base two, rather than our familiar base ten decimal system. A binary number is well suited to the electrical circuitry of the computer. These circuits are bi-stable, having only two possible stable positions. A circuit is either positive or negative; a light bulb is either on or off. Therefore, a transistor or circuit, in one state, corresponds to a 1, and in its only other possible state corresponds to a 0. Thus, circuits using these bi-stable, on or off devices, may be combined to perform arithmetic functions using binary numbers. A *binary coded decimal system* is a further refinement of binary arithmetic wherein each digit of the decimal number is expressed in a binary digit, either 0 or 1. For example, in binary, each digit is worth twice that of the number to its right, starting with 1, as in: 16 8 4 2 1. To convert from binary to decimal, the decimal equivalents of the binary numbers are added together whenever a binary 1 appears, as in:

binary number	1	0	0	1	1	
decimal value	16	8	4	2	1	
add values of 1	16			2	1	= 19

Again, using the above binary notation, the decimal number 362 would be written in binary as: 101101010, this representing each digit with a value twice that of the number to its right, starting with number 1, and not adding any 0 values. Thus, reading from right to left, add $0 + 2 + 0 + 8 + 0 + 32 + 64 + 0 + 256 = 362$. To code this in binary decimal, each decimal digit—units, tens, or hundreds, is coded in binary, as follows:

	hundreds	tens	units
decimal number	3	6	2
binary number	0011	0110	0010

Further refinements may be made in binary to express letters. For instance, if 01 represents the first third of the alphabet A through I, 10 the second third J through R, and 11 the final third S through Z, then a table could be constructed showing all the numbers and letters in binary. In the table below: 01-0011 stands for letter C; 10-0100 is the letter M. Blanks represent special symbols or characters.

BINARY TABLE

Alphabetic and Numeric Code

	Zone 00	Zone 01	Zone 10	Zone 11
0000	zero	—	—	—
0001	one	A	J	—
0010	two	B	K	S
0011	three	C	L	T
0100	four	D	M	U
0101	five	E	N	V
0110	six	F	O	W
0111	seven	G	P	X
1000	eight	H	Q	Y
1001	nine	I	R	Z

Exhibit 47

The computer prints out processed data using high-speed printers. However, the computer processes the data electronically at much faster speeds than the electro-mechanically operated printer. One of the limiting factors, therefore, in processing computer-generated reports is the slower output speed of the printer. This may be overcome by using auxiliary storage units, like tape storage, to retain data. Only summary information need be printed out, speeding up the report process.

Another limiting factor is the printer itself. It must operate under the strict constraints established by the computer program, on a line by line basis and in sequence. You cannot rotate the paper carriage back to an earlier line as you can with a typewriter. Therefore, it is best to keep reports simple and to show only key data. Since the computer printer operates at relatively fast speeds and can be programmed to print out a great deal of data, computer reports tend to have too much data, to be confusing and unreadable. Keep them simple!

As with any discipline, precise language must be developed to identify the concepts involved. A Glossary follows, of special terms which generally identify the "hardware," "software" and operations of a computer system:

GLOSSARY

Access Method: A means of moving data between a computer's memory storage and its attached devices (card, tape, disk etc).

Alphanumeric: A character set containing an alphabetic letter, digits and sometimes other characters such as asterisks and punctuation marks.

Assembler Language: A low level programming language written in a one for one relationship with machine code. It is translated to machine code at time of compile.

Asynchronous Transmission: An irregular pattern or flow of data such that each character or block of characters is transmitted arbitrarily. A start and stop signal defines each character or block to the computer.

Baud Rate: The number of bits or units transmitted per second.

Binary Coded Decimal (BCD): A four bit binary coded definition of a decimal character where the weights 8-4-2-1 are used. e.g. 0101=5 and 0011 0101=35.
Note: 110101 in pure binary notation would equal 53.

Bit: The smallest definable unit or element in a computer. Represented by either a 0 or 1 in a pure binary system.

Byte: A set of eight binary bits that can represent many values.

    e.g. in binary   0-255
         in octal   0-377
         in decimal 0-99
         or an alphabetical character.
    Note: These are not all the values.

Channel: A device that connects the processing unit and I/O (input/output) devices.

Character: Usually used to define a single numeric, alphabetic or special value. It is also used for the control, organization or definition of data.

    e.g. character string
        character density
        character block
        character set
        etc.

Cobol: (COMMON BUSINESS ORIENTED LANGUAGE) A high level computer language that uses an English-like method of coding. This code is processed by a compiler prior to running on a machine.

Compiler: A program that converts or translates a program written in a business language to machine language.

COM Unit: (COMPUTER OUTPUT MICROFILM UNIT) A computer peripheral device that converts computer output to microfilm or fiche.

Core: A term used to define main storage in a computer.

CPU: (CENTRAL PROCESSOR UNIT) The control processor of a computer.

CRT: (Cathode Ray Tube) A TV-like device to display images produced by a computer.

Cycle Speed: The time required to complete an event, ie: a cycle of processing.

Data Base: A term usually used to define all the available data in a corporation's computer. It can, however, be used to define a set or portion of the whole.

DBA: (DATA BASE ADMINISTRATOR) The person responsible for the control and utilization of the Data Base.

Distributed Data Processing: Computers or terminals deployed where they can be used more effectively (usually where the action takes place). These computers or terminals are usually interconnected with a central processor for the gathering or dissemination of data.

Emulation: Either special machine features or programming techniques used to execute programs written for another computer. It should be noted that this method is slower than processing in native mode.

File: A set of related records treated as a single unit. Sometimes defined as a data set.

Fortran: A high-level programming language whose primary function is mathematical problem solving. It, like other languages, requires a compilation prior to running on a computer.

Front End Processor: A computer (usually a Mini) that is attached to a large scale computer. Its task is mainly to control input and output (I/O) of data transmission, relieving the large scale system of the I/O handling.

Hardware: A term used to define data processing equipment.

Hexadecimal: Synonymous with sexadecimal. A base sixteen notation or numeration where the characters 0-9 and A-F are used to define the value.

High-Level Language: A language that is not limited to one computer, but can be compiled on different systems.

Integrated Circuit: Sometimes referred to as a CHIP, made of silicone or some other crystalline material treated to support combinations of interconnected circuits.

Memory: The main storage area of a computer where data and problems are held for fast access.

Mini-Computer: With the advent of large memory sizes on 'Mini'-computers the distinction between them and 'MAINFRAMES' or 'MAXI'S' is a gray area. A mini can be loosely defined as a computer built specifically for real-time processing.

Microprocessor: A computer that has its arithmetic logic unit (processor) on a single chip.

Multi-Point Network: A data communications configuration where more than two terminals are interconnected.

Multiprogramming: An operating mode where two or more programs can be executed concurrently in a single processor.

Operating System: The resident software that controls the execution of programs.

Parity Check: A redundancy check for error detection which tests that the sum of the bits is either even or odd.

Partition: An area in main storage that is allocated to the processing of a task.

Processor: A term that can define either a hardware unit or software.
a) A unit in a computer that interprets or executes instructions.
b) A program that compiles or assembles (see compiler).

Program: A term used to define a piece of software that performs a series of actions to achieve a desired result, or the writing of the actual software.

Real-Time: Describes a system that operates in a conversational mode with a person manning a terminal device.

Routine: A set of instructions having an entry and exit that is usually used frequently by a program. It may be a subset of that program or one that is of a general nature used by multiple programs.

Simulation: The ability of a computer to imitate another. This is usually done by software. This gives the ability to run programs on a system that was designed for another without altering them.

Software: Programs that give the computer the ability to operate, in contrast to hardware.

Spooling: The use of auxilary storage to buffer the data passing between a processor and its peripheral devices.

Storage Device: A unit in which data can be placed, retained and retrieved as required. e.g. card, tape, disk, drum etc.

System: Can refer to a hardware configuration, a set of programs or a method of accomplishing a task.

Table: Data arranged in a logical array to be used as an argument to accomplish a task.

Task: A basic unit of work defined in a system which can be either manual or computerized.

Time Sharing: A mode of operation that allows multiple users to concurrently share the resources of a computer.

Virtual Storage: A method which allows a program to be written that is larger than the available area in main storage. This is accomplished by the system breaking the program into sections (called pages) and storing them on an auxiliary unit. When the program requires a specific section (page) that is not currently in storage, that page is brought into the next available space, the page that was in that space being put back into the auxiliary unit (This is known as paging). The address of the new page is redefined to the actual address of the area into which it was brought.

Word: A set or string of binary bits or bytes combined to form an entity. The number of bits or bytes in a word depend upon the type of computer.

e.g. IBM 370 or 360, 32 bits or 4 bytes = 1 word

IBM system 7,   16 bits or 2 bytes = 1 word

ORGANIZING FOR DATA PROCESSING

The data processing function involves manual as well as automated data processing. The organization of this function will depend, primarily, on whether operations are centralized or decentralized.

In decentralized operations, often called distributed data processing, mini-computer-based terminals at remote sites can raise overall data processing efficiency and can cut costs. This method is most effective for a large firm with widespread operations and many profit centers. It may be totally inefficient for a highly centralized operation. Distributed processors, or mini-computers, can perform prosaic and yeomanlike functions in isolated points, on a continuing basis. They can then use standard telephone lines to transmit data to a main central processing unit (CPU). This releases a large portion of the central, more expensive computer's operating time for more complex overall operations.

The so-called "intelligent" terminal permits this type of operation. The terminal incorporates a mini-computer which can be programmed to lead the terminal operator through the entire keying process, which a central computer cannot do in remote, batch controlled systems. Moreover, this can be done inexpensively, and with good error-checking capability. The mini-computer can maintain limited tables and files to permit look-ups of master files, such as account numbers, credit limits, or year to date information.

In brief, a decentralized system would serve better than a centralized data processing system when: profit centers are many and widespread; centralized systems are too busy, overloaded with detailed work; centralized processing takes too long to feed information back to users; there are too many errors occurring in processing centrally, requiring turn-around communication with outlying offices and consequent processing delays; the danger of centralized equipment break downs is too great, requiring expensive back-up equipment; there is a need to tailor programs to local needs.

Decentralized or distributed operations do not imply lack of central control. *The surest route to disaster in distributed processing is a helter, skelter melange of terminals, each programmed by a local group, with improper interfaces to the central data processing department.* This would lead to the transmittal of data to central offices from distributed points which were thought to be similar, but which, very probably, would have different input criteria. All data might carry the same label, but it would be different and, therefore, not reliable. While decentralized managers should be encouraged to develop local applications in a self-contained manner, these should be subject to centralized data processing controls. Those controls would include computer, as well as management constraints.

An Organizational Chart follows for a headquarters organization in a company using decentralized data processors, feeding inputs into and controlled by a central management organization:

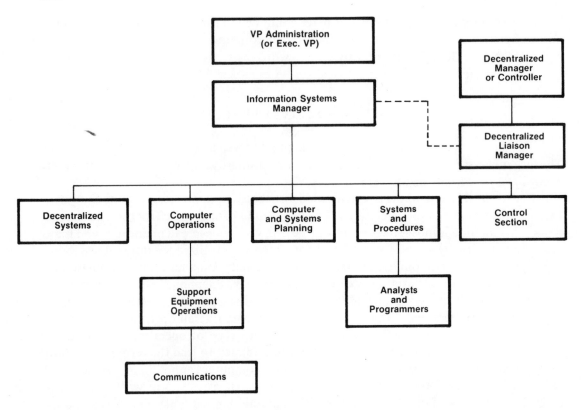

Exhibit 48

**Organization of a Centralized EDP Control Function
(in a Decentralized Company)**

COMPUTER REPORTS AND APPLICATIONS

In computer applications which have been established without a uniform data base, it is difficult to change programs or even to obtain new reports. A Data Base Management system (DBMS) is essential to collecting data from various decentralized locations or from diverse master files. This is a software system, sometimes available from computer manufacturers or software vendors, which establishes guidelines as to how data should be kept on the file. A program merely requests a certain type of data and DBMS can find it within the established data base. This enables the accurate retrieval of a variety of data which can be assembled into a variety of reports. In essence, DBMS is an overall system to consider the overall data requirements of the organization, without which flexibility in applications and reports cannot be obtained.

Additional flexibility in applications and reports can be realized from the utilization of time sharing terminals. These may augment central or decentralized processors. Many time sharing vendors provide pre-programmed access to a variety of applications. It is not necessary to program your own applications from scratch, and the cost of time sharing is far less than the cost of original programming for these special applications. Many of these services are available from banks, public accounting firms, management consultants, or outright time sharing vendors. Typical financial analysis programs include: return on investment, regression analysis, ratio analysis, trend analysis, comparative balance sheet and income statement analysis, capital project evaluation, depreciation scheduling, discounted cash flow and present value analysis, statistical sampling programs, forecasting using financial models, and risk analysis for new products or pricing levels. Learning to program inputs for time sharing terminals takes about three full days of training. The time is worth the effort for the reporting flexibility it achieves.

The types of reports to which the computer best addresses itself are those requiring the accumulation of masses of data. Typical is the rolling forward of data and the print out of accumulated amounts, as in year to date payroll information. The computer can also keep count of transactions, at the same time it accumulates. Hence, it can compare shipping dates to order dates, count the number of days to ship each order, and accumulate that information. A report could then be printed stating: 1,000 orders shipped in 2 days; 1,200 orders shipped in 3 days; 600 orders in 4 days, and 30 orders in 5 days. The report could, further, calculate percents in each category and compare them to last month's results, or year to date or both. It could also accumulate the dollar value of orders in each category and the average value per order shipped in each category . . . . . . all this as a by product of recording an invoice to a customer. The features of computer reports, then, are accumulated data, print outs of masses of data, comparisons of earlier periods, calculations of relationships of data in categories or percents. All of these features are found in reports on Accounts Receivable, Inventories, Payrolls, Accounts Payable, and Financial Statements.

The characteristics of reports should conform, as nearly as possible, to the principles set forth in Chapter 12. This means, in general, that computer reports should try not to look like computer reports, but like management reports. A few of the "don't's" of computer generated reports are listed below:

Don't:

1.   have cover pages with computer-drawn logos. (These look nice but serve no purpose and waste programmer's time, paper, and the reader's time.)

2.   show computer technical information to the report user, such as time to run the program, invalid data, or program number identification. (Show only that information and those numbers that have meaning to the reader. If the computer people need such information, print it out on a separate page and tear it off the report which is distributed.)

3.   use computer jargon on any reports.

4.   circulate reports on computer sheets. (They are bulky, hard to file and retrieve. Instead, reduce computer sheets to 8½ x 11" letter size copies.

5.   distribute detailed print outs of data to managers. (Managers want summary, exception information. Leave the reams of paper in the computer room or the control clerk's desk.)

6.   neglect to show assumptions and distribution on each report. (The user needs to know the basis of the data and who else is reading the report.)

CONTROLLING THE SYSTEM

Control means getting the system to do what it's supposed to do and, indeed, squeezing more out of it. The good system supplies timely reports, in a format useable by the reader, at the least cost. Control starts with good management.

Data processing departments should operate under defined management by objectives programs. The techniques of management by objectives are described in Chapter 13. It is a good idea, moreover, to rotate data processing managers from one department to another. They then bring to the department a hands-on knowledge of other user departments and a broader company perspective.

Good management achieves control using the proper data processing techniques. These include company surveys, hardware monitors, and reporting systems:

Company surveys are a simple and accurate way to evaluate the system. You merely ask users of the system what they think of it. No matter how skilled are the professional managers in the data processing department, nor how sophisticated the equipment, if the users of the information are not satisfied, the system is no good. There are three basic questions which need to be asked:

1. Are the user departments satisfied with the timeliness, quality, and quantity of information and reports supplied by the data processing people?

2. Is the department working on the right problems whose solution is most important to the company, and who determines what is important?

3. Does the company or the data processing department consider alternative solutions to the users' problems, including manual procedures and outside services?

The responses to these questions will help the manager to determine the direction of his effort in building and controlling the data processing system. Surveys should be taken every six months. The results should be summarized and circulated to top management, showing comparisons to previous surveys and forecasts of the results expected for the next survey. Some abbreviated analytical comment should be on the report to alert management to the reasons for problems and the expectation for solutions.

Hardware monitors will help the data processing manager to determine whether his system is being used most effectively. We all know that systems generally cost two to three times what we expected them to cost, and installations take two to three times longer than we anticipated (Gotthilf's Rule), but, often, they don't give us the results we desire in the format we want. This happens because many computer people build the reporting system around the comptuer technology rather than the users' requirements. Monitors will help to determine the effectiveness of the system. Monitors, in effect, are computer programs which capture data from the computer and analyze it. Sometimes, a mini-computer is used to capture and process the data. Otherwise, data is collected on magnetic tape and then analyzed through the main processor. Data which flows from peripheral equipment, card readers, tape, or disk drives, is collected using sampling techniques. The mini-computer or main program will measure different functions, such as the extent of utilization of memory, times required to accomplish specific tasks, and which information channels were used. In some cases, computer manufacturers themselves are incorporating hardward monitors in their new systems.

The result of all this monitoring is real-time reports, easy to analyze, showing big computer systems which computers and communications systems are not being fully utilized, enabling work to be shifted to them. This is also useful analysis in determining whether to up-grade to a newer system or to correct software systems to provide a more efficient direction of the flow of messages.

Good *reporting systems* are an essential element of controlling the entire data processing system. Such a system includes circulating a listing of all output reports, showing budget reporting date and expected output date. The report should be designed to show late dates in a separate column, for exception viewing. If there are too many late dates in that column, on a recurring basis, the entire system is not working. This, notwithstanding, the listing must be circulated to all user departments so they can schedule their own work around the anticipated report delivery date.

SELECTING BETWEEN ALTERNATIVE SYSTEMS

Alternative systems or decisions include whether to lease or buy, to time share or use an outside service bureau, and whether to charge user departments on a profit center basis. Good managers, those who understand their business and manage by objectives, may be relied upon to make the right decisions for the company, at the right time. Decisions should not be written in concrete. Alternative courses of action, not good for today, may be right for tomorrow.

The lease or buy decision may relate to hardware or software. As to the latter, the decision is really a make or buy decision, to do it in-house or buy a package from an outside company. The outside cost is a given. The in-house cost depends on whether you have or can recruit the available personnel to do it inside. There is also the additional cost of existing staff which must be assigned to the project and the effect this could have on routine work responsibilities. An important consideration, too, is what to do with new staff you might hire, after the project is completed.

Lease or buy decisions relating to hardware are of two types. The first considers an operating lease (no ownership, no residual value, no depreciation or investment tax credit benefits) versus an outright purchase. Having made that decision, the second alternative is whether to finance lease the hardware (a long-term ownership lease which covers the major part of the expected life of the hardware, with residual value and tax advantages).

The finance lease or outright purchase decision is a relatively straightforward one. A finance lease is nothing more than a loan, actually an installment purchase of the machine. The effective interest rate on the finance lease is readily calculated using standard techniques, and compared to the cost of other methods of borrowing. The operating lease, however, is a pure rental of the equipment, and the decision depends on financial and other factors.

The financial decisions relating to an operating lease are based on the discounted cash flow techniques described in Chapter 3 which recognize the time value of money, and the decision would be made which results in an interest rate which is more favorable when compared to other types of financing. The cost of the asset, the inflow, is compared to the various outflows—these are the lease rentals, the residual value of the hardware which is lost through leasing, and the tax benefits which are given up. The tax benefits lost are the Investment Tax Credit, which is recognized in the year it is taken for tax purposes, and Depreciation expense, which is picked up each year using some accelerated method, minus the lease rental expense, times the effective income tax rate. The resulting discounted cash flow analysis will produce an after-tax interest cost to the company which is compared to other alternative costs of financing and the company's anticipated return on investment.

Other than the financial cost, the company must consider the risk of obsolescence in making a buy decision. Computer technology is purported to have a six to eight year generational cycle, and it might not be prudent to buy toward the end of the life cycle of a particular model. The residual value would be less, and there would have to be the expectation that the next computer model would have significant advances in technology that could rapidly obsolete your model. Technology advances on new computers usually come with little increase in cost. If, however, the company operates in a stable data processing environment which can be predictably handled over future years with one particular model of equipment, the buy decision could be the right one, even at the end of a generational cycle.

The use of time sharing services and outside service bureaus offer interesting alternatives to user departments. Financial considerations include the cost, compared to doing it inside, the disruption in existing in-house projects, whether there is even in-house expertise sufficient to do the job, and the speed with which the end result is required. In a related vein, companies may avail themselves of facilities management programs, wherein an outside service will assume complete responsibility for the in-house computer operation. In general, outside services offer the smaller user more flexibility and a greater variety of programs than he could normally afford himself. Big system users, however, can often use the outside service to augment peak processing requirements a few times each month by plugging in to another big system on a time sharing basis. As stated earlier, the financial and subjective elements will be considered by responsible managers who may be expected to make the right decisions, at the right time, based on their stated management objectives.

A frequently considered alternative is whether to charge other departments for information and services supplied by the centralized data processing department. This could include computer time as well as systems support. Top management is often in favor of doing this, as it creates revenue for the data processing department, enabling it to function as a profit center, generating revenues, costs, and a bottom-line. Unless a system is totally centralized and susceptible of complete control, it is generally not a good idea to allocate data processing costs or to charge for work delivered, even if the charges are arms-length. Overcharges create fictitious profits for the data processing department and even fair charges, or undercharges, can be viewed by the user as an unnecessary expense. The user can sometimes obtain the same services outside, at lower cost, and this results in needless expense for the company and incomplete utilization of its own data processing facilities. A better method is simply to budget carefully data processing department expenses, based on the user's expected requirements. This requires good management control, controlling and monitoring the system for efficient utilization, and establishing a good budget. Expenditures would then be compared to budget for financial control.

THE COMPUTER AND FINANCIAL ANALYSIS

1. Its enormous memory and high output and printing speeds make the computer a valuable tool for the financial analyst.

2. Organization for the data processing function may be centralized or decentralized, depending on the size and dispersion of company operations.

3. Computer reports should have the characteristics of manual reports which make them user oriented, rather than being simply masses of data.

4. The computer system is controlled through user surveys, hardware monitors to measure effective utilization of machines and programs, and timely listings of the flow of reports to user departments.

5. Alternative decisions should be made as to whether to lease or buy equipment, to make or buy software, to time share or use outside service bureaus, and whether to operate the data processing department as a profit center. Decisions should be changed as conditions and circumstances change, rather than being considered indelible.

CHAPTER 10

Decision Making For Tomorrow

... subjective factors can be measured using constraint analysis which measures whether this would be a good business ... to be in ...

EVALUATION OF RESEARCH AND DEVELOPMENT PROJECTS

It is difficult to determine how much many companies are spending on research, development and engineering, because in published financial statements, such as annual reports, this cost is often included in selling, administrative, and general operating expenses. There is evidence, however, that the total outlay for research, both by government and by private industry, has been expanding at a rapid rate, in recent years.

The phenomenal success (and its resultant publicity) which certain industries such as chemicals, drugs, and semi-conductors have derived from research did much to trigger this trend. One reads that some companies just assume that every dollar spent on research today would yield a dollar of profit per year after the developmental period. This conclusion is far from valid of course. Building a laboratory and installing a staff of scientists does not insure instant success.

On the other side of the coin, however, it is the companies with good solid research and development facilities and programs which are now, and will continue to be, the leaders in their respective industries. A continuing flow of profitable new products, the creation of more jobs, and higher standards of living are some of the results of research effort. In addition, there are important intangible advantages of research which contribute to public interest and to the advancement of knowledge, for which there is no apparent financial reward.

This points up the need for the evaluation of research and the development of techniques which will relate research activities and costs to corporate goals and policies—not only for today, but for the future.

ECONOMIC VALUE OF RESEARCH AND DEVELOPMENT OUTPUT

Engineering, research, and development appropriations involve risks and tie up money; therefore, care should be exercised in deciding what kind of programs are undertaken. Management should know where and how well all research areas are spending time and money. In the first place, research should be evaluated for its over-all contribution to the corporate profits. Secondly, it *can* be evaluated if accurate costs are maintained for its different phases and if proper plans for research activities are matched to over-all corporate plans, including market opportunities.

The question of how to place an economic value on research breaks down into the following considerations:

1. The determination of cases where dollar valuation is appropriate.
2. The techniques for placing a dollar value on technology.
3. The use of qualitative appraisal in cases where dollar valuation is inappropriate.

Since profits are the most practical measurement of the whole organization's effectiveness, the evaluation of research expenditures might attempt to relate its contribution to the actual profit the company may (or may not) make by exploiting each specific technological project.

Profit-adding technology may be exploited in a number of ways. It may lead to:

1. New products or processes.
2. Cost reducing materials, processes, techniques.

_____Product A B C_____   Division

Date ___October 15, 19xx___
Requested By ___C.B.___

Auth. No.	Total Cost	Project Title	Approved	
OK 193	$250,000	Hi Speed XYZ Machine for Product "A"	By P.H.	
			Date October 30, 19xx	

PROJECT SCOPE AND OBJECTIVE

Design and build a new XYZ machine capable of operating at speeds up to 500 pieces per hour including an automatic ware take-out device and conveyor to the inspect and pack stations.

RELATION TO CORPORATE MARKETING AND/OR OPERATING OBJECTIVES

This equipment should enable us to maintain or exceed present quality standards, increase production capabilities and provide manufacturing cost reduction.

TIME TABLE OF INVESTMENT

Fiscal Year	19xx	19xx	19xx		Total
Time Period	6 Mos.	12 Mos.	4 Mos.		Project

EXPENSE

1. Development	35,000				35,000
2. Engineering		40,000	10,000		50,000
3. Market Development					
4. Pre-Operating			25,000		25,000
5. Other					
Total Expense	35,000	40,000	35,000		110,000

CAPITAL

6. Land					
7. Buildings					
8. Mfg. Equipment		75,000	65,000		140,000
9. Mobile Equipment					
10. Other					
Total Capital		75,000	65,000		140,000
Total Investment	35,000	115,000	100,000		250,000

Estimated Increase in Annual Net Sales	$950,000
Estimated Date of Commercial Production	May 1, 19xx
Estimated Increase in Annual Net Profit	$ 75,000
Cash Payback Period	3.2 Years
Discounted Cash Flow Profitability Rate	28.4 %

Exhibit 49

Research Project Authorization Request

3. Improved quality in present products.

4. A preferred patent position or royalty income.

5. A material which allows the company to eliminate costly interruptions in supply.

QUANTITATIVE EVALUATION OF R & D PROJECTS

Of the available techniques, the discounted cash flow system is suggested as the most satisfactory way of rating an investment opportunity, whether it be a capital investment or a research project. The discounted cash flow system handles all pertinent financial variables: the amounts of income and investments, their relative timing, the cost of capital tied up in the venture, and the risk of the investment. The concept of this technique is covered in Chapter 3, and samples of forms which might be adopted are illustrated in Exhibits 14, 15, 16, and 17. Exhibit 49 illustrates the type of project authorization which could be adopted to summarize the information and obtain formal approval.

Product development projects should be evaluated as soon as the project enters the development phase, or as soon as the application of the technology becomes known. At this point a company can begin to forecast investments, product introduction costs, and operating revenues. The forecasts begin with general sales and profit forecasts, and are refined as technical development proceeds.

Cost reducing projects can similarly be valued as soon as their technical outlines become reasonably complete. Such developments might include new processes, materials, components, or techniques which reduce the unit costs of producing present product lines. Again the valuation process relies on investment and return forecasts, supplemented by the discounted cash flow technique.

The type of research project authorization request illustrated in Exhibit 49 can be used as more than just an instrument to obtain management approval for a specific expenditure. In this particular example, let us say that product "A," as presently manufactured, is a break-even or loss item, profit-wise. Knowing this, the item is not promoted or pushed by the sales force, but orders are accepted because the item is part of some product group and must be made and sold if only as an accommodation to the customers. The sales and marketing people advise that if costs could be reduced and the item would be vigorously promoted, the company's share of the market could be greatly increased. The additional sales could come not only from present customers, but new customers might also be developed.

Let us assume that the equipment required to manufacture this product is not commercially available but must be custom built. Also, that the present equipment not only is inefficient and costly, but does not produce the quality necessary to compete effectively in the total market. Obviously we must turn to our research, development, and engineering people for the design and construction of a superior piece of equipment which would increase our sales and profits, or risk losing an important segment of our present business.

An economic evaluation of this proposal should be made, so that the authorizing authority can become acquainted with the situation and compare this proposal with other projects competing for the available or budgeted development dollar. Some type of formal instrument, as illustrated in Exhibit 49, should be utilized. It records the description, explanation, and goal of the project. It shows the amount of the investment needed, the type of expenditure, whether capital or expense, and the timing. It tells who requests it, who authorized it, and when. It predicts the estimated improvement in revenue, and gives a financial rating expressed by cash payback and profitability rate.

The use of this form imposes a discipline on the various management people involved to organize and define the problem, and to formalize the estimation of costs and results. It necessitates the collaboration of production, sales, accounting, and marketing people with the engineering function. This results in a team effort which should be beneficial to the total corporate welfare.

QUALITATIVE EVALUATION OF R & D PROJECTS

There are other types of research for which cost and profit calculations are not appropriate. Some examples are in the following list:

1. Research for the public good.
2. Research on materials or processes to help the company survive special situations.
3. Product improvement research of a continual and general nature.
4. Certain fundamental research.
5. Strategic—essential projects with intangible financial benefit.

The result of such research generally defies dollar evaluation. However, management should be able to judge these areas objectively enough to avoid losing effective control over the research operation. A good budget program can be of help here.

Pursuit of knowledge in a given field, without any regard for its eventual specific applications, presents evaluation problems. In certain cases, fundamental research could lend itself to direct dollar valuation. This would happen whenever a fundamental breakthrough opens the way to a series of exploitable new developments with predictable results and measurable markets.

Some of these *subjective factors can be measured using constraint analyses which measure whether this would be a good business for anyone to be in,* and, if so, would it be a good business for us to enter? The exhibit below considers the various factors which affect each question:

R & D Constraint Analysis Chart

Industry Factors	Projects A B C	Company Factors	Projects A B C
Profit/Sales poten-tial	— — —	Capital and Debt	— — —
Growth rate/year	— — —	Marketing strength	— — —
Competition:	— — —	Manufacturing strength	— — —
reaction	— — —		
patent protection	— — —	Know-how and patents	— — —
life cycle	— — —		
Applications	— — —	Skills:	
Market Penetration	— — —	leadership	— — —
		all other	— — —
Political/Social			
Anti-trust	— — —	Totals	═ ═ ═
Economic	— — —		
Environmental	— — —	Rate projects from 1 to 10	
Social	— — —	Discard projects below 70	
		Proceed if score is over 80	
Total	═ ═ ═	Use caution from 70 to 80	

Exhibit 50

There are twelve factors, six each for the industry and the company, with a rating on each factor from 0 to 10, for a maximum possible total of 120. Where there are sub-sets under major factors (competition, political/social, and skills), the sum of the scores under each sub-set should add to no more than 10. Projects will generally succeed with a score of 80 or more, unless extraneous influences, such as governmental constraints, are unexpectedly introduced. The chances for success deteriorate rapidly below 70. Additional factors can be substituted which may be more germane to certain industries or companies. The factors are briefly analyzed below:

Industry factors:

1. A rating of 10 should be based on the expectation of a 10% annual increase in sales, to be achieved in a reasonable time, say three to five years, and an ROI (see Chapter 3) of 30% or more.

2. A top score should be based on 10% sales growth, after inflation, per year.

3. How will competition react, will patents keep competition out, and will the product have a long run or last just a few years?

4. Is there only one product or application from the research, or several, over which to spread the risk?

5. Can we penetrate the market with a break-through product, or is this merely state-of-the-art? Will we attain major market share?

6. Consider federal regulation constraints, pollution, social structures, and economic trends. If there are neither positives nor negatives in this category, assign it a 5.

Company factors:

1. Is capital and debt available and how much is required? The lower the requirement, the less risk, and the possibility of more competition. Hence, assign less points. If there is strong cash flow indicated with high capital and debt needs, score 10.

2. Score 10 for a good fit with existing marketing capabilities. Building from scratch is risky and costly.

3. Existing manufacturing facilities require less capital or debt and shorten the entry time to commercial introduction. Score 10 for this.

4. Know-how includes patents, design, engineering, manufacturing, marketing, and administrative skills.

5. Be certain that several suppliers of materials are available or that long-term supply contracts can be negotiated as an inflation hedge.

6. A project has the highest chance of success with a strong top-manager, supported by middle management and skilled production workers.

ANNUAL PERFORMANCE RATING WITH COMPETITION

It is only natural that most companies want to compare their overall performance with that of other companies in the same or related industries. This will enable corrective actions to be taken to better position your company within its industry in the future.

Exhibit 51 not only shows balance sheet and profit and loss statistics, but also many different types of comparison ratios. For easy interpretation of these ratios, the items have been numbered. Arithmetical formulas by which we calculated these ratios have been included. Exhibits 52 and 53 are graphic trend charts of selected categories from Exhibit 51. Note that the illustrations only cover two competitive companies and two key indicators. In actual practice, about six selected companies would give a broader comparison. When setting up your own analysis, you may omit some of the categories included in the exhibit and add others (e.g., ratio of receivables to annual sales.)

VALUE OF COMPARISON ANALYSIS

One of the best methods of evaluating the general situation of your business is your relative standing with your competition. Factors like current ratio, inventory turnover, and profit margin should be compared to those of companies in the same industry. If your firm is increasing turnover and improving profit margin at a faster rate than the industry average, or your prime competition, this should indicate a high management effectiveness. You may wish to use this technique in evaluating a possible new vendor which you may be considering as a major supplier, and whose ability to perform would have a serious impact on your own business. You may wish to study a new big customer before you tie up large sums of capital in inventories for him. Last but not necessarily least, this technique should be a big help to an investor in making a choice between several companies in the same industry.

XYZ CORP. vs. SELECTED COMPETITORS

		XYZ CORP.	*A CO.*	*B CO.*
1 Cash		12,464,639	3,488,059	8,747,387
2 Short-Term Securities		-	2,974,474	10,110,645
3 Inventories		36,731,307	6,061,478	18,746,350
4 Total Current Assets		76,914,085	17,437,102	49,459,042
5 Investments (At Cost)		6,004,676	18,326	-
6 Net Fixed Assets (At Cost)		115,992,255	17,727,297	29,507,900
7 Accumulated Depreciation		74,805,688	11,871,558	33,233,294
8 Total Assets - Net		200,174,615	35,302,250	79,269,778
9 Total Assets - Gross	(7+8)	274,980,303	47,173,808	112,503,072
10 Total Current Liabilities		27,508,234	4,509,068	15,662,696
11 Long-Term Debt		-	2,731,025	-
12 Preferred - No. of Shares Outstanding		161,522	60,959	49,000
13 Preferred - Par Value		16,596,385	3,047,950	3,947,230
14 Common - No. of Shares Outstanding		5,088,248	1,319,852	2,962,150
15 Common - Par Value		5,088,248	6,599,260	18,513,438
16 Retained Earings		100,091,016	13,064,777	38,368,306
17 Net Sales		291,538,690	52,632,661	142,858,900
18 Cost of Sales (Mfg. - Shipping - Delivery)		198,460,832	41,285,844	111,706,971
19 Cost of Sales (Research & Engineering)		-	-	-
20 Cost of Sales (Selling - Administrative)		49,764,230	4,565,914	12,815,162
21 Total Net Profit After Taxes		16,225,313	3,048,205	7,001,597
22 Stock Dividends - Preferred		605,718	152,400	152,381
23 Stock Dividends - Common		8,116,156	1,003,574	4,143,685
24 Earnings less Preferred Dividends	(21-22)	15,619,595	2,895,805	6,849,216
25 Market Price of Stock		46	33	38
26 Working Capital	(4-10)	49,405,851	12,928,034	33,796,345
27 Stockholders' Equity (Common)	(15+16)	105,179,264	19,664,037	56,881,744
28 Yield - Common Stock	(30÷25)	3.5%	2.3%	3.7%
29 Book Value - Common Stock	(27÷14)	20.67	14.90	19.20
30 Dividends Per Share - Common	(23÷14)	1.60	.76	1.40
31 Current Ratio	(4÷10)	2.80	3.87	3.16
32 Inventory Turnover	(17÷3)	7.94	8.68	7.62
33 Profit Margin	(21÷17)	5.6%	5.8%	4.9%
34 Return on Gross Assets	(21÷9)	5.9%	6.5%	6.2%
35 Earnings Per Common Share	(24÷14)	3.07	2.19	2.31
36 Price Earnings Ratio	(25÷35)	15	15	16
37 Gross Asset Turnover	(17÷9)	1.06	1.12	1.27
38 % Cash to Net Assets	(1÷8)	6.2%	9.9%	11.0%
39 Current Asset Turnover	(17÷4)	3.79	3.02	2.89
40 Cost of Sales Ratio to Sales	(18÷17)	68.1%	78.4%	78.2%
41 Research Cost Ratio to Sales	(19÷17)	-	-	-
42 Sell. & Adm. Cost Ratio to Sales	(20÷17)	17.1%	8.7%	9.0%
43 % Net Working Capital to Sales	(26÷17)	16.9%	24.6%	23.7%
44 Cash Flow Per Common Share	(48+21÷14)	5.36	3.13	4.16
45 Opr. Exp. Ratio to Mfg. Cost	(19+20÷18)	25.1%	11.1%	11.5%
46 % Earnings on Invested Capital-Common	(35÷29)	14.9%	14.7%	12.0%
47 % Cash Flow on Invested Capital-Common	(44÷29)	25.9%	21.0%	21.7%
48 Annual Depreciation		11,070,054	1,086,488	5,320,627
49 Cash Flow to Gross Fixed Assets	(48+21÷6+7)	14.3%	14.0%	19.6%

Exhibit 51

Financial Comparison, 19—

SOURCES OF DATA

There are large standard financial services which publish daily, weekly, monthly, and yearly summaries about whole industries and individual companies. If you do not subscribe to one or more of these services, they are almost always available through stock brokers, banks, public libraries, and, in some cases, college libraries. All the financial data listed in Exhibit 51 was taken from various individual companies' annual reports.

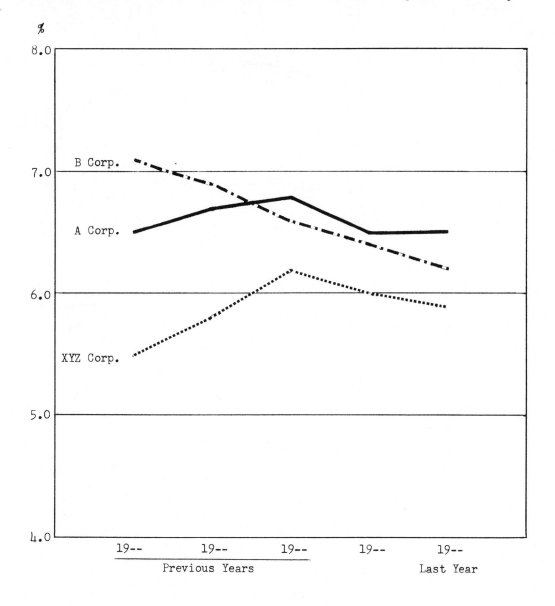

Exhibit 52

Return On Gross Assets

Annual reports can usually be readily obtained direct from the company or through a stock broker. In studying an annual report, be sure to read the footnotes following the financial statements for explanation of any possible restrictions, such as pledges or commitments of specific assets to specific liabilities. Also, the reading material in the annual report usually offers clues as to the product mix and degree of diversification, which is not revealed in the total company financial condition and operating performance.

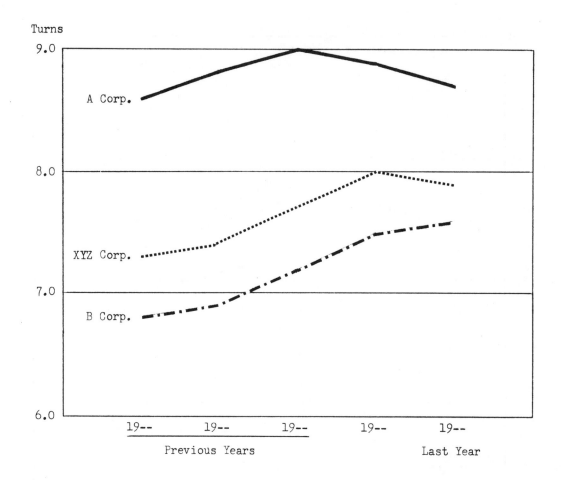

Exhibit 53

Inventory Turnover

TIME PERIODS STUDIED

It is recommended here that this comparison analysis with competition should be made annually. It should be pointed out, however, that one year's data does not tell enough about a firm. It is recommended that a file be built up on each selected competitor containing at least the last five annual reports. From these, then, it is possible to prepare the type of report illustrated by Exhibits 52 and 53. Although we have used only two indicators for illustrative purposes in trend comparisons, most companies will no doubt wish to use additional comparison categories and more competitors.

PRACTICAL PERFORMANCE BENCHMARKS

Financial statements and reports can produce benchmarks which can quite accurately reveal the quality of a company's management, as well as a prognosis of future success or failure.

If the management of a company has no respect for facts such as projected sales, operating problems, capital requirements, and many other key indicators covered in this book, it probably will be reflected in the quality of its decisions. In the absence of any other information at all, the internal or published formal financial statements over a period of just a few years can be quite revealing.

In Exhibit 51, the first twenty-four items were obtained from the various companies' annual reports. For item 25, the market price of the stock, we merely took the closing stock quotation on the last day of the year. If desired, you could use some average figures for the 12 month period. This market price was then divided by item 35, the earnings per common share, to obtain item 36, the price earnings ratio. (The New York Stock Exchange calculates P/E ratios, during interim fiscal periods, based on the last four published quarterly reports, hence, a rolling four quarters.) This figure should be of interest to a company's management, because it reveals to some extent what value the financial community, or at least the investing public, places on the company and its future prospects. This is certainly important because the goals of management and the stockholders have much in common. If the corporate objectives of management do not serve the best interests of the stockholders, it will eventually show up in the price/earnings ratio. Wall Street tends to evaluate the price of a company's stock based on its P/E ratio, although, as explained in Chapter 3, ROI is a better indicator.

Current ratio, which is current assets divided by current liabilities, is a significant figure, both as a trend indicator in an individual company and in comparison with the industry. As a general rule, a high current ratio would be desirable. The components of this factor, however, must be closely analyzed. If a low current ratio figure is caused by an abnormally high liability item of accounts payable, this might signal a poor working capital position. Conversely, a high current ratio figure might not be as favorable if the cash position is built up at the sacrifice of normal growth and expansion. It would not be good business to pile up cash and securities at a much lower yield than the same money would bring from new ventures or expanded facilities. Even more dangerous to your future is the hoarding of cash resources while your competition is building new plants or stores all around you.

Probably the most attention in industry comparison ratios is paid to the profit margin, item 33, and the return on gross assets, item 34, (Exhibit 51). Earnings per common share is extremely important as a trend figure within an individual company over the years, but not too meaningful between companies unless it is expressed as the price/earnings ratio, as noted earlier in this chapter. An analysis of other items in Exhibit 51 such as asset turnover, cost of sales ratio to sales, selling and administrative cost ratio to sales, and many others should certainly provide clues as to poor or deteriorating profit margins and return on investment.

CASE HISTORIES AND EXAMPLES

The successful or unsuccessful conduct of a business enterprise is brought home to us most vividly when we read about specific companies in our daily newspapers, financial papers and services, business magazines, and news magazines. We read about numerous business failures and business successes. We read about successfully consummated mergers and other proposed mergers which have been blocked by government agencies. Some of the companies' names are so familiar and known to us as to be household words. Others are virtually unknown to anyone but those people involved or interested in their specific industry.

To the student of management science, it is of prime interest to ascertain the reason for either failure or success. It seems to us that in many cases the reasons appear to be so fundamental and basic that it is difficult to understand how some companies could drift into trouble without taking corrective action long before the situation became so critical. One explanation might be that the management of a failing company either was not kept informed or did not utilize the type of key financial intelligence advocated in this book.

It seems a paradox that the rate of business failures in prosperous times sometimes is greater than in some recession periods. One of the obvious reasons might be over-optimism based on total economic conditions with disregard of specific situations. An analogy might be that just because the Dow Jones Average goes up, every stock in the market does not go up. It is emphasized here that we are referring to terminal business mortality, not year-to-year ups and downs. A certain amount of period fluctuations in sales and profits can be expected under the most competent of managements and in most every industry, and should not be occasion for undue alarm.

In recent years it seems that everybody needs just about everything, and many companies "get by" with mediocre quality and service. However, when industrial capacity catches up with basic needs, we enter an era of higher costs, lower prices and tougher competition. It is in this economic climate in which only the alert and knowledgeably-managed company succeeds, or even survives.

While company growth is usually desirable, and sometimes necessary, over-expansion can be the road to bankruptcy. We recently read of a medium-sized manufacturing company that built several new plants and never obtained the additional sales to utilize them. They took their growth trend of a period of prior years and arbitrarily projected their sales forecast into the future at the same rate, without first making a realistic current market survey. To make matters worse, their sales actually dropped off, and their increased overhead could not possibly be supported by their decreased volume.

An antiquated or inadequate cost accounting system can grease the skids for even old established firms. This is especially true when there is a diverse product mix, and management cannot distinguish between the winners and the losers. A company can win contracts through low competitive price bids and enjoy a lush sales volume and sooner or later find that they are either working for nothing or losing money. We know of a furniture manufacturing company which produced a wide range of different kinds of furniture and produced a satisfactory profit on their normal product mix. One particular line became very popular, and its sales volume increased radically in proportion to the rest of the lines. The company went into the red almost immediately. Cost studies revealed that this particular line showed a deficit in gross profit margin. Chapter 6 recommends monthly sales analysis and profit contribution data by product or product line.

Sometimes diversification is the answer for a company whose traditional product is losing ground in the market place for some reason not related to quality or service. For example, a dairy products company with the best reputation in its field might be losing sales because of the rising consumer demand for low cholesterol and low calorie substitutes. It might be a serious error to branch out into the manufacture of electronic components, if they did not have either the know-how or the sales channels to be successful. In this case, it would seem to be more feasible to manufacture margarines, unsaturated cooking oils, and the like and continue to serve their same customers, even though it might appear that there is some contradiction within their total product. Personally, we consider this a realistic approach and see no conflict. We know of a farmer in Indiana who has recognized this problem, reduced his herd of cattle, and planted several acres of soy beans. It is just a matter of becoming more customer-oriented and less rigidly product-oriented.

In Chapter 2, we stressed the importance of inventory management. This is another area where management vigilance is important. Many manufacturing firms have slowly and sometimes almost imperceptibly drifted into deep waters by unwise inventory build-ups. There are few industries which can operate on a "make and ship" practice. Most companies must have substantial inventory stocks to adequately serve their customers. This is probably one of the stickiest problems in the management policy and decision-making area. However, beware of the production control and customer service executive whose idea of an ideal inventory situation is to have such an abundance of everything carried in stock that the execution of a customer order merely entails shipping from the shelf in the warehouse. Besides having too much working capital tied up in this category, there is the ever present risk of obsolescence in a fast-changing market. Another dangerous practice can develop in a company which uses large quantities of high cost raw materials which fluctuate widely in price. There is a temptation here to load up on a commodity during a lower price period. It is questionable whether this type of speculation is wise or appropriate in a manufacturing firm.

There are many case histories on record of firms which have successfully reconstructed their companies because of technological developments or changes in consumer needs and attitudes. In some cases this has resulted in the dropping of entire product lines, divestiture of plants, and even divisions. Other cases have involved acquisitions of other companies and ventures into new fields having little or no affinity to their traditional and original product.

LONG-RANGE PROFIT PLANNING

Every company should operate with some type of long-range Plan. The size of the company would be a factor only in the format and procedure employed. It is important that smaller companies plan, as well as large companies that are more complex and decentralized. The smaller companies have some advantage in that they are usually closer-knit, can adapt to sudden changes more rapidly, and can employ a less formal type of long-range planning procedure.

DEFINITION AND FUNCTION OF PLANNING

A business Plan might be defined as a systematic and formalized procedure for directing and controlling future operations toward stated objectives for a future period of time, usually longer than a year. (That one year Plan is usually called the Budget.) A good Plan would probably cover the determination of the long-range objectives of the company, plus the development of a strategy for attaining operational programs for obtaining desired results. In general, a satisfactory and useable Plan would broadly consist of a clear statement of the basic company purpose and a carefully selected strategy by which to accomplish this purpose. It should help to guide the company toward a desired future position. In the preparation of the Plan, assumptions would have to be made, objectives stated, policies established, and future actions determined. The time period covered in a Plan can be one year or twenty years. In most companies and industries, five years appears to be the most practical, with the first year in considerable detail (see Chapter 12 on budgeting) and the next four years much more general. Actually, many companies have discovered that the short-term Budget can be made much more accurate and effective if it is integrated with a longer-range Plan.

NECESSITY FOR LONG-RANGE PLANNING

More than ever before, current business decisions are based on future forecasts and plans. "Future" does not mean just the rest of this year, but for next year and the next five years as well. In the coming years there should be almost unprecedented opportunities for many industries and companies to boost profits and to expand. Because of ever increasing competition, the companies which employ foresight and planning will have a far better chance to reap the benefits than those which improvise as they go along. Planning ahead may not only be the road to success and growth, but even to survival. Changing business conditions, sudden technological changes, large capital outlays, intense competition, and the administration of complex large-scale organizations are making some sort of planning function a necessity. As the population continues to increase, we realize that so much of what is happening now had been predicted. Certainly much of what will happen in the future can be predicted now to some degree. The obvious fact that planning for a future period involves a considerable degree of uncertainty does not invalidate planning. The intent of business planning is not the accurate foreseeing of the future, rather, it is the identification and recognition of a range of fairly predictable alternative situations, and the formulation of plans to meet them.

ADVANTAGES OF FORMALIZING A PLANNING PROCEDURE

The advantages of a formalized procedure are obtained both from the making of Plans and from the follow-up. Long-range profit planning forces consideration of what direction the future might take, and what management should do about it. In a sense, planning formalizes the entire creative managerial process, for it is simply a method of putting down on paper what management intends to do in the future. One might say that one of the most important benefits of formalized planning is to be derived as much from the actual process of making plans as from their implementation or enforcement.

The preparation and presentation of the Plan forces all levels of management to prepare a positive plan for the future, and provides top management with an opportunity to review and evaluate the plans of the total company. This procedure should reveal any unrealistic plans, and they can then be re-evaluated and revised as indicated.

The development and operation of the Plan require the active participation of the line managers in all areas of the business. The planning process thus provides an excellent opportunity and medium of communication between line and staff personnel. This should result in a high degree of coordination and cooperation between line and staff, and, by promoting better understanding of each other's functions, responsibilities, and problems, should be beneficial to both. See Chapter 12, for the technique of communicating with managers.

A SUGGESTED PLANNING PROCEDURE

It is not suggested that there is only one right way to prepare a long-range Profit Plan. There is no standard format for planning. Certain basic concepts are generally applicable to most companies, both large and small, but in practice there are many different ways of carrying out the planning. The method of planning to be used must be tailored to the needs and characteristics of the individual company.

It is believed, however, that it would be germane to this chapter to include a brief outline of how a Plan might be constructed. First of all, it is recommended that the Plan cover a period of five years, commencing with the next fiscal year's or calendar year's Budget. The coming year's Budget could be detailed by month as well as in total, the next year or two, perhaps, by quarter, and the rest of the years in total annual figures. If desired, the first Plan year could be considered as a short-term Plan, and the total five year period the long-range Plan. It is recommended that the entire five year Plan be completely re-evaluated and revised every twelve months, as very few industries are static enough to permit the use of the same Plan for more than one year. In a company where the calendar year is the fiscal year, the Plan would probably be prepared in the fall months and presented to management just prior to year end. Secondly, it is recommended that the Plan be divided into sections representing major corporate functions. For example, a Plan might consist of the following parts:

1. Basic purpose and objectives of the company.
2. Marketing plans.
3. Manufacturing plans.

4. Research, development, and engineering plans.

5. Capital investment plans.

6. Financial projections.

Each one of these sections should be covered in enough depth to be meaningful and useful.

These sections could consist of written statements accompanied by schedules of data when applicable or pertinent. It is suggested that schedules of figures, such as sales, costs, profits, capital expenditures, and the like cover the past five years of actual experience by year, the estimated current year, and the next five years by year. This will be valuable for trend and growth illustrations, and could be portrayed in both tabular and graphic form. In every case, the supporting schedules should be prepared in easy to read and understandable form. Whenever possible, the familiar formats used by the company for current financial, sales, and production figures should be adapted for the Plan data.

Long-range profit planning provides a means for coordinating these diverse activities. This is especially important for large multi-divisional companies that operate on a decentralized basis and have widely dispersed plants and offices, and for companies engaged in various different and sometimes unrelated lines of business. Changes in living habits and shifts in consumer needs and spending patterns can exert considerable pressure on companies to make changes in market programs. These changes should be reflected in the Plan. Other segments of the business, such as manufacturing operations and research effort, should then also follow the marketing program, provided they are compatible with overall company policy and objectives.

BASIC PURPOSE AND OBJECTIVES

A broad statement of a company's objectives may appear to be sufficiently self-evident that it can be omitted from a formal Plan presentation. However, some companies feel that it gives direction and uniformity of purpose to the total Plan. It is in this first step in the Plan that a company expresses its broad policies and business philosophies, and specifies the direction of its future operations. Broad statement should be made in this section as to what kind of business the company wants to be in, what markets it wishes to serve, and how big a share. A statement might be made as to what direction future growth should take, whether it should diversify into new products and new markets and, if so, whether by internal development or outside merger. Also, it is in this section where management may wish to comment on their attitude toward employee welfare, community relations, good will, and the like. All these goals, however desirable they may be, must be secondary to the one prime goal, which is *to maximize profit*. Without an adequate profit, none of the multiple secondary goals, however lofty, could be achieved.

MARKETING PLANS

The starting point for the marketing section of the Plan would probably be a sales forecast by product line for the future period. This could be based on the actual company sales of past years grouped by product classification. This analysis would draw heavily on the type of data illustrated in Exhibits 38, 39, 40 and 41 (in Chapter 6). Industry and trade volume of like sales could be considered here, if available. In some industries, these are possible to secure through trade associations, trade publications, and various business magazines. Sometimes, considerable intelligence in this area is picked up by a company's own salesmen in the field. From the perspective of a sales forecast, the historical figures should be re-classified if there were significant changes in products, competition, or distribution methods. Although a good sales forecast should begin with known facts it must be recognized that the economic climate of past years, when those facts were created, could be different from that of the future. An example of other factors which might be considered are:

1. The current outlook for the economy as a whole.
2. Possible factors affecting the outlook for your own particular industry or trade.
3. Special sales plans for your own company during the forecast period.
4. Any known plans of other companies in the industry or trade.

With the above information as a starting point, the sales and marketing plans for the future gradually evolve. Perhaps at this point, general management could meet with the sales staff, marketing research staff, and sales promotion staff for discussions and decisions which might include the following:

1. A review of the current level of sales volume by product lines, sales branches, and geographic areas.
2. A discussion of the company's potential market by current product lines in areas already covered satisfactorily, and in areas where there is possible additional sales volume to be obtained.
3. Consideration of possible entry into new products, new markets and new areas.
4. Consideration of possible changes in distribution methods, additional sales personnel, expense budgets, and incentive plans.
5. Review of advertising budget and sales promotion emphasis.

A marketing strategy meeting of this scope provides an excellent opportunity for management to make an objective appraisal of those product lines which have been profit producers over the years, but which might now be on shaky ground. Sentiment should be rejected in such cases, and a dynamic action planning program should be initiated to adjust to changing conditions, if indicated.

MANUFACTURING PLANS

As soon as the marketing plan has been approved, and the planned sales volume and product mix established, the manufacturing plan can be prepared. Manufacturing capacity must be matched with sales demand as expressed in the market plan. Since the planning and obtaining of manufacturing equipment and facilities often cannot be accomplished in a short period of time, management must anticipate its requirements so as to provide a lead time of as long as a year in some cases. Usually, in this situation, a very large cash outlay for equipment is required and a definite commitment made which cannot be reversed without substantial loss. On the other hand, the decision to order new or additional machinery which requires a long lead time cannot be deferred until the customer's order is in hand. This could be one of those situations where management faces a "moment of truth." A good, dependable long-range planning program can do much to minimize the risk in this decision-making area.

The marketing plan will also indicate the anticipated future activity levels of the manufacturing process. This will enable the production management to determine overall manpower and facility requirements. In addition, consideration should be given in the manufacturing plan for possible changes in plant layout, automation, replacement of worn out or obsolete equipment, wage increases, improved manufacturing efficiency, cost reduction programs, better quality control, and the like. These plans cannot be confined to general statements or observations, but should be spelled out so that the information can be translated into financial terms as well as being in a form appropriate for inclusion into the total corporate Plan. For example, the facilities needed should be identified and itemized together with cost estimates for use in the capital spending plan, the balance sheet projection, and the source and application of funds statement. Improved efficiencies and cost saving programs, offset in part by wage increases, should be reflected in the profit and loss statements. Inventory levels must be determined and valued because of their effect on the balance sheet and cash flow situation. Future manpower requirements and types of skills should also be included in the production or manufacturing plan presentation. Manufacturing problems requiring engineering services should be brought out so that consideration can be given in the research, development, and engineering plan program.

RESEARCH, DEVELOPMENT AND ENGINEERING PLAN

In developing a total corporate long-range Plan, all of the company sections and functions must dovetail, and in the final analysis be expressed in financial terms and total company objectives. Only part of the research and development plan needs to relate to the other parts of the corporate Plan. There should be many projects under way in this area which have not progressed far enough to be reflected in the marketing and manufacturing sections. This is not a contradiction to what we have said thus far. Actually, it is a desirable situation because hopefully many of the projects which will be commenced and included in the research plan will appear in the market plan in some near future time. Many products today have a much shorter life expectancy than was the case even a decade ago. This makes the research and development plan most vital to the success of many businesses.

In the preparation of the research, development, and engineering plan, it is recommended that the proposed projects be described as specifically as possible, except, of course, some of those in the fundamental research area. At any rate, the plan should group the projects and programs into categories, and also contain cost estimates. The cost estimates will find their way into the financial statement projections and also into the annual Budget for top management review and approval. The total cost of the research, development, and engineering effort can be related to planned sales and compared to similar historical ratios to assist management in setting the size of the total Budget in this area. An example of the type of categories the projects might be grouped by are as follows:

1. Fundamental and basic research.
2. Applied research.
3. Product development.
4. Process improvement and technical services.

Explanations of these categories are covered earlier in this Chapter. These four general categories can be separated further into sub-categories, if desired.

CAPITAL INVESTMENT PLANNING

The capital budget or fixed asset spending plan is obtained from the various facility needs as received from the manufacturing plants, plus special expansion plans as might be envisioned by general management. This list of planned capital expenditures has important financial implications, both in the balance sheet projections and, of course, in cash flow calculations. The profit and loss statement is affected by the calculated depreciation which would accrue from the additional fixed assets. It might be emphasized here that a blanket approval of a capital budget for planning purpose should not be construed by the plant managers as a carte blanche to order costly equipment indiscriminately. Each capital item of substantial amount should be processed through the procedure recommended in Chapter 3 as the need arises.

FINANCIAL PROJECTIONS

The plans and programs of the various segments and functions of a business which have been considered in this chapter must, of course, be translated into their financial consequences on the future period under study. All of these actions and programs have been, or should have been, planned with the net objective of favorably influencing future profits. In order to insure that this end result is attainable, pro-forma (giving-effect to) financial statements will have to be constructed from the information and data included in these separate but integral functions.

The starting point would probably be a Profit and Loss Statement. Here, again, the very first step must be the long-range sales forecast or plan. Sales volume determines the basis or level of activity and indicates the contribution margin necessary to support the period or fixed costs which were expressed in the various proposed or planned operating budgets. The product mix of the planned sales is necessary to develop the cost of sales or manufacturing costs. The ratios used might be based on current or past actual experience influenced by future estimates of wage increases, fringe benefits, better efficiencies, and other similar expectations for the long-range period. Selling, administrative, and engineering costs for the profit and loss plan statement would be obtained from the budgets and plans of the various departments and divisions concerned.

A pro-forma Balance Sheet plan would probably be the next step in the financial section. This should include both the asset and liability side. On the asset side, the major items would probably be accounts receivable, inventory balances, and fixed assets. On the liability side, estimated accounts payable balances, reserve accounts, and retained earnings (profit after tax from the P & L) might be of major significance. The section on balance sheet forecasting in Chapter 2 and a format designed after Exhibit 11 should be helpful in constructing this Plan statement.

In addition to the information from the Plan Balance Sheet and Profit and Loss Statements, other supporting data can be prepared for management presentation. These additional statements in the financial section might include Plan performance statistics, such as profit margins on sales, return on investment, inventory turns, current ratio, future cash requirements or surpluses, list of planned capital expenditures, debt or capital requirements, and any other statistics which would be used to measure future plans and performance. A Statement of Changes in Financial Position should be presented.

It becomes apparent that by preparing all the plans by the operating sections of the business, and then constructing financial statements from the information thus received, the final profit margins and earnings per share projected for the future period might fall short of top management's desired objectives. If this should be the case, and if we wish to follow the procedure outlined in this chapter, there is no other recourse but to review the entire Plan and possibly lower the corporate goals in some areas, or seek to effect economies in other ways to achieve a better profit picture for the future period.

Another alternative might be to obtain from top management the earnings figures or ratios and work backward in the preparation of other data. In this procedure, for example, department heads would probably have to be told what budget they would be given to work with instead of being asked to submit a budget and plan they felt they needed. As stated before, there is no standard method of planning to fit every company, and these matters must be decided upon on an individual basis. It is usually best for top management to submit a broad statement of its objectives to Division Managers prior to their initial formation of operating plans.

ASSIGNMENT OF RESPONSIBILITY FOR THE PLAN

Some large companies have separate full-time planning staffs, which may contain not only economists, accountants, and marketing experts, but also people with broad technical knowledge of the business as well. In other companies, the actual planning is done by the line managers who will have the subsequent responsibility of carrying out the plans and obtaining the objectives. In this case, there will usually be staff individuals or groups assigned to assist each line manager in the construction of his own part of the plan, and aid in coordinating all the plans of the various departments and functions. Regardless of who prepares the Plan, or how it is constructed and expressed, its success will depend to a great extent on the degree of top management support it receives. It is in those companies where the annual Plan originates with top management, and is considered as a fundamental aspect of the company's operating routine that the fewest problems are encountered in the Plan's inception and implementation.

PERIODIC COMPARISON OF PLAN VERSUS ACTUAL PERFORMANCE

At the end of each year, the actual operating results should be compared to the same period in the Plan. Actual sales, profits, and capital expenditures can be compared with the annual Plan, and the reasons for the differences explained. This is one of the opportunities for analysis of possible changing conditions and for revising strategies, when indicated. The Plan should be flexible and help to select the best of various alternative actions, not a strait jacket to prevent freedom of constructive action. I am sure that no one expects future events to conform exactly to a Plan which obviously contained a substantial degree of assumption and prediction. This variance of actual to Plan would be more likely to strengthen the process of continuous strategic planning rather than detract from the value of the original Plan.

OPERATIONS RESEARCH AND ANALYSIS

The procedures and forms illustrated and explained in this book are essential to operations research activities. Obviously, no system of management information or financial analysis reporting could be so all-inclusive as to provide automatic solutions to every business problem which might arise. On the contrary, the financial and operating intelligence contained in these recommended procedures will, no doubt, reveal problem areas which might otherwise go undetected. For this reason, many companies will require some sort of staff assistance to the decision-making executive. The manner and degree of staffing for problem solving should depend upon the size of the company, the degree of diversification, the amount of decentralization, and the inherent complexity of the business. A problem solving staff could consist of from one man to a good sized department. A staff unit could be an operations analysis department and/or an operations research team. If desired, the controller's department could augment his staff with any additional skills or knowledge needed to include operations analysis and operations research activities.

The staff unit, however organized, would be responsible for defining and researching specific problems, and presenting them to management with definite recommendations or alternative action plans from which future operating decisions could be made.

OPERATIONS ANALYSIS VERSUS OPERATIONS RESEARCH

Operations analysis is a means of grouping together various problems and problem solving techniques. An "operations analysis" department would operate in a staff capacity, conducting studies and surveys for the purpose of assisting management in determining or adjusting basic plans and programs for the maximum benefit of the overall company business.

Operations research is usually a procedure with heavy emphasis on mathematical devices and techniques. Pure operations research is usually expressed in mathematical terms, much like any other science. One of the devices of operations research is the construction of models, either actual or simulated, to describe a process and predict the results of various changes or innovations. The mathematical methodology of operations research can solve certain specific problems which are so complex that they cannot be solved by quantitative analysis. Conversely, there are many problems which can be solved by quantitative analysis, logical thinking, or plain common sense. A practical example of operations research techniques was the effort by a large city to evaluate the causes of and reduce car thefts. The details of each theft—neighborhood, time, whether locked or keys left—were recorded and analyzed. The analysis revealed that most thefts were simply managed because car keys were left in the ignition. The city initiated a city-wide poster and radio campaign encouraging drivers to remove their car keys when they parked. Car thefts were significantly reduced, as a result.

ADVANTAGES OF AN OPERATIONS ANALYSIS STAFF

The application of scientific management is a growing practice. No manager or chief executive can possibly be an expert in all specialized fields. Therefore, a good staff of specialists and experts can be of great assistance to him in his management control and decision-making processes and responsibilities. The original and basic theories, concepts, and rules of business organization and management are not outmoded, they are merely enhanced and augmented by these new and more sophisticated techniques.

A major advantage of an operations research and analysis staff is that it permits the time and effort of one or more qualified persons to be spent in studying various specific business problems in detail, free of the pressures or obligations of routine day-to-day operating responsibilities and duties. It provides a complete and explicit statement and analysis of the problem in depth, and with a minimum of bias. This process in itself often leads to the solution of a problem. Another plus which sometimes accrues from the detailed and penetrating examination of a specific problem is the accidental solving of an entirely different problem, or the coincidental discovery of some other unrelated profit opportunity or improved operating method. This serendipitous by-product of operations research in depth sometimes proves much more valuable than the successful solution of the original problem. This same phenomenon also occurs in technical research and development operations.

SUGGESTED PROCEDURE FOR AN OPERATIONS RESEARCH ASSIGNMENT

In applying operations research methods to a problem or situation, the following general procedure might be used:

1. Prepare a written statement of the specific problem and the objectives of the solution. Check with everyone concerned as to his agreement with the interpretation of the problem and the objectives.
2. Collect, in as much detail as available, all data and information pertinent to the problem or situation.
3. Sift through all the data, rejecting the information not important or helpful, and study and analyze all data which appears to contribute to pertinent knowledge and a possible solution.

4. Apply whatever mathematical or statistical techniques appear to be indicated or appropriate. Techniques which are referred to here include "value analysis," network techniques (such as "PERT" and "CPM"), "scientific sampling," and any other method which lends itself to the problem at hand.

5. As the information and intelligence from all this data is being studied and analyzed, various alternative solutions should begin to emerge or evolve.

6. Test the validity of the various problem solutions in as many ways as is possible or practical. One way is by actual trial under regular operating conditions. Another way is by constructing a simulated model of the problem or situation, and mathematically measuring the various possible changes or actions needed to obtain a reasonably legitimate inference.

7. Recommend a solution or a number of alternative solutions to the decision-making management.

8. When a solution is approved, install the new procedure or method, and supervise and audit its function until it has been proven out before turning it over to the operating personnel.

9. Communicate all the information to management in the traditional language of business and accounting . This includes the original statement of the problem, the objectives, the problem solving methods, and the recommendation.

LIMITATIONS OF THE OPERATIONS RESEARCH APPROACH

Operations research and analysis methods are not applicable to all corporate or operating business problems. In order to successfully utilize an operations research approach, a problem or situation should be:

1. Capable of being described in physical terms, such as units or dollars.

2. Capable of being measured so that cost of performance data can be accumulated and operating conditions evaluated.

3. Complicated enough so that operations research methodology is indicated and can be justified. If a problem can be solved by management judgment, know-how, or past experience, it may not be economical to incur the expense of an operations research approach.

4. Important enough to warrant a study. It is possible for a problem to be so insignificant that an intuitive or even arbitrary decision would be adequate.

VALUE ANALYSIS

Value analysis is an organized and systematic approach to cost improvement. Basically, it is a scientific method of getting the same performance from a product at a lower cost. It is a deliberate effort to improve the value of a product or product component by examining and eliminating unnecessary cost of any kind in the entire cycle of product design and manufacture. In order to achieve maximum benefits from this procedure, the analyst should extend his investigation beyond the consideration of the item itself, and examine the *function* of the product or product part. That is, in addition to looking at the cost reduction problem just from the specific viewpoint of how an item can be produced more economically, a broader examination should be made which questions how the cost of the function required can be cut, while retaining the same quality and service requirements, or even improving them.

The terms and objectives of "value analysis" and "value engineering" are practically identical, and many companies use the terms interchangeably. Generally, "value analysis" pertains to the systematic review of existing products and parts to see if cost saving changes can be made. "Value engineering," on the other hand, is usually associated with the original design, making the same kind of analysis before actual production begins. This should eliminate unnecessary costs in advance.

Chapter 7 dealt with financial analysis for cost reduction. In that chapter, value engineering was mentioned as one of the areas of cost reduction opportunities. Value analysis and value engineering are closely related to what we might call more conventional cost reduction, but they differ from it in at least two ways. First, in their heavy stress on precisely expressing the function of products and product components in terms of dollars; and second, in their use of not only a company-wide participation approach but also an organized and specifically delegated responsibility concept.

In this chapter we are suggesting, at least by inference, that the value analysis function and responsibility be assigned to the operations analysis staff or department. Actually, this responsibility could very well be assigned to general engineering, industrial engineering, purchasing, or manufacturing. The prime concern here should be to put it where it will do the most good to whatever department is best capable of fully exploiting it. Setting it up as a separate and additional department, however, should not be necessary. Value analysis can be organized and adapted to an existing organization structure. No matter what department the value analyst becomes a part of, he should have ready access to and cooperation from *all* segments of the business. At the same time, the authority of the value analyst should be limited to that of an advisor and consultant. His real job should be to supply information and recommendations regarding particular products and processes to the proper management people who are responsible for the decision-making. In any case, the skilled and qualified value analyst should encourage understanding and participation by other personnel in this function in as broad a scope as possible. A formal value analysis program should help to produce an attitude of cost consciousness throughout a company.

The value analysis procedure seems to consist of a discipline of constant and repeated questioning of the value and contribution of functions and things. This usually involves a step by step procedure to make a penetrating scrutiny of every part and every operation in the manufacture of a product. Actually, the questions are usually very basic and practical, and might proceed as follows:

1. Exactly what is the function, process, or thing?
2. What does it really do or provide?
3. Could it be eliminated altogether?

4.   Could it be replaced with something cheaper but just as effective?

5.   Are the quality specifications, such as dimensional tolerances, far more rigid or tight than necessary for customer acceptance or end use requirements?

In the process of obtaining answers to these questions, the Value Analysis Specialist will probably have frequent consultation with engineering, manufacturing, and marketing people.

It should go without saying that the most substantial savings accrue from the areas where the largest expenditures are involved. Stated another way, "don't spend a lot of time and money improving something which at best will result in an insignificant profit return." The value analysis technique, in its purest technical form, must also be tempered by good common sense and reason. There are many nonutilitarian functions to which it is difficult to apply a dollar value, such as employee morale, corporate public image, prestige, customer relations, community status, and the like. In other words, items like deluxe rest rooms, comfortable office furniture, better than average equipment, company airplanes, air conditioning, and the like might not fare too well with value analyses, directed by a rigid criteria, and oriented only to easily measureable dollar value and return. This is just another reason why the management must make the decisions in these matters. No object, function, or design is ever improved that probably couldn't be further improved with unlimited time and resources. Here again is where management exercises its prerogative and responsibility by saying, "this product is now good enough, so let's get the show on the road."

PROFIT PROTECTION TECHNIQUES FOR TOMORROW

1.   R&D projects can be evaluated using discounted cash flow techniques and by quantifying and measuring the factors which would affect the company and the industry.

2.   In addition to evaluating your company on the basis of internal operating controls, it is also desirable to compare its performance with that of other companies in the same or similar industries.

3.   A formal, long-range profit plan can translate management strategies into maximum profits.

4.   Operations research specialists, particularly in large companies, supplement the financial and operation information system in reducing costs and attaining corporate goals.

CHAPTER 11

Key Factors and Proven Techniques in Evaluation of Mergers and Acquisitions

Intelligent ... financial evaluation of a proposed acquisition ... calls for application of all the conventional financial yardsticks, ... and then applying analytical and intuitive judgment.

Many corporate managements have been or will be involved, sooner or later, with a question of mergers or acquisitions, either as a purchaser or a seller. Because the numerous financial implications inherent in acquisitions present a corporation problem, management people would do well to acquaint themselves with the problems and techniques involved in the acquisition process.

A dominant company, or "buyer," usually refers to this transaction as an acquisition, while the subordinate company, or "seller," prefers the term merger. In a merger, the acquired corporation is dissolved or "merged in" to the acquirer, and the acquiring corporation continues to operate under its corporate name and identity. A "consolidation" takes place when the two corporations combine into one new one and both the corporations are dissolved.

Mergers may be made to obtain diversification, increase manufacturing capacity, round out product lines, buy time in the development of marketing organizations, increase the corporate base for competitive reasons, or a wide variety of other reasons, as listed below.

The basic assumption is that the companies combined will be more successful than each operating individually. This chapter is intended to provide a method of evaluating this possibilty or goal before any irrevocable steps are taken.

Companies acquire other companies for as many reasons as there are companies. A few of the most common reasons, and a brief discussion of each, follows:

1. New Products—Instead of developing your own new products through research and development, a company can be bought which has already developed the desired product.

2. Vertical or Horizontal Integration.—Vertical integration is the purchase of companies from whom you buy or sell, thereby saving the profit which others normally make on your company. Horizontal integration involves companies making a different product but selling it within your industry, usually to the same customers. Cost savings are explicit in horizontal integration.

3. Personnel—A company may seek to buy a marketing force, a research capability, manufacturing expertise, or top management through an acquisition.

4. Profits—Acquisitions are often made of companies which have a good earnings track record or the potential for good earnings. The trick, here, obviously, is to discount those earnings at a yield which makes the acquisition feasible. You can't overpay for future earnings.

5. Tax Benefits—Under some circumstances, companies can be acquired which have net operating loss carry-forwards which can be utilized by the acquirer. This cannot be done if the primary purpose is the utilization of the tax losses, but given other benefits, the tax considerations could sweeten the purchase price and make for an easier acquisition.

6. The Seller Must Sell—The death of an owner, with improper tax planning, may force the sale by the deceased's estate. There are, often, time considerations which impel the estate to make a quick sale. The buyer may be getting a bargain purchase.

7. Realization of Goals—The buyer may simply be in a position to acquire a company in a field in which he has always wanted to be. This may be nothing more than the realization of early dreams.

8. Fixed Assets—As with personnel, a company may seek to buy the assets, physical plant or manufacturing facilities of the acquiree. This may be done because the assets cannot be built or purchased elsewhere for the equivalent cost, or because assets of this excellence cannot otherwise be obtained. This would pertain to the acquisition of a retail store with a preferred location, or a factory in a highly skilled labor area.

9. Listed Stock—A private company may desire to go public. One of the routes is acquisition of a smaller company, already listed. Similarly, "going private" may be accomplished through merger.

10. Diversification—While this may be accomplished to a limited degree through integration, the company may desire to protect future earnings by diversification of markets, product lines, and technology.

11. Future Benefit—Long-range planning may indicate a change in marketing effort to an industry which will grow at a greater rate than ours.

12. Balance Sheet Advantages—The seller may have a strong current ratio which, when consolidated with ours, would improve our position. Similarly, it may have a debt to equity ratio which, on consolidation, would improve ours.

13. Liquidity—Related to the balance sheet advantages, the seller may have cash, high receivables and inventory, a segment of the business which could be sold off—all of which he will sell to us for stock. This liquidity may be obtained at less cost than through the issuance of new stock or debt.

14. Source of Supply Maintenance—Related to integration, but usually done because of a supplier's weak financial condition. The company may acquire a supplier in distress. Or, a supplier may be acquired to prevent a competitor from obtaining it.

15. Market Protection—A distributor or dealer may decide to sell out. The new buyer might not buy our product and an acquisition might be indicated.

COMPLIANCE WITH REGULATORY GOVERNMENT AGENCIES

When considering a merger, it is important that the financial and legal departments of the corporation plan together. This is necessary because there are many problems with both financial and legal implications. For example, an acquisition may appear to be ideal from a financial standpoint, but legal counsel may conclude that it should not be consummated because of possible anti-trust problems.

In planning a merger or an outright acquisition, in addition to all the non-tax factors which must be considered, analyzed, and evaluated, the tax effect of the transaction should be determined, and if deemed desirable, firmed up by a Treasury ruling before any further action. In most cases, the tax positions of both the buyer and seller may have to be reconciled before a merger can be consummated.

Many business and governmental factors influence selection of the form of acquisition. They include, in part, statutory and regulatory requirements, accounting techniques, and the impact of taxation. At the present time the major consideration is probably the legality of the acquisition under the anti-trust laws.

SELECTION OF A PARTNER

Over the years, many companies have chosen the acquisition route for diversification and expansion. Many different methods can be used for determining the best candidate for acquisition. Whatever method is employed generally includes a great deal of detailed analysis. Information should be obtained concerning the prospect's plant, its personnel, its products, and any other aspects of its profit potential. As much financial data as is available should be collected and interpreted. This analysis should be carried out as unobtrusively as possible to avoid rumors and premature disclosures.

When decisions are ready to be made, key factor summaries should be prepared for management, supported by the quantitative material. The detailed analysis should not be presented at the board of directors level because of the natural difficulty of digesting a large volume of data and untangling possible numerous overlapping decision elements.

A certain amount of initial screening of merger candidates can be accomplished quite readily once the basic objectives and requirements have been established. Some companies which are obviously unsuitable can be eliminated from consideration without comprehensive analyses. Chances are there would remain three or four almost equivalent companies, with strengths and weaknesses in different areas. Accordingly, the problem is one of weighing and balancing the different factors to make the best decision.

The employment of the techniques suggested in Exhibits 54, 55 and 56, plus the various discounted cash flow analyses and forecasting techniques in preceding chapters, should prove quite helpful to this type of decision making.

STATISTICAL ANALYSIS TO EVALUATE A MERGER PROGRAM

Exhibit 54 provides a checklist for evaluation of a company under consideration for acquisition. Although this checklist calls for a great deal of accounting information and statistical data, it also points up the fact that a successful merger program calls for a lot more than the arithmetical application of financial intelligence. The suggested yardsticks of sales and profit performance should be tempered with exceptions, explanations, and attendant circumstances which need to be considered. Historical performance measures the past. It also helps to predict the future as it provides a solid base for projection. For a merger candidate, however, the future performance depends to some extent on factors which cannot be measured statistically, mainly the potential inherent in the new relationship after the merger. Also, a company with an adverse trend may be just about due to turn for the better. Conversely, a company which has been doing exceptionally well may be levelling off, and even be approaching a downturn.

The recommended yardsticks of past performance relating to asset management, sales growth, profit trends, and cash position do not provide all the necessary information, but they do provide a very important part of it. After a merger candidate has been selected from the screening processes and comparison ratios as recommended in Exhibit 54, the next preliminary step might be to measure the immediate effect on the two companies' financial statements as of the time a merger would be consummated.

CHECKLIST OF INFORMATION FOR EVALUATION OF A COMPANY UNDER CONSIDERATION FOR ACQUISITION

Exhibit 54

A. GENERAL DESCRIPTION OF BUSINESS

1. What is the general nature of the business? Give brief description of the product line and the market it serves.

2. How big is the company? Latest annual sales figures in dollars, and value of total gross assets.

3. Why is this company a candidate for acquisition? If privately owned, does owner wish to retire? If publicly owned, does company wish to broaden their base and become part of a larger complex? Any other reason?

B. HISTORY OF COMPANY

Obtain as much information as possible concerning date formed, by whom, where organized, and amount and source of original capital.

C. STRUCTURE OF COMPANY

1. Corporation, partnership, or proprietorship.

2. Financial structure—amount and ownership of common stock, preferred stock, bonds, and notes.

3. Organization chart—lines of authority and numerical size of personnel in various categories.

D. FINANCIAL STATUS

1. Balance sheets with supporting detail of appropriate items.

2. Income statements including trends in sales, gross margins, and profits.

3. Cash and working capital requirements.

4. Inventory data by category and including slow moving and obsolescence factors.

5. Credit reputation with supporting Dun & Bradstreet reports, bank references, and supplier relationships.

6. Property mortgages and notes.

7. Accounts receivable and bad debt situation.

E. PRODUCTS

1. Description of products and product lines. (Including catalogs and circulars.)

2. Price and cost data.

3. Any new products on the drawing board and their potential.

4. Patent and license situation.

5. Quality, style, and price in relation to competition.

6. Risk of substitution in material and style of present product.

7. Possibility of product diversification.

F. DISTRIBUTION

  1. Characteristics of Sales Department.
      a. Number of people and method of selling.
      b. Territories and coverage.
      c. Branch offices.
  2. Use of distributors and manufacturers agents and contractual relationships, if any.
  3. Markets.
      a. Domestic and foreign.
      b. Market background information.
      c. List of major customers.
      d. Estimate of potential market.
      e. Geographical concentration.
  4. Sales Analyses.
      a. Itemize products and product lines.
      b. Itemize markets and major customers.
      c. Order backlog and size.
  5. Advertising program.
  6. Customer relations and reputation for service and quality.

G. COMPETITION

  1. Name of major competitors.
  2. Description of competitive products.
  3. Competitive position in total market.

H. PURCHASING

  1. Principal materials used.
  2. Sources of supply.
  3. Purchasing methods—discounts, etc.
  4. Importance of inbound freight costs.

I. MANUFACTURING PROCESS

  1. Comparison of facilities and processes with competition.
  2. Patentable processes.
  3. Degree of automation.
  4. Flexibility to meet possible changes in requirements.
  5. Ratio of material to labor.
  6. Maintenance requirements.
  7. Type of quality control.

J. RESEARCH AND ENGINEERING

  1. Comparison of size and quality of laboratories and staffs with competition.
  2. Amount of research work contracted to outside engineering firms.

K. EMPLOYEE RELATIONS
  1. Union situation and labor contracts.
  2. Wage rate comparison with competition and community.
  3. Labor supply in area.
  4. Fringe benefit plans.
  5. Labor turnover statistics.
  6. Number of shifts in operation.
  7. Appraisal of working conditions.
  8. Group insurance program.
  9. Retirement program.

L. EVALUATION OF PERSONNEL
  Special skills, abilities, education, reputation, and income.
  a. Top management.
  b. Administrative personnel.
  c. Plant supervision.
  d. Maintenance personnel.
  e. Engineers and scientists.
  f. Sales force.
  g. Office force.
  h. Production employees.

M. FUTURE PROSPECTS AND PROBLEMS OF ANY KIND WHICH MIGHT BE PREDICTED

N. EVALUATION OF PHYSICAL ASSETS
  1. Land.
    a. Market value, assessments, easements, adjoining property, and space to expand.
    b. Tax rates.
    c. Accessibility to roads, streets, and railroad terminals.
    d. Adequate parking area.
    e. Landscaping.
  2. Buildings.
    a. Market value.
    b. Age and type of construction.
    c. Fire protection.
    d. Shipping and receiving facilities.
    e. Amounts of insurance and rates.
    f. Taxes.
    g. Systems—light, heat, water, ventilation, aisles, and conveyors.
    h. Lockers and wash rooms.
    i. Cafeteria and lunch rooms.
    j. Building codes and zoning laws.
    k. Sewer and waste disposal.
    l. Inventory storage facilities and shelving.

3. Machinery and Equipment.
    a. Complete list of all equipment identified by original cost, manufacturer, age, net book value, condition, and replacement value.
    b. List of obsolete or unused equipment.
    c. Arrangement for work flow.
    d. Machinery on order.
    e. Machinery designed by company itself.
    f. Lift trucks and other material handling equipment, including tote boxes.
    g. Tractors and trailers, officials' cars, panel trucks, pick-ups, etc.

O. ACCOUNTING POLICIES AND PROCEDURES
    1. Inventories.
        a. Categories.
        b. Costing practices.
    2. Fixed asset or property record accounting.
        a. Type of appraisal cards.
        b. Grouping of categories.
        c. Straight line or accelerated depreciation.
        d. Guidelines and investment credit.
    3. Type of cost system.
        a. Job cost.
        b. Standard cost—absorption or direct.
        c. Selling price determination.

12 MONTHS ENDING JULY 1, 19xx
(In Thousands of Dollars)

	A	B	AB
Net Sales	58,200	6,000	64,200
Cost of goods sold	47,900	4,860	52,760
Sell & adm. expense	5,400	900	6,300
Interest on long term debt	300	—	300
Total Cost	53,600	5,760	59,360
Profit before tax	4,600	240	4,840
Federal tax	2,300	120	2,420
Profit after tax	2,300	120	2,420
% Net profit to sales	4.0	2.0	3.8
Total gross assets	56,100	8,500	64,600
Asset turnover to sales	1.04	.71	.98
% Return on gross assets	4.1	1.4	3.7
No. of common shares	1,740	500	1,940
Earnings per share	1.32	.24	1.25
Market Value per share as of 6/30/xx	30	6	30
Price-earnings ratio	23	25	24

Exhibit 55

Merger of Company "A" and Company "B"
Pro-Forma Income Statement

Exhibits 55 and 56 illustrate the type of pro-forma financial statements which provide a snapshot of the new company at the time the merger is consummated. Actually, this should be and can be done before the final decision is made, and might be very valuable. For example, if it appears that a merger will result in excessive dilution of the capital stock of the acquiring company, much of the advantage will be foregone. For example, too great an immediate dilution might indicate that it would be better economics to reject the merger approach and develop the new product line yourself, starting from scratch.

Exhibit 55 shows a brief simplified pro-forma income statement for Company "A," the acquiring company, Company "B," the merger candidate and the new merged Company "AB," for the most recent 12 month period. From a purely statistical standpoint, this proposal does not look too attractive. For example, Company "A" has twice as good a profit on sales and three times as good return on gross assets. Because of the size of the two companies, however, the combined earnings of the two companies would have lowered Company "A's" profit on sales by .2% or 5% and the return on assets by .4% or 10%. The earnings per share would have been .07 cents lower or 5.3% less. Obviously, then, there must be strong considerations other than mere accounting logic or immediate financial gain to motivate this merger. Needless to say, the future prospects of the new "AB" company must have been important to Company "A's" long-range and perhaps even short-range plans. Investigation might reveal that company "B" has a product or a process that can be better exploited through merger with the larger Company "A" than could possibly be accomplished by Company "B" as presently constituted.

Exhibit 56 is the pro-forma balance sheet demonstrating the effect of the merger. For purposes of simplification we have merely added most balance sheet items together to arrive at a new total for the combined companies, except for the stock and surplus items. In actual practice, there could be some substantial changes in the new "AB" company balance sheet within a year or less after the merger was consummated. For example, an outside property appraisal company might be employed to revalue all the fixed assets. If some of the product lines of the old "B" company were dropped, it might result in scrapping and writing off some of the equipment. Some of the inventories might be disposed of and the total value thus reduced. You will note that "B" company originally had 500,000 shares of common stock @ $2.00 per share on their books. This item disappeared and the new common stock becomes the original 1,740,000 shares plus the 200,000 shares used to purchase "B" company, or 1,940,000 shares for the new "AB" company. At the par value of $5.00 per share, the original amount of $8,700,000 is increased by $1,000,000 (200,000 shares @ $5.00) to a new amount of $9,700,000. The actual purchase price agreed upon was $6,000,000, payable in stock in the amount of 200,000 shares at the then listed market value of $30 per share. The difference between the par value of $5.00 and the listed market price of $30 for 200,000 shares was $5,000,000, which then showed up in the liability and stockholders equity section as capital in excess of par value.

AS OF JULY 1, 19XX
(In Thousands of Dollars)

	A	B	AB
Cash & securities	2,900	250	3,150
Receivables	5,900	1,000	6,900
Inventories	7,600	1,250	8,850
Total current assets	16,400	2,500	18,900
Land, bldgs. & equipment	39,700	6,000	45,700
Less accrued depreciation	14,800	1,200	16,000
Net fixed assets	24,900	4,800	29,700
Total Assets	41,300	7,300	48,600
Accounts payable	1,900	400	2,300
Accrued wages & expenses	2,000	350	2,350
Accrued income taxes	1,700	150	1,850
Total current liabilities	5,600	900	6,500
Long term debt	4,800	---	4,800
No. of preferred shares (in thousands)	60	---	60
Value of preferred @ $50.	3,000	---	3,000
No. of common shares (in thousands)	1,740	500	1,940
Par value of common stock	8,700	1,000	9,700
Capital in excess of par value	---	---	5,000
Retained earnings	19,200	5,400	19,600
	30,900	6,400	37,300
Total liabilities and capital	41,300	7,300	48,600

Purchase price - 200,000 shares of common stock @ current market value of $30. per share. (Par Value $5.)

Exhibit 56

Merger of Company "A" and Company "B"
Pro-Forma Balance Sheet

You will note that the new balance sheet shows retained earnings amount greater than "A" company originally had, but much less than the total of "A" and "B"; the difference being reflected in the capital in excess of par value account. As stated earlier in this chapter, you cannot just add numbers across in this type of transaction.

The accountants have a heavy responsibility in gathering and presenting statistical data for appraising and screening merger candidates. When the actual merger wheels begin to turn, however, it is time to call in the legal and tax experts, whether from your own organization or from the outside.

PURCHASE OR POOLING OF INTERESTS

Acquisitions may be treated as Purchases or Poolings of Interest, for accounting purposes, in accord with APB Opinion No. 16. In a pooling, an acquiring company takes the assets of a merged company into its own books at their original cost. This has sometimes allowed a company to issue stock at a worth much more than the original cost of the acquired assets and then to sell the assets at present value and take the difference as a profit. It has also been possible to include the profit of an acquired company in an annual report, even though the pooling occurred at the end of the fiscal year reported on. Opinion No. 16 requires that either the pooling or purchase method be used, not a combination; pooling may be used only if companies combine through an exchange of common stock, subject to certain restrictions. All other business combinations must be accounted for as purchases. In purchase accounting, any difference between the price paid and the value of tangible and identifiable intangible assets acquired, as goodwill, must be systematically written off against future earnings for a period not to exceed 40 years. Moreover, under Opinion No. 16, it is not possible to include the profits of an acquired company in net income reported to stockholders if the pooling took place after the end of the year reported on.

The previous example illustrates the accounting for a pooling of interests, as distinguished from purchase accounting. In this case, the assets, liabilities, and equity interests of the stockholders are combined. The final capital of AB company is the sum of the capital of A plus B, although a new account, capital in excess of par value has arisen and retained earnings has been reduced. No goodwill has been recognized on the merger, even though A paid far in excess of the net worth of B. This accounting recognizes the principle of the pooling and continuing of interests of both companies, even though A is dominant.

DETERMINATION OF ACQUISITION PRICE

A major problem in agreeing to a merger or acquisition is establishing a value for a cash purchase, or an exchange ratio if payment is to be made in stock or other securities. In acquisitions involving purchase accounting, potential future earnings, if substantial, can result in a "good will" or "intangible asset" classification on the new balance sheet.

Other values, such as book value and appraisal value enter into the negotiations. Be sure to utilize the other methods for determining value, including discounted cash flow, capitalization of earnings, and computation of the relative value of one company in terms of the other. The combination of all values should be weighed in the final decision. This preliminary evaluation can only indicate a range within which a transaction could be agreed upon.

For any company whose acquisition would be of substantial benefit, it might be realistic to assume the need to pay a takeover premium. The basis for an acquisition should be the inherent pluses of merging together, rather than the search for a bargain. It might even be futile to conduct a search for the "perfect acquisition."

A first step would be to determine whether dilution of earnings per share will result from the acquisition. In the example at Exhibit 56, will an acquisition at a price of $6,000,000 (200,000 sh. at $30) cause dilution of earnings per share for A, after the acquisition? Obviously, yes. The price of $6,000,000 is 50 times B's earnings of $120,000 as seen in Exhibit 55, but A's stock is selling for only 23 times earnings. What price could be paid to prevent dilution? This can be expressed by the formula:

$$Pb = Pa \left(\frac{1 + B}{1 + A}\right)^t$$

If A will grow at A% per annum and a company to be acquired, B, will grow at B% per annum, then in order to prevent dilution of A's earnings per share (eps) in year t, A should buy B at a price/earnings ratio less than or equal to Pb, where Pa is A's price/earnings ratio. Thus, for example: Let,

1) A grow at 30% per annum.   A = .30
2) B grow at 20% per annum.   B = .20
3) Time frame be 5 years.   t = 5
4) A's P/E ratio be 23.   Pa = 23

Therefore,

$$Pb = 23 \left(\frac{1 + .20}{1 + .30}\right)^5 = 15$$

Thus, A should pay no more than 15 times B's earnings, or 15 × $120,000 = $1,800,000. By paying $6,000,000, A will dilute earnings. Obviously, A has agreed to pay more based on considerations other than earnings, as discussed just above, or as may be inherent in the Reasons for Mergers discussed earlier in this chapter.

A second step would then be to determine the purchase price using the methods in Exhibit 57.

Method 5 capitalizes profits 30.3 times (100% ÷ 3.3%) and then deducts the average net assets. This results in a higher goodwill figure by assuming profits should be capitalized at the same normal rate of return, 3.3%, used for the investment in net assets used in method 4. Actually, profits are more tenuous than assets, and the payback should be over a much shorter period, using capitalization rates of 20% (5 years), 33.3% (3 years), or 50% (2 years). Use of those shorter periods would produce a negative result, indicating that nothing should be paid for goodwill, or that the profits being produced by the net invested assets are not sufficient to justify paying book value for those net assets. This is probably true in the case of Exhibit 55, as the return on gross assets is only 1.4% for B, and this is hardly a sufficient return on any investment, absent other considerations for the acquisition.

Methods of Determining the Purchase Price

Data:	Net Assets of B	$6,400
	Net income of last 5 years	58, 69, 83, 100, 120
	Average net income last 5 years	86
	Net income of next 5 years	144, 173, 207, 249, 299
	Average net income next 5 years	214

1) *"Years' purchase of past annual profits"*

Profits of second preceding year	100
Profits of first preceding year	120
Total, and price to be paid for Goodwill	220

2) *"Years' purchase of average past profits"*

Average profits of last 5 years	86
Multiply by number of years of purchase, say	5*
Goodwill	430

*This assumes a 20% capitalization rate for
profits, that the purchase price will be
returned over a 5 year period.

3) *"Years' purchase of average future profits"*

Average profits of next 5 years	214
Multiply by number of years of purchase, say	5
Goodwill	1,070

Methods 1, 2, and 3 are variants of each other. They suffer the disadvantage of providing for no return on the $6,400 of net invested assets. As a result, the computation produces a higher goodwill amount than those below:

4) *"Years' purchase of average excess profits"*

Average profits of next 5 years	214
Deduct normal return on investment in net assets (see Exhibit 1 - $6,400 x 3.3%)	211
	3
Multiply by number of years of purchase, say	5
Goodwill	15

5) *"Capitalized profits, minus net assets"*

Capitalized value of average profits of next 5 years, or total value of business (214 ÷ 3.3%)	6,485
Deduct agreed value of net assets, other than goodwill	6,400
Goodwill	85

Exhibit 57

Once the goodwill has been calculated in the above examples, the calculated goodwill is added to the value of the net assets, $6,400 M to determine the total purchasing price. In the case of Exhibit 56, the purchase price is $6,000 M (200,000 shares × $30/share). This is less than the value of the net assets, obviously due to the low percent of net profit to sales, 2%, and the 1.4% return on gross assets, as seen in Exhibit 55.

Intelligent and equitable financial evaluation of a proposed acquisition is a very difficult task. It calls for the application of all the conventional financial yardsticks, interpreting much non-financial information about markets, products, personnel, and real estate, and then applying analytical and intuitive judgment.

DETERMINING THE METHOD OF PAYMENT

Having determined the price, the method of payment will depend on:

1. The tax consequences to the seller.
2. The buyer's financial position.
3. Liquidity and p/e ratio of the buyer's stock.
4. The earn-out contract.

Each of these methods is discussed below:

1. The seller may be seeking a tax-free sale or may desire to receive stock in exchange for his business which he can hold for appreciation and subsequent disposal at capital gains rates. In this event, the goal is to structure a *Tax-Free Reorganization.* The seller exchanges his shares for ours, and we pick up his assets at his tax basis. Convertible securities, if given, must not be converted for five years, to retain the tax-free status.

The IRS Code allows for a tax-free Statutory Merger or Consolidation. In a merger, A is merged into B and B survives. In a consolidation, A and B combine to create a new C, which is the consolidated company. There are three types of Tax-Free Reorganizations:

Type A-Cash—The shareholder gets cash, up to 50% and stock. The cash received is taxable as a capital gain.

Type B-Stock swap or tender offer—The buyer must issue only voting stock and receive an 80% minimum of the acquired company, and a parent-subsidiary relationship is then established. You cannot buy shares for cash even shortly before the tender offer. You cannot give a guaranty as to the future value of your stock, and you may not pay the finder's fees of the selling company or the non-taxability of the reorganization will be destroyed.

Type C-Acquisition of assets—The buyer must acquire substantially all of the assets of the seller corporation and must give only voting stock. Some or all of the liabilities may be assumed, but you must obtain at least 90% of the net assets (assets minus liabilities). Thus, the selling company may retain only 10% of net assets to pay off any dissenting stockholders.

The issuance of contingent stock (all shares not being issued presently) may destroy the tax-free reorganization, as the seller is receiving something other than voting stock. This would defeat a stock swap, Type B, or acquisition of assets, Type C. But the IRS will allow contingent shares to be issued if:

a. The maximum number of shares to be issued is pre-determined.

b. At least 50% of the maximum shares are issued at closing.

c. The contingent share payout does not exceed five years.

d. There is a contract (not a certificate or warrant).

e. There is a good business reason for the contingent issuance, such as not being able to determine the value of the purchase and needing future earnings as a guide.

When contingent shares are issued, the imputed interest rules on deferred payments may come into play. Section 483 imputes a higher interest rate, giving the seller an interest deduction, but this causes taxable interest income to you, the buyer. You may avoid this by 1) specifying a 6% interest charge, the minimum prescribed amount, which will result in lower taxable income for the buyer, or 2) issuing the shares into escrow, pending their possible return if the future earnings level is not met, thus completely avoiding the interest income imputation. While in escrow, the seller must have voting rights to the shares, and dividend rights.

A spin-off may be accomplished prior to the tax-free merger or acquisition. This is the disposal of unwanted assets or a segment of the business. Usually, if the business is over five-years old and there is a business purpose for disposal, a spin-off will be tax-free. If the merger follows too closely on the spin-off, it may be taxable. It would be best to go for an IRS ruling as to non-taxability of the deal, prior to spin-off.

A variety of types of security may be given to effect the merger, as long as they are voting securities. Warrants are not stock, however, and if given with voting stock, they must be valued and would be dividend income to the seller, not capital gain.

Voting preferred stock is also acceptable. Class A preferred, paying a cash dividend, or Class B preferred, paying a stock dividend, may be used, and the dividends would be taxable dividend income to the holder. A convertible preferred is sometimes used, convertible into common in increasing amounts, say 4% each year, in lieu of the cash dividends. The increments of 4% would be a taxable dividend to the holder. There are advantages and disadvantages to convertible preferred which are discussed below.

2. *The buyer's financial position* may be such that he needs immediate cash, even more than the 50% in a Type A Merger. In this event, a taxable acquisition may need to be structured. The buyer may acquire stock, or any of the assets, but instead of giving voting stock, you give more than 50% in cash or other securities, with the following tax considerations:

a) The seller has capital gain but you may use the installment sale method and pay less than 30% in the year of sale, thus postponing 70% of the tax. No contingent payout is permitted on the installment method. In computing the 30%, allow for imputed interest which IRS will apply on any deferred payment. This could make the entire sale taxable at once. You may also use a convertible debenture. This is taxable to seller, but it carries a lower interest rate to the buyer and does not dilute earnings until conversion. If the buyer puts certain restrictions on the bonds, such as making them non-negotiable for a period of time, they may not be taxable until the restrictions lapse. The gain to the seller is locked-in until conversion. The conversion feature on bonds creates a contingent aspect, as the value of the bond fluctuates based on its conversion feature. As a consequence, the installment sale method may not be used.

b) If the seller sells assets—he will effectively lose his capital gain treatment on that portion of the assets (put into service after 1961) which have depreciated. Thus, he must recapture depreciation as ordinary taxable income. Similarly, he would have an Investment Credit Recapture, which would have to be paid, whether or not he had any taxable income.

c) A Calendar Year Reorganization (Section 337) may be undertaken by seller, with usually no tax to his corporation. Inventory or assets may be sold with no gain being recognized, except for the ordinary income, taxed at the corporate level, as a result of recapture of depreciation, described above.

d) If the seller is willing to be taxed on the sale, and the buyer wants a higher, or stepped-up tax basis, you must buy assets, rather than capital stock.

e) Finder's Fees and the SEC Registration Costs are deductible to the acquiring corporation, and the IRS has ruled that they are not taxable to the selling corporation.

Note: Non-taxability applies only to finder's fees and registration costs, nothing else. If you pay the seller's accounting or legal fees, it can make the entire sale taxable in an otherwise tax-free reorganization.

The *Cash Tender Offer*—fully taxed to the seller, is often used where there are numerous stockholders, or where the buyer is not negotiating directly with management but approaches the stockholders. It has these advantages:

• You need not make SEC disclosure of the offer unless you have $1 million in assets and 500 or more shareholders, but this disclosure is less burdensome than the disclosure on a merger or stock swap, which may need stockholder approvals and 20 days advance notice on exchange. This needs disclosure, but only at the time of the tender, and the SEC will not usually examine the offer until you exercise the tender.

• The disclosure does not need independent public accounting audits and certifications of financial statements.

• The disclosure does not need extensive information as to the nature of your business. You are, thus, less vulnerable to attack or resistance by a recalcitrant management group.

• Your total investment can be much less than in a merger. You do not need to acquire "all" of the stock, or even the 80% minimum for a stock swap.

- You may withdraw within 7 to 60 days for any reason.

- You need not name the exact source of your funds, such as the bank who makes the loan for purposes of the tender.

- You need not disclose your "ideas" to manage the newly acquired company nor tell of the "minor" changes you plan.

It has these disadvantages:

- Under SEC 16, a 10% holder must file with the SEC in 10 days, just as if you had taken the company over in a tender. You must give ten years of information, the source of your funds, the amount of shares held, name of your partners or group or syndicate. The 10 days begin on the date of your option, contract or committment, not on actual receipt of the stock.

- You must accept, pro-rata, during the first 10 days when you get more stock than you desire. This gives management more time to fight the tender—up to 10 days.

- If a complete disclosure is not made, the SEC or management may sue. This obviates the blind tender offer.

- The disclosure must relate your plans to sell, merge, liquidate or change the corporate structure. If you do not so disclose and you later do a merger, even though not intended to be done at the time of the cash tender offer, you expose yourself to litigation.

- The offer is subject to the 1967 "corporate takeover bill" and to the SEC rules which followed that bill.

These management defenses are available:

a. The Buy-In. The tenderee can use its own funds to buy-in its own stock on the open market. The courts will allow this if management shows that the tenderer will hurt the company. Management normally cannot buy-in after notice of the tender, unless it files the number of shares it will buy and its source of funds, in a notice to all shareholders and the SEC.

b. Management may advertise, say the price offered is too low, tell plans, make promises. The SEC will look at the offer to be sure it is not false or misleading. The SEC may, in fact, sue the tenderer, which will prejudice the stockholders.

c. The tax consequences may be adverse to stockholders, who may not be prepared to be taxed on their gain.

d. Management may quickly merge with another company.

e. Management may alert the Justice Department which has been taking a more active advance role in acquisitions.

f. Alert management is sensitive to the possibility of a takeover and may even have boiler-plate press releases prepared, mailings to shareholders, and signed and sealed documents (undated, already in Washington), to be completed for quick SEC filing, charging anti-trust violations by the tenderer.

g. Stock held by employees in Employee Stock Option Plans, the Employee Stock Ownership Trust, the hands of management, can be marshalled for a solid block. Loans may be made to employees to exercise large blocks of key employee stock options, or stock may be given away, free to employees, in amounts based on seniority. These all provide excellent employee benefits in return for which management is assured of employee support in the takeover fight.

h. Large blocks of stock may be held by friendly institutions, known to the alert company. The company may have held many meetings, over the years, with these institutions.

i. The company may enlist the aid of its national union to resist the tender. If labor resists, on a national basis, the tenderer may withdraw.

j. Management, with shareholder approval, can raise the percentage of votes required to approve a merger, to call a special stockholders' meeting, to remove a director, from the usual 51% to 70% or 75%.

k. Long-term employment contracts with top executives will present the tenderer with the problem of managing the company as it will be bound by the contracts.

l. The company may stagger the board of directors, for example with 3 out of 9 directors due up for election in any year. Using this device, the acquirer would need at least 2 years to gain control of the board.

m. The certificate of incorporation may be amended to require 5 to 8 directors for a quorum, with chairman having the tie-breaking vote.

n. Standby directors can be named in advance, and voted on at the annual meeting, who would fill any vacancy, automatically, in proscribed order.

o. The company may reorganize itself into a different state, like Delaware, which makes corporate takeovers more difficult. In fact, ten states have anti-takeover statutes which, in general, provide that the target company may call for a state securities hearing on the fairness of the proposal, providing for an automatic 30-day delay. The states are Virginia, Idaho, Indiana, Ohio, South Dakota, Kansas, Minnesota, Nevada, Wisconsin, and Hawaii.

p. Litigation on anti-trust arguments, securities regulations, or other regulatory agencies is a common defense. Even if ineffective, the suit allows time to counteract the offer.

Convertible Preferred Stock, if voting, may be used in a tax-free reorganization and if non-voting, in a taxable purchase. In general, like convertible bonds, it carries a low equivalent interest rate (dividend) but may be more attractive than bonds. It has these advantages:

- You postpone dilution of earnings.
- The conversion price may be above the common based on the fact of the preferred dividend.

- The seller receives income, via the dividend, over a period of years (which may be a strong psychological point in making the purchase), without the necessity of giving income to all common stock holders.

- The seller is protected against the volatility of the buyer's stock. The preferred dividend gives him down-side protection.

- Earnings per share should be increased. You will earn more on the preferred (on the seller's business which you bought for your preferred), than you pay out to the seller in preferred dividends. The leverage should increase EPS and the market value of the buyer's stock.

It has these disadvantages:

- Pro-forma earnings per share, giving effect to conversion, must be shown in the Form 10-K and in the Annual Report, if the conversion price is below market value.

- If a major portion of the value of the preferred is attributed to the common stock, the preferred may be considered a residual security, not a senior security. Moreover, since the common stock may fluctuate, then the value of the conversion feature may fluctuate, and the preferred may be considered as a residual security one year and not the next. If considered as a residual security, earnings would be reduced by the amount attributable to the residual security, further reducing pro-forma EPS.

- The convertible preferred, if not registered, has no market and provides no down-side protection. Registration is expensive.

- It may be hard to buy back convertible preferred later, especially if you divest yourself on the acquisition.

- The risk is greater, as you are committed to an after-tax dividend, which you cannot convert to debt. Some preference stock may circumvent this risk by 1) paying no cash dividends. 2) setting a convertible feature which compounds annually at over 3% (meaning you get 3% more common, compounded, each year). 3) setting a conversion price that compounds equal to the amount above, thus, 1 : 1 in year 1, then 1.03 : 1, in year 2, etc. 4) redeeming up to 3% of the total issue each year at par. The IRS has ruled that the yield to the seller is ordinary income, but this is no worse than any dividend he might receive. On the other hand, the buyer does not reduce EPS (as the redemption is not an expense but a capital transaction).

- If the dividend is too low, and less than 75% of its value is in the preferred stock itself, its issuance may not be attractive to the seller.

3. The *liquidity* of the buyer (or lack of it), coupled with a high *price/earnings ratio* on his own stock may dictate that a common stock, or convertible into common, purchase be made. The buyer may determine that he can offer far more than a competitive bidder, and still not dilute his earnings or book value per share. If goodwill arises, however, and the transaction is treated as a Purchase, rather than a Pooling of Interests, the Purchase Accounting Rules of APB Opinion No. 16 require that goodwill first be attributed to assets at an appraised value. This means that if assets are appraised at higher than book value, their value will be "stepped-up" to the extent of goodwill (for accounting purposes only, not for tax purposes), and they will be depreciated based on this higher value, thereby reducing earnings after the merger, without any tax benefit. This could possibly cause dilution of earnings per share.

In this case, the determined purchase price could be paid through a Pooling of Interests, rather than a Purchase. The pooling would be tax-free or taxable, based on the same considerations as any purchase, and no goodwill would arise.

Warrants may be used in lieu of stock. The warrants may trade at 25% of the price of the common stock. Their issuance, thus, creates value. Warrants are not considered an underlying security since they are not stock and, therefore, do not dilute EPS. Warrants may also be used together with debentures. This creates fixed interest charges and makes the company more vunerable to cyclical downturns. The high fixed interest charges could be offset by acquiring a company with large cash flow, say an insurance company, despite its low earnings. It might be bought for below book value (if you offer a good growth stock in exchange). In this case, purchase, don't pool. This creates negative goodwill which can be written-up to book value over the years, thereby creating income. Having served the above purpose, the low income, high cash flow company may then be spun-off, tax-free. It is probably worth more as a separate entity than in consolidation. The price for which it is sold is then plowed back into new, future earnings.

Don't neglect Cash. In times of a depressed stock market and low p/e ratios, stocks lose appeal and the seller may prefer cash. Many buyers, with high liquidity, during depressed markets, make the most advantageous acquisitions.

When liquidity problems do not permit the luxury of cash acquisitions, a good technique is to buy assets for preferred stock, and earnings (minus the preferred dividend) for common stock.

4. The *earn-out* contract, being a key motivator for the seller, in arriving at a higher price than he would otherwise receive, also determines the method of payment.

The earn-out contract, as well as all the negotiated details, needs to be set out in a memorandum which will memorialize the agreement, prior to going to actual legal contracts. The memorandum should be in letter form, should tell the details of the purchase, and, in fact, should have a brief reference to every clause which will ultimately be in the contract down to the minutiae of assignability of the contract, which state law will prevail, whom the old owner will report to.

The guideline for preparing the memorandum should be an actual contract. If none is available from a prior acquisition, make one up for this purchase, but don't allow the seller to see it until after the memorandum is prepared and agreed to. Changes to the memorandum may be quickly incorporated into the actual contract, and you are much more likely to get quick approval on the contract when the seller later tells his lawyer he has already agreed to a specific point.

If there is any misconception on either the acquirer's or the acquiree's part, this will surface in the memorandum. Sometimes, in fact, the seller may seem to have been very amenable and anxious to sell, during the verbal negotiations. But when the memorandum arrives, shock sets in! He suddenly realizes he is selling his business, his life's work. He may have second thoughts or even try to strike a better deal. Better to face these now than have him walk out of the closing. Therefore, the memorandum should be direct and to the point, covering all points, but not so severe and rigid (as in a contract) that it will scare him off.

POSSIBLE RESULTS OF A MERGER

The accomplishment of a merger or acquisition presents management with one of its most important responsibilities. The element of risk stems from the long-term effects of such a transaction. Marriage to the wrong company could result in deterioration of strength and position, if not disaster. Conversely a successful acquisition can lead to many benefits for both principals, open entirely new product areas, and provide a foundation for a good profit and for healthy growth opportunities.

In any merger, one company must be dominated and be the acquirer, and the other company must accept a subordinate position.

During the initial period, in which both sides are learning to live together, many new formations may lose some of the personnel whose talents were one of the factors which motivated the acquisition. Mergers and even rumors of mergers create anxiety and feelings of insecurity among all levels of an organization. The acquiring company's need to effect economies might be anticipated by the selling company's personnel, and its most valuable people might find other connections.

Mergers may also have damaging repercussions on tax liabilities, balance sheets, and the legal and accounting situation of the resultant company.

Those companies which turn to acquisitions as a desperate attempt to rescue a sinking business are most likely to acquire even more difficult and seemingly insoluble problems. Those companies who use acquisitions as an integral part of a disciplined and orderly long-range planning program have a good chance to obtain subtantial benefits.

ACQUISITION AIDS

1. Mergers and acquisitions should not be resorted to as an expedient solution to business problems.

2. Mergers shoud be made for a definite reason, ideally as part of a long-range plan.

3. The best reasons for mergers are to obtain diversification, increase production capacity, round out product lines, acquire "instant" marketing organizations or outlets, meet or outpace competition, smooth out cyclical situations, or acquire some new capability.

4. During the consideration and evaluation of merger candidates, delve far deeper into the company than is revealed in their financial statements, as suggested in Exhibits 54 and 57.

5. Before the consummation of a merger, both principals should insure compliance with the regulatory government agencies. Competent legal assistance and good tax advice could eliminate many possible difficulties.

CHAPTER 12

Fine Tuning Financial Analysis Through Modern Budgeting Techniques

The yardsticks for Return on Investment and Earnings Per Share are interrelated and are readily expressed ... in this schematic ... equation ...

The basis for all financial analysis, as it pertains to company operations, is the Plan of operations, otherwise called the Budget. The Plan provides, to the extent required in the business, profit planning, programs for capital investing and financing, the expenditure of research and development funds, sales forecasts, expense budgets, and cost standards, together with the necessary procedures to effectuate the Plan.

This is called, alternately, the Profit Plan, the Budget, the Operating Control Plan, the Operating Plan, or, simply, the Plan.

The following definitions are generally intended in accounting and budgeting parlance to distinguish the concepts involved:

a. Budget—The quantified plan of operations for given fiscal periods, expressed in the form of financial statements with sufficient supporting schedules to enable measurement of actual performance to budget.

241

b. Forecast—This is less extensive than the budget, being a prediction of one aspect of the budget at a specific point or over a period of time, such as sales for the year, or cash balance at the end. As the term is used here, it does not refer to "financial forecasts," which may be the same as budgets, but usually refers to an objective, logical, supported statement of the most probable financial results. A financial forecast differs from a budget as the latter involves motivations, control, and performance evaluation considerations as principal elements.

c. Estimate or Projection—An estimate based on assumptions that are not necessarily the most likely. A projection is often developed in answer to "What would happen if ...?" The assumptions of the budget result in estimated or projected financial statements.

d. Operating Plan—The Budget, as defined above.

e. Profit Plan—The initial profit target as expressed by the Chief Executive Officer and as reflected in the bottom line of the Budget. This, therefore, becomes the Forecast of a number, stated either pre-tax or after-tax.

THE BUDGETING CONCEPT

Every business, large or small, budgets. It is sometimes accomplished informally. Perhaps the retail store owner estimates what his sales will be on the Columbus Day holiday; how will they compare to last year?; is the weather forecast good?; do I have sufficient inventory on the shelves to handle the expected traffic, and if the day starts out badly, shall I announce some immediate mark-downs to encourage an impulse spurt in sales? All the basic budgeting elements are found in that exercise, and though loosely embraced, all budgeting techniques include the following:

1. A Profit Plan
2. A Budget
3. Communicating the Budget
4. Budget vs Actual (BVA) performance

These formal steps are necessary in large corporations to establish a framework related to the extended span of control in such companies.

THE PROFIT PLAN

The Profit Plan for a public company is implicitly determined by the market place and is reflected in the price/earnings ratio for the Company's stock. These market expectations are signaled to the Board of Directors and the President who examine them in light of their long-range goals. They, then, set their profit objective and pass it on to subordinates for implementation—to responsible officers for manufacturing, research and development, personnel, and administration—to financial and marketing division officers, and to the Controller for mechanical processing.

The profit objective should be tied to sales growth and will be quantified with these yardsticks: sales growth, gross profit margin, operating expenses to sales, pre-tax margin, after-tax margin, return on average net worth, return on total assets, and return before interest to total assets. The President may, further, specify certain minimum standards for liquidity and turnover of assets which are pertinent to the individual company being budgeted, such as receivables, inventory, accounts payable, and working capital.

The yardsticks for ROI and Earnings Per Share (EPS) are interrelated and are readily expressed in the diagram below. This schematic device, as a budgetary tool, impresses users with the importance of all items in the equation—income, revenues, assets, interest cost, equity, and shares outstanding:

Return on Investment and Earnings Per Share

Return on investment, total assets and stockholders' equity are illustrated below in various functions, as they relate to each other:

PRIOR YEAR TO DECEMBER 31, 19xx

	Pre-interest margin		Turnover		Earnings-interest index		Resource leverage		Book-value per share	= EPS
	Net income plus tax-adjusted interest	x	Revenues	x	Net income*	x	Total assets (avg.)	x	Stock-holders' equity (avg.)	= EPS
	Revenues		Total assets (average)		Net income plus tax-adjusted interest		Stock-holders' equity (average)		Number of shares	
Applicable Numbers $(000)	$\frac{808}{10,000}$ x		$\frac{10,000}{15,530}$ x		$\frac{800}{808}$ x		$\frac{15,530}{9,030}$ x		$\frac{9,030}{7,007}$	= 11.4¢
Results	8.1% x		.64 x		.99 x		1.72 x		$1.29	= 11.4¢

Return on assets to debt and equity ——————— 5.2%

Return on assets to equity ————————————— 5.1%

Return on stock-holders' equity ————————————————— 8.9%

Earnings per share ———————————————————————— 11.4¢

*After Preferred Dividends

Exhibit 58

THE BUDGET

The Controller, or his responsible budgeting manager, will establish, coordinate and administer the budget using a Budget Calendar and employing a Budget Committee.

The Budget Calendar is merely a formal document which is published to all managers setting forth the budget schedule. Each step in the budgeting process is listed and a completion date is shown. Typical steps are: budget forms issued; goals are communicated; home office budgets are sent to superiors for approval; field office budgets are sent up for approval; all departments send approved budgets to budget department for processing; data processing sends printed budget to accounting; corrected budgets are reprocessed and distributed; budget committee reviews, approves, and/or adjusts budgets; data processing adjusts budgets and forwards to accounting; budget section issues approved budgets. The budget section monitors the noted dates and coordinates with all divisions to hit the target dates. This will often require the budget manager to inveigle, cajole, and perform as a generalist to remain on target.

The Budget Committee gives final budget approval. This could be a committee of one, consisting of the President, but more often involves three to five corporate officers. Every arm of the organization must be represented on the committee, either by the directly responsible manager or his superior. By definition, therefore, the President could serve alone. If he does not, then every officer reporting to him should be a committeed member. The committee should be chaired by the President or a financial officer, who can best interpret the financial goals established in the Profit Plan by the Board or the President. The Controller or Budget Manager need not be committee members, as one of them will be at every Budget Committee meeting, anyway, to present, analyze and interpret the Budget for members of the committee.

The Budget Committee should also approve the Budget Calendar.

Stable companies, without seasonal aspects to their operations, may allow up to 120 days in their Budget Calendar. Volatile companies should focus on a 60 to 90 day advance period.

COMMUNICATING THE BUDGET

The Budget started with communication of the President's profit objectives to officers responsible for sales, manufacturing, administration, research, distribution and finance. The Profit Plan is tied to sales growth and is expressed in the form of yardsticks, as previously described. The question now arises as to whether budgets should be submitted, first, by the various departments or divisions who are responsible and, then, be compared to the Profit Plan or whether the Profit Plan should be submitted to the departments with instructions to budget so as to achieve the Profit Plan. In other words, do we budget from the bottom, up, or from the top, down?

The answer is a little of both. Successful budgeting requires total involvement of the people who are expected to achieve the forecasted results. If a plan is submitted for these people, the operating personnel, and if their performance is to be measured against this plan, they should cooperate in setting the goals by which they will be measured.

The philosophy of employee involvement cannot be overdone. Setting performance goals for employees without their concurrence in the attainment of these goals is certain to result in failure. However, employees should not be permitted to set goals which are not consonant with corporate objectives.

In other words enlightened management, sensitive to stockholders needs, through the Board of Directors and the President, is in a position to determine the most likely attainable Profit Plan. This is imparted to officers who distribute the plan to subordinates, sometimes explaining, exhorting, selling, demanding some of each—as to the total soundness of the Profit Plan. The plan is then passed down to the lowest level manager who has profit responsibility, with similar exhortations.

At this point, training sessions should be held to inculate managers with the reasons and needs for budgeting. The following may serve as a checklist of points to be raised in the training session:

- The Budget is an estimate of anticipated costs and expenses. A study of this helps us to understand our business better, to coordinate the efforts of all divisions, to provide top management with overall visibility of operations, and to avoid surprises.

- The Budget is not restrictive. It allows for flexibility and improvement. It provides estimates of costs and expenses if goals are exceeded and, similarly, provides for reductions in expenses if goals cannot be met.

- The Profit Plan or objective is the sole important goal to be achieved. Failures to attain the stated goal are analyzed each period to determine the necessary corrective actions and to permit us to achieve the required goals in the future.

- Bad habits and poor management are eliminated. Errors are corrected, at once.

- Every management decision is directed toward achievement of the Profit Plan as expressed by the Budget.

- Forecasts of sales and expenses are based on past performance, plus planned changes and expected level of business activity. These forecasts recognize population trends, indicators of business activity, employment trends, personal income levels. They are not guesses but intelligent estimates of future activity.

- The Budget is a Statement of Policy, expressed in an overall profit objective. It is not a working guide or a tool for managing. Its objectives may be qualified into useful "rule-of-thumb" guides, such as the published yardstick.

- The Budget is the tool which provides additional profits by using the processes of analysis and advance planning.

- Additional profits result because the key to successful operations lies only in the analysis and advance planning by all division managers before final Budget approval.

- Large businesses have an attenuated span of control, and it is difficult to properly communicate corporate goals. The Budget compresses the communication process into the quantified expression of a Profit Plan. Small businesses profit, equally, by an intensive study of past operations and future prospects.

- Day-to-day decisions are avoided as decisions are pre-assessed through budgetary planning as to their effect on the entire business.

- Budgetary planning requires that plans be written and that the manager be held responsible for their execution. This instills the habit of analysis and advance planning.

- Participation by managers in the budgeting procedure creates thorough familiarity with the overall objectives of the enterprise, and thorough involvement. No one is left out or by-passed. Each manager can suggest and obtain the benefit of others' counsel. The final Budget represents the combined judgment of all managers in the best ways to attain the Profit Plan.

- The Budget not only coordinates efforts along the most profitable lines but helps in controlling operations through the issuance of periodic comparison reports of Budget to Actual performance.

- The Budget uses "responsibility" accounting. It is as improper, however, to over-budget as it is to underbudget. For example, if each manager under-budgeted in order to look better in actual performance, the Company would not have enough cash budgeted to meet its attainable goals.

- The Budget uses the direct cost concept, with each manager being responsible only for those costs which he can control. There are no allocations or corporate pool charged in to any profit center.

Following these training sessions, the distribution of forms, the Budget Calendar, and the explanation of corporate goals may commence. This is best done in a general meeting with immediate subordinate managers who, in turn, will hold similar meetings with their immediate subordinate managers. In this way, the importance of the budget—its timing and its goals—is given a personal touch with each immediate manager. It is not relegated to a written directive. These meetings will stress the concepts which were presented in the training sessions:

1. *Responsibility Accounting*—requires creating profit centers at decentralized locations where costs may be controlled by a responsible manager. The local manager becomes responsible for the sales and administration of his office, as well as the generation of costs and profits. He is, therefore, "responsible" and he, himself, creates the operating plan for his office and is responsible for its results. The Budget Department merely supplies this manager with a print-out of his own budget, set forth in a readable format, and then reports the results of actual operations to the manager, together with a statement of variances from the Budget. The manager must explain and comment on these variances to his superior who, in turn, is held accountable for his subordinate's performance. The system of responsibility, thus, channels up from the lowest level of managerial control to the highest. Responsibility Accounting requires that the Chart of Accounts be made to conform to the responsibility concept, enabling costs to be recorded in the right profit centers.

2. *The Profit Center*—is the lowest level on the Organizational Chart at which the manager exercises control over revenues and expenses. Each box on the chart, described in the chapter on Organizing for Financial Management, represents a Profit Center, presided over by a manager who controls its expenses and is responsible for its revenues.

3. *Direct Costs*—are used in attributing expenses to the Profit Center. A Direct Cost is defined, for Budget Purposes, as "any cost which would be eliminated if the Profit Center, itself, were eliminated." This definition is necessary as there often are costs endemic to the operation of the Profit Center which are not necessarily immediately controllable by the manager. They are, though, ultimately controllable. For example, rent expense in a remote sales office, say with a five year lease, may not appear to be under the control of the branch manager. It is, though, ultimately, as the office could be sub-let, if necessary, and salesmen could travel from their homes.

The Direct Cost definition must be communicated to all managers to avoid arguments over what costs are charged into their Profit Center. This definition implies a degree of ultimate control which relates to the very existence of the Profit Center and is, thus, not an arguable concept as it relates to charging expenses into the cost center.

Stated another way, remove a box from the organizational chart and any costs that follow it are Direct.

The Direct Cost concept avoids allocation arguments. Do not allocate, apportion, or charge-in to the Profit Center any costs which are not Direct Costs. There have been too many regretful cases where a local manager has purchased outside services at a lower cost than that he would pay to a corporate department. It is difficult to assail his logic due to the artificial allocation of corporate charges.

4. *Intercompany Transfer Price*—is the concept used to charge corporate pool and home office expenses to Profit Centers, without the necessity of allocations. Under this concept, the Profit Center is charged for merchandise purchases at some famliar yardstick price, such as lowest dealer price. The price includes a normal mark-up and element of profit for the home office, but is the same price at which an independent, non-company owned dealer would purchase. The Field Manager cannot argue the logic of this charge, since if he cannot operate profitably on this basis, the Company would be better off to close the field office (which is not a Loss Center, rather than a Profit Center) and franchise an independent dealer. All Profit Centers are compared on this same basis, using the yardstick price, permitting gross profit margins to be compared against each other.

5. *The Organizational Framework*—described in the chapter Organizing for Financial Management consists of the tools necessary to communicate and administer the Operating Plan. These tools are the essential ingredients of the communication process. They consist of:

Organizational Charts	Personnel Policies
Chart of Accounts	Publication Control
Accounting Manual	Exercise of Authority
Position Descriptions	Philosophy of Management
Standard Operating Procedures	Management by Objectives
Operating Policies	Internal Auditing

These tools set the parameters for the job, avoid duplications by other managers and fix responsibility for broad areas. We have often been asked why you can't merely tell a manager he is responsible for profits in his area, and that's it. Why do you need to go to the trouble and expense of the Position Description? The comment has merit. Profits are the goal, but where there is more than one responsible manager, more than one profit center, these corporate goals become interwoven, and each manager has functional responsibility to each other manager. Corporate policy in the form of social consciousness, anit-trust adherence, corporate image, and overall corporate posture are ingredients in attaining overall profits. Each manager may achieve his profit goal, but the corporation may lose a damaging patent infringement suit which could destroy its profits. The organizational framework approaches all these ends from a corporate, not an individual standpoint.

6. *Divided or Functional Responsibility*—is the concept of "dotted-line," rather then direct responsibility. Communicating the Profit Plan and corporate goals requires an appreciation that every manager has dotted line responsibility to every other manager. In a sense, each serves the other and reports to the other, both up and down and across the organizational ladder. The Position Description shows specific Organizational Relationships, but inherent in each manager's job are the unwritten relationships to all other managers. This is the concept of cooperation by which corporate goals are attained.

A sub-set of Communicating the Budget is the review of previously submitted budgets and re-communicating the need for revisions. The Budget Committee, as stated earlier, is composed of the President and/or key officers of the corporation. When individually submitted budgets are viewed in total perspective by the Committee, they may not meet the corporate stated Profit Plan. It is no easy task to have to go back to managers who have labored over their budgets for weeks and convince them that revised estimates are required to meet the overall corporate goals. If, however, the communication process has carefully included the explanation of the budgeting process during the training sessions described on page 245 of this chapter (the first checklist point), managers will understand the concept of overall profit objectivity. They can be readily convinced to make a revised contribution to the accomplishment of the Profit Plan. This may mean that one division manager may have to make a disproportionate effort, for which he obviously will expect to be rewarded.

BUDGET VS. ACTUAL (BVA) PERFORMANCE

The completed, approved Budget is presented to top management in the form of financial statements, to include:

P&L Budget
Balance Sheet
Statement of Changes in Financial Position

and supporting schedules and data:

Sales Budget
Cost of Sales Budget
Expense Budget

Employee Forecast

Financial Ratios and Yardsticks

Capital Expenditures Budget

R&D Budget

P&L Explanations

General Budgeting Instruction Manual

The format of these financial statements, of course, will vary with the individual business, but they should usually be presented in a manner which conforms to the format of internal statements normally presented to top management. Similarly, top-line corporate budgets should conform to published financial statements in appearance. If the Budget is presented in this manner, it will permit future comparison of actual results to be done quickly and easily.

The periodic comparisons of actual performance to Budget is an essential ingredient of any formal budgeting system. This allows for mid-stream corrective action which assures that the organization will reach its Profit Plan. Review techniques must be established to measure performance to Plan and variances from Budget need to be accounted for and controlled. This requires establishing a Reporting System. Such a system should have the following features:

REPORTING SYSTEM FEATURES

1. Reports should be original for your company. Do not copy someone else's reports—they are not tailor made. They must meet the needs of your organization as developed by your own evaluation.

2. The accounting system must provide for the generation of non-financial reports, which meet the needs of operating managers, as well as the financial reports which are published and used by top management.

3. Operating reports should compare performance to Plan, should highlight deviations, suggestion action, and relate current position to the ultimate goal.

4. Show summary information without all the detail.

5. Design the report to be useful. Determine whether last month or last year comparisons are the more meaningful.

6. Use graphs and charts to add sauce to your presentation.

7. Use acronyms for report titles to create enthusiasm and to facilitate familiarity by the user. Use PABST, instead of Product Analysis by Sales Territories.

8. Show the distribution on all reports, so each reader will know who else received it, without having to look it up. Don't waste the user's time.

9. Show major assumptions on the face, or attach to each report. Avoid the reader's having to ask questions or research the underlying assumptions. Facts change with different assumptions.

10. Publish only necessary and key reports. Don't flood the company with unneeded reports. Don't distribute it to anyone who doesn't need it.

11. Publish reports on a timely basis: daily reports on the next day; weekly reports with three days, and monthly reports with ten days of the close. Timely reports, using broad assumptions for missing data, are better than late reports which are more accurate. Use flash reports.

12. Watch the cost of reports. Design them for broad distribution, not just a few individuals.

13. Information on reports should follow organizational lines of responsibility. Report by Profit Centers in accordance with the Responsibility Accounting concepts described earlier.

14. In the presentation of data, segregate controllable from non-controllable expense. Similarly, avoid allocations of expenses, or show them as separate totals.

15. Make statements easy to read: Use 8½″ × 11″ paper, not computer sheets; limit columns of figures to not more than three columns to a group; leave plenty of white space on a page; omit all cents and thousands of dollars where not meaningful; show year to date figures.

16. Provide binders for repetitive, important reports, to allow them to be retrieved and used more easily.

17. Date and show the originating author's or department's name, to facilitate feedback comments or questions, and to help identify the report months or years later.

18. Use trend reports when the data is more meaningfully presented that way.

19. Present results on an exception basis that only emphasizes good and bad performance.

In addition to standard reports in columnar or graph form, a good reporting system will utilize *the narrative report*. This should be prepared as a monthly flash report by each manager. It flows up organizational lines to higher managers, resulting in summaries which find their way up to the top division officer or President before the regular month-end data processing or financial reports are ready. For example, on the last day of the month, local sales managers would report to their regional managers; the regional managers would summarize these reports and synthesize them, on the second day, for zone managers. The zone managers would summarize these for the general sales manager by the fourth day. Similar narrative reports would have been flowing in to all division managers at headquarters, and these would be summarized for the Executive VP by the sixth day, at which time final summaries would be sent to the President. Narrative reports are merely summaries which explain what the financials will show when they are ready. They pre-explain variances and make projections for next month. They tell a better story than the numerical report. Such reports should be not less than one half page nor more than two pages long. Less then one half page is not informative enough. More than two pages tends to be verbose and full of excuses for poor performance.

A variant on these monthly reports are quarterly earnings reports released to stockholders and regulatory agencies and the Board of Directors by the President. These contain a President's letter or comments which further synthesize the monthly narrative reports, interpreting them for the users.

Staff meetings belong under any discussion of reporting the results of operations. In this context, staff meetings mean any meetings involving managers concerned with attaining budgeted objectives. Thus, a line department, like a field sales office, may have a staff meeting attended by the branch manager, office manager, and service manager, representing all the concerned managers. Or, a headquarters staff manager, say a field administrative manager, may hold a staff meeting with line office managers for Budget review purposes. These meetings may be planning meetings, to work on submission of a new Budget, or action meetings, to discuss Budget versus actual, BVA results, to discuss variances, and to plan corrective actions.

Staff meetings should be held immediately after the monthly BVA reports. If the reports need interpretation, a Budget department or Controller's representative may be present. It is useful to prepare flip charts or to use overhead transparancies to spice up the meetings. Preparing the charts leads to a well-thought-out agenda and helps to involve the attendees. These meetings should be chaired by the responsible manager of each box on the Organizational Chart. Meetings should consist of three to five persons. Under three is not a meeting—it's a discussion between the manager and a subordinate and will not produce a free exchange of ideas. More than five can cause the meeting to break down into a forum, everyone trying to get a message in, just to make points.

Zero base budgeting is a management technique which uses all the budgeting concepts discussed previously but, in some companies, can be a considerable improvement over typical budgeting techniques. ZBB starts from scratch. Managers, at the lowest Profit Centers on the Organizational Chart, are required to justify every expenditure as if it were being done for the first time.

The manager must isolate every function he controls, say a mini-computer, and then write an outline of why the function exists and what it costs. This is called a "decision package" and serves to identify the minimum expenditure level below what is currently being expended, plus an expanded level were more funds to be made available. This package also examines alternative ways of accomplishing the task, such as using an outside service bureau, or time-sharing. Lastly, the manager ranks all his decision packages by priority and forwards them to his superiors. Higher managers, in turn, go through the same exercise of identifying expenditures, describing them, costing them, and ranking.

The process, if well done, permits an analysis of every facet of the business which is not usually found in the standard budgeting exercise. Standard budgets include "slack" or built-in cushions to protect the manager. Many managers also tend to "build empires" and surround themselves with subordinates who are easily dispensed with in times of budget cuts. ZBB avoids slack and empire building by carefully analyzing budgets, from the bottom up. It analyzes, carefully, the interrelationship of all departments in the organization and gives top management the opportunity to make decisions based on an overview of a particular department or segment of the business as it relates to the whole.

Zero base budgeting is difficult and costly to install. It requires a carefully designed budget manual and intensive personnel training to make it work. The added cost, however, and the temporary disruption may be an investment in better budgeting which contributes to better corporate management in the long-run. The ranking procedure gives higher management the opportunity to concentrate heavy analysis on those functions that have shown poor results.

Performance auditing and the "sunset concept" can supply similar results to ZBB (cost justification from the first dollar), often at lower cost. Performance auditing is nothing more than operational auditing with the added feature that it reviews, not only the effectiveness of the operation being audited, but its economy. This economy review requires the participation of the local manager in analyzing his operation and developing output measurements. Like ZBB, performance auditing can concentrate on those areas of the business which show poor results.

The sunset concept merely recognizes that an activity will automatically be discontinued on a given date—the sun will set every few years. The activity will not be revitalized until it undergoes the same scrutiny it would receive in a performance audit or in evaluating a decision package in a zero base budget system. As a consequence of the review process, outdated programs and associated costs can be cut.

BUDGETING POINTERS

1. Budgeting starts with the Profit Plan (the bottom-line) formulated by the Board and the President. It is translated into an Operating Plan called the Budget, which results in projected financial statements. All levels of management must be involved in the planning process.

2. Budgeting techniques require communication to all levels of management through careful training, and the Operating Plan is prepared with each key manager being responsible for a Profit Center, exercising control over his direct costs of operation.

3. Actual performance is compared to Budget through a reporting system which includes monthly staff meetings, narrative reports, and carefully constructed charts, graphs, and analytical columnar reports.

4. Reports are designed to suit the particular company. They are circulated in a timely manner and contain information which is related to organizational responsibility.

The Budget is a control program which involves the broad management concept of planning corporate moves in advance, and then comparing performance to the plan. It is not concerned with the details of every transaction but only with the end result—profits. Budgeting is management accounting of the highest order, not based on the output of a green eye-shaded Uriah Heep, but, rather on the planned performance of the management group in setting goals and realizing them, utilizing the sophisticated planning tools of responsibility and budgetary accounting in achieving them.

CHAPTER 13

Streamlined Organizing For Systematic Financial Management

Those responsible for creating revenues or incurring costs are decision makers whose performance should be tracked and reported.

In the previous chapter, we discussed Financial Analysis Through Budgeting, involved with establishing the Plan for the control of operations. Inherent in planning for this control function is the implementation and administration of the previously established Plan. You've got the Plan. Now make it fly! This means you need an organizational framework to be sure people receive the Plan, read it, understand it, are involved in it, and perform up to it. You'll want to establish budget review techniques to measure performance against the Plan. This will involve the use of variance reports and budget review meetings. But, first, you need the framework. The framework necessary to communicate and administer the Plan for the control of operations, to ensure that the right people make the decisions and that the wrong people don't, consists of the following:

Organizational Charts

Chart of Accounts

Accounting Manual

Position Descriptions

Standard Operating Procedures

Operating Policies

Personnel Policies

Publication Control

Exercise of Authority

Philosophy of Management

Management by Objectives

Internal Auditing

These devices are available to even the smallest company. They are quickly and easily constructed and once completed, they attest to the internal control which is exerted by responsible management. They provide for the right decisions to be made by the right people, in a timely manner, and they make the Operating Plan work.

ORGANIZATIONAL CHARTS

It is a business axiom that a company's success depends on having a sound organization. An organizational chart serves to define:

Responsibility

Delegation of authority

Span of control

Job functions

Reporting relationships

Profit and cost centers

Decentralized/centralized philosophy

Every organizational chart denotes these items, either specifically or inherently. The responsible positions are indicated. The lines leading from the top boxes indicate delegation of authority and span of control. The placement of the boxes, in relation to other boxes, implies the job function and reporting relationships. Each responsible box becomes a profit or cost center, and the flow of the lines will tell a good deal about the operating philosophy of the company. It is important for the organizational chart to be kept current, to be maintained with identifying names and titles, thereby painting a picture for every employee which associates the individual with the job—it is worth a thousand words.

One would suppose (as would your independent auditor), the lack of even a simple and updated organization chart would indicate that there are unresolved questions of responsibility, authority, and reporting relationships—and if this be so, the organization, obviously, is unable to perform up to its promise.

In constructing an organization chart, the following principles should be considered:

1. Each person should report to only one supervisor.
2. Responsibility for performance of assigned duties must be accompanied by corresponding authority.
3. Each person's responsibilities should be clearly defined.
4. Charts must start at the lowest level which determines expenses and/or revenues.
5. Charts should top out with the recipients of profits, be they owners, stockholders, or trustees—not with the President.
6. Functional (dotted line) relationships should be drawn.
7. Only a few subordinates (usually no more than six) should report to each superior (unless the subordinates all perform essentially the same job).
8. All essential functions should be charted.
9. Adequate checks and balances must be provided.
10. Committees should be identified and charted.
11. Names of individuals should be slotted and kept current.

These principles are evident in the organizational chart in Exhibit 59. The top corporate chart is illustrated, together with downward explosions into marketing profit centers managed by Branch General Managers and Area Managers.

The designation of profit or cost centers is tied to the concept of responsibility accounting. *Those responsible for creating revenues or incurring costs are decision makers whose performance should be tracked and reported.* Each such responsibility is indicated by a box on the organizational chart. Only direct revenues or costs should be considered in each profit or cost center. There should be no allocations of revenues or costs. Allocations are usually subjective, if not arbitrary, and cause arguments. Sometimes, too, they cause extraordinary decisions to be made. A case in point would be the allocation of central computer service costs to outlying departments. If the allocated costs are excessive, the outlying department might purchase computer services on the outside, thereby incurring a hard dollar expense which was never contemplated.

In determining which costs or revenues are "direct" to the responsible reporting unit, the concept of discontinuance of operations is employed. These costs or revenues which would be eliminated if the operation were discontinued are considered to be direct. This definition, obviously, precludes allocations from other departments. Moreover, for this purpose, it is irrelevant whether costs are fixed or variable since both types are direct to the profit center. Rent, for example, in a sales office is a fixed cost in that it does not vary with sales. It is, however, direct to the profit center, as it would be eliminated if the sales office were to be closed. In defining direct costs, timing should be ignored. The rent obligation might continue for years after the office was closed, but eventually the rent cost would disappear and it must, therefore, be considered a direct cost.

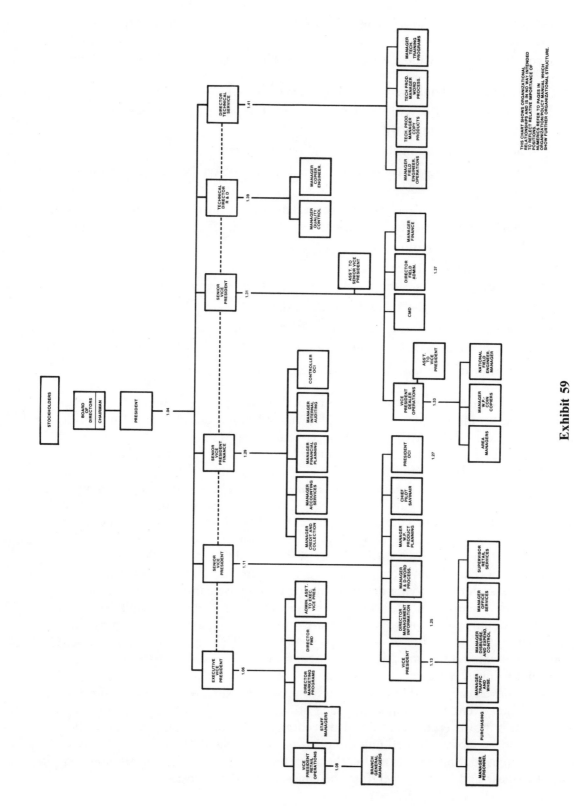

STOCKHOLDERS

BOARD OF DIRECTORS CHAIRMAN

PRESIDENT
1.04

EXECUTIVE VICE PRESIDENT
1.06

SENIOR VICE PRESIDENT
1.11

SENIOR VICE PRESIDENT FINANCE
1.29

SENIOR VICE PRESIDENT
1.31

TECHNICAL DIRECTOR R & D
1.39

DIRECTOR TECHNICAL SERVICE
1.41

DIRECTOR MARKETING PROGRAMS

DIRECTOR FMD

ADMIN. ASST. TO EXEC. VICE PRES.

VICE PRESIDENT RETAIL OPERATIONS
1.08

STAFF MANAGERS

BRANCH GENERAL MANAGERS

MANAGER R & D-WORD PROCESS.

DIRECTOR MANAGEMENT INFORMATION
1.25

MANAGER PRODUCT PLANNING

CHIEF PILOT SAVINAIR

PRESIDENT OCI
1.27

VICE PRESIDENT
1.13

MANAGER PERSONNEL

PURCHASING

MANAGER TRAFFIC AND WHSE.

MANAGER DISBURSE. AND EXPEND. CONTROL.

MANAGER OFFICE SERVICES

SUPERVISOR RETAIL SERVICES

MANAGER CREDIT AND COLLECTION

MANAGER ACCOUNTING SERVICES

MANAGER FINANCIAL PLANNING

MANAGER INTERNAL AUDITING

CONTROLLER OCI

VICE PRESIDENT DEALER OPERATIONS
1.33

AREA MANAGERS

MANAGER W.P.- COIN COPIERS

NATIONAL FIELD ENGINEER. MANAGER

ASST. TO VICE PRESIDENT

ASST. TO SENIOR VICE PRESIDENT

CMD

DIRECTOR FIELD ADMIN.
1.37

MANAGER FINANCE

MANAGER QUALITY CONTROL

MANAGER COPIER ENGINEER

MANAGER FIELD ENGINEER. OPERATIONS

TECH. PROD. MANAGER COPY PRODUCTS

TECH PROD. MANAGER WORD PROCESS.

MANAGER TECH TRAINING PROGRAMS

THIS CHART SHOWS ORGANIZATIONAL RELATIONSHIPS AND IS IN NO WAY INTENDED TO REFLECT RELATIVE IMPORTANCE OF POSITIONS. NUMERICS REFER TO PAGES IN ORGANIZATION/POLICY MANUAL WHICH SHOW FURTHER ORGANIZATIONAL STRUCTURE.

Exhibit 59

Organizational Chart

Once the direct cost determination is made, using the discontinuance of operations analysis, the costs may be classified further as fixed, variable, or semi-variable, using standard cost accounting techniques, to enable "direct cost" analyses to be made, as that term is characteristically used in determining contribution margins in cost/volume/ profit studies.

CHART OF ACCOUNTS

The accounting chart of accounts should be designed to capture the information, revenues and costs, generated by each profit or cost center on the organizational chart. A typical chart of accounts would have the following designations:

Chart of Accounts
FYE 4/30/

First Digit (High Order) - Position in Financial Statements

1. Assets
2. Liabilities
3. Capital Stock and Surplus
4. Sales and Operating Revenues
5. Sales Returns and Allowances and Discounts
6. Cost of Sales
7. Operating Expenses
8. Non-Operating and Royalty Income
9. Non-Operating, Royalty, and R&D Expense

Second Digit - (Sub-Position in Financial Statements)

1	1. Current Assets
	2. Fixed Assets
	3. Deferred Assets
	4. Other Assets
2	1. Current Liabilities
	2. Long Term Liability
	3. Other Liabilities
3	1. Capital Stock Issued
	2. Capital Surplus
	3. Retained Earnings
4, 5, 6	1. Electrostatic
	2. Xerograpic Products
	3. C Paper
	4. Diffusion Products
	5. Other Operating Revenues or Expenses
	6. Discounts
7	1. Selling Expenses
	2. Service Expenses
	3. Traffic and Warehouse Expenses
	4. General and Administrative Expenses
8, 9	1. Royalties
	2. Interest
	3. Research and Development
	4. Miscellaneous

Third and Fourth Digits - (Major Descriptions)
Fifth and Sixth Digits - (Minor Descriptions or Branches)
Seventh Digit (Low Order) - (Reserve for Future Use)

Exhibit 60

Once the chart of accounts is designed, changes in future years should be made reluctantly. An unchanged chart allows for meaningful comparisons over different years.

To assure that expenses are properly coded for distribution into the ledgers, an accounts payable voucher should be utilized which requires each vendor's invoice to be entered, capturing the vendor account number, dollar amount, and chart of account coding. This will facilitate data processing and provide the needed accuracy. All coding in excess of a specified amount should be double checked by an assistant controller to verify that entry has been properly made as specified in the accounting manual.

These seemingly elementary steps are essential building blocks for a reliable reporting system, without which financial analysis would be unreliable.

ACCOUNTING MANUAL

An accounting manual is a reference guide which enables the chart of accounts coder to assign the expense to the proper account category. For example, the broad category of selling expenses might contain sub-headings for training expenses (to train salesmen) and travel and entertainment expenses (intended for expenses related to customers). The manual would specify that travel expenses to training schools are to be coded to training expense, rather than to travel and entertainment expense. Similarly, car rental expense incurred by a salesman in calling on a customer would be coded to travel and entertainment expense, rather than to car rental expense, the latter being reserved for car rentals at field sales offices required for administrative purposes.

Advantages:

1. Insures adherence to company policy where alternative coding situations exist.
2. Prevents variable practice regarding the coding of alternatives.
3. Helps train new employees.
4. Provides a basis for audit by both internal and independent auditors.
5. Identifies alternative situations, in advance, by the act of codifying all accounting situations in a manual.
6. Creates a uniform system for all personnel and all offices.
7. Provides documented advice to all manual users that these are policies of top corporate management.

Format:

1. Table of Contents and Index—to facilitate use by accounting personnel.
2. Introductionary Instructions—to explain how the material is arranged, whether by subject matter or Chart of Accounts, the former being preferable. A good idea is to use both.

3. Policies Section—to explain policies and procedures which affect the coding (for example, what is the basis and life used for depreciation? or how to inventory fixed assets and what book entries are to be made).

4. A Definition—to explain each account

5. Inclusions—to state the nature of all items to be included.

6. Exclusions—to list specific alternative situations to be avoided.

7. Classification—to provide specific instructions for coding to the Chart of Accounts.

8. Loose-leaf Binding and Correction Checklist Page—to facilitate additions, updates, and corrections.

9. Forms Section—to illustrate each form which serves as input into the accounting system.

10. Tabs and sub-dividers—for easy reference

11. Outline Format—with main headings and sub-paragraphs, for easy reading. Use charts, graphs, and diagrams where possible.

Avoid These Pitfalls:

1. Don't use individual names. Use titles. Otherwise you'll have to correct a page every time an employee turns over.

2. Do not squirrel the manual with the Chief Accountant. Distribute it to everyone who needs it and should use it.

   a. Keep a log of users for distribution of corrections.

   b. Number and log in each copy so you can retrieve it on employee terminations.

The accounting manual is sometimes called an accounting dictionary. It defines the expense, permits it to be coded accurately and, with the chart of accounts, is a necessary ingredient of a reliable reporting system enabling meaningful financial analysis.

POSITION DESCRIPTIONS

The position of each box on the Organization Chart is an indication of the character of the job, shows the reporting relationships and, generally, summarizes the details which are found in the Position or Job Description. Just as every procedural narrative has a flow chart to affirm its logic, so, too, does the Organization Chart affirm the logic of the Position Description. One does not exist without the other.

It is necessary to distinguish between Job Descriptions, as defined above, which are broad statements of duties and responsibilities, from the detailed job descriptions or Work Duties which should be prepared for each job in each department. Work Duties spell out in specific detail just how a job should be performed. Each department head should maintain a Work Duties sheet for each job under his aegis, with a copy in the Personnel Department.

Position Descriptions should be:

1. Current.
2. Prepared for each box on the Organization Chart.
3. Reviewed by immediate superiors.
4. Filed in a Position Description Manual for ready reference by all managers.
5. Prepared in a uniform manner using published guidelines.

The dotted line appearing on the organizational chart represents the secondary line of responsibility which one manager has to another. Such relationships should be carefully considered in constructing the Position Description and in showing the reporting relationships. This relates key managers to each other and is the cement in the organizational building blocks.

STANDARD OPERATING PROCEDURES

We have seen that each employee, within the department, has a detailed Work Guide prepared for his job, and his superior has a Job Description which broadly states his responsibilities. To effectuate the duties set out in Work Guides and Job Descriptions, the Director of Administrative Operations, under the aegis of the Controller, will prepare the Standard Operating Procedures for the Company.

The following guidelines should be followed in writing Standard Operating Procedures:

- Codify all procedures in a manual.
- Use a simple numbering system for identification. For example, the first Accounting procedure is A-1, the second is A-2. Purchasing is P-1, P-2, etc.
- Use a Table of Contents, divided in sections by major area, such as Accounting, Purchasing, Order/Billing, Data Processing, Office Services, Personnel.
- Index all procedures.
- Exhibit all forms as part of procedures, and prepare a Forms Index.
- Cross-reference "Procedures Applicable to Other Departments" with a Contents listing which shows, for each department, those procedures which are not primary to it, but which involve this department. For example, an Accounting procedure involving Accounts Payable is primary to the Accounting Department but secondary to Purchasing which must send a copy of a Purchase Order to the Accounting Department.
- If the manual becomes too bulky, divide it into separate binders for ease in handling, using the categories in the basic numbering system.
- Always separate field procedures from home office procedures. Use separate manuals.

- Require the Controller to approve all procedures before publication and for him to obtain other necessary approvals where other divisions are involved.
- Keep procedures current.

Helpful Hint: A change in a very detailed procedure may mean a re-write of the entire procedure. This takes time and could delay the publication of the change. Speed this up by using a special form titled "Procedures Change Order" (referred to as a PCO). This looks like a simple interoffice memo but uses a special PCO masthead. The change is described and a printed legend on the bottom of form states that the Procedure No. XXX will be up-dated soon.

- Use a special form for all procedures, to enable all personnel to identify them, immediately, as procedures. Forms may be color-coded, for emphasis, by category or department.
- Use a Correction Checklist to up-date the Procedures Manual.
- Always start the procedure with a Purpose, a General Narrative, and show its Applicability.

Helpful Hint: Summarizing the Purpose, Narrative, and Applicability makes it unnecessary for every employee to take the time to read every procedure (some procedures run 10 to 20 pages). Only the first few paragraphs need be read to ascertain whether one is involved.

- Give extensive and detailed instructions on how to complete forms properly, supporting these with an illustration, cross-referenced to the detailed instructions.

OPERATING POLICIES

Standard Operating Procedures are the blueprints which are behind the broad statement of duties set forth in the Position Descriptions. These procedures may be said to be the steps in the "how to" of the job. The Company needs to augment these SOP's with a Policy manual.

Each Policy is not a "how to" but, rather, a statement of the prudence or wisdom which should be exercised in certain of the organization's affairs, consonant with the broad and overall philosophy of its management. This statement of management's material interest is expressed in the form of policies which may run the gamut from anti-political activities to zero defects in performance.

The Policy Manual is the highest authority for conduct in the corporation. It takes precedence over all other publications.

This manual is best arranged by subject matter which conforms to the company's structure (sales, service, finance, administration), with sub-sets for broad categories.

Subjects often covered in policies are listed below:

Alcoholism-Drugs.	Illegal payments.
Anti-political activities.	Labor claims.
Anti-trust.	Law suits.
Compensation Plans.	Legal review of contracts.
Conflicts of interest.	Maintenance agreements.
Contributions.	Meeting minutes.
Credit terms.	New products.
Employee stock options.	Personnel.
Equal opportunity employment.	Promotions.
Exercise of authority.	Public relations.
Extension of credit and pricing.	Responsibility to auditors.
Gifts.	Stockholder and broker releases.
Gifts from suppliers.	Zero defects.

As indicated before, the statement of Policy represents management's expression of the prudent way to conduct its affairs in the particular matter addressed in the Policy. However, the saying and the doing are not always the same.

Case in Point: A company had a published Policy directing its employees not to down-grade its competitor's products. The Policy was intended to avoid anti-trust actions. Unknown to the management, its salesmen persisted in stating that the use of competitor's supplies in its equipment caused malfunctions—not borne out by the facts. The company was sued by the competitor, lost on a treble-damage judgment with a cost running into the millions of dollars. The solution—training should have been conducted for field managers in the very good reasons for this policy to encourage continuing adherence.

PERSONNEL POLICIES

Some companies separate policy matters relating to their personnel from the standard Policy Manual and publish these policies in the form of a Personnel Policy Manual or a Personnel Handbook.

This type of manual is to be distinguished from operating procedures involving personnel which are printed in the SOP Manual. Such a procedure might involve the steps and paperwork in giving an employee a raise—an operating procedure. However, the prudence or wisdom in giving overall raises would become a matter of Personnel Policy. This is sometimes expressed in a Wage Administration Program which establishes wage levels for all classes of employees and determines when raises may be given. Other subjects which could be included in a Personnel Handbook would serve as orientation (for new employees), as well as to sketch prevalent policies.

Usually, there is a welcoming letter from the President, a history of the Company, its objectives, a description of its organization and operations, fringe benefit descriptions, insurance and medical programs, death benefits, and vacation policies.

PUBLICATION CONTROL

There are a variety of other manuals which a business may issue. These have the force of procedures or policy manuals and, so, affect the administration of the Operating Plan.

Consequently, the Controller or other responsible operating officer, must exercise jurisdiction over their publication—if only to insure that they are kept current and are properly circulated to all concerned managers.

Typical of these manuals are:

Price Lists	Service and Parts Manual
Sales Programs	Marketing Directives

As with any Policy Manual, the basic decision regarding the issuance of the Policy may not be the Controller's or the designated operating officer, but the responsibility for publication and circulation is his. More importantly, the lack of publication could be a serious omission which could adversely affect the successful administration of the Operating Plan and the generation of operating reports needed for successful financial analysis.

The designated operating officer (usually the Controller or Administrative officer) should require that, despite the source of authorship, the distribution and mechanics of publication of all manuals remain within his jurisdiction, possibly through the Manager of Office Services or the Systems and Procedures Department. This would enable controlled publication to those who need to know, would verify that overall policies are considered and adhered to, that proper approvals have been obtained for new policies, and that circulation is timely.

An important element of controlling publications is a system to provide that manuals are kept current, that changes and up-dates have been filed, and that old procedures have been discarded. This is particularly important when there is a personnel change in a particular job. The old employee may be doing the job correctly, but with an out-dated manual. The new employee may very well pick up the obsolete procedure because the manual is not current. The method of accomplishing this currency of publications is through the use of a *Correction Checklist.*

The Correction Checklist is simply a sheet of pre-printed numbers, in sequence. Every correction issued to a manual is given a sequential correction number. This number is merely crossed off the Correction Checklist. Any uncrossed off numbers indicate that a correction has been missed and that the manual is not current. The Checklist is kept in the front of each manual for ready reference, and it is used for organizational charts, position descriptions, and the various manuals described in this chapter.

Forms control is, perhaps, the most elusive part of publication control and requires the greatest effort. By definition, the other publications are controlled by the responsible decision makers—the sales manager is certain that the price lists are kept current; the national service manager cannot operate without an up-to-date parts manual—but, it seems that every manager, every assistant manager, and even every responsible clerical employee is bound by a propensity to design and circulate his own forms. They may be typewritten and photocopied or mimeographed but, somehow, they are widely distributed throughout the organization. Every such form creates input and the input often initiates a decision, albeit improper. For example, a purchasing department clerk may create a form to be completed by requesters of office supplies—how many paper clips did you use in the last six months; what do you expect to use in the next six months? He has, by the unauthorized initiation of this form, effectively implemented a six month buying decision. No consideration has been given to quantity price breaks and the company's overall return on investment. We may be better off with a two month supply or a one year supply, depending on the price differential and our own cost of money as expressed in our ROI. To avoid this happening, forms control belongs in the purvey of the Controller or the top administrative officer. This means his final approval or endorsement is required on every new form, changed form, or discontinued form. This approval, given from a vantage point which is not available to the purchasing clerk, gives consideration to the overall organizational relationships and decision making responsibility of each officer or division manager.

EXERCISE OF AUTHORITY

Whether operations are conducted on a centralized or decentralized basis, decision-making authority must be vested in subordinates, to avoid higher managers having to examine every piece of paper. To this end, a Standard Operating Procedure should be established which sets decision-making limits—limits of authority.

Helpful Hint: Psychologically, these limits are better received by employees if they are not titled Limits of Authority, but, rather, Exercise of Authority, to connote the employee's judicious use of his delegated authority.

These constraints should be observed in preparing the limits:

- Every possible expenditure should be listed.
- All decision makers should be included, in columnar form.
- Functional (dotted-line) authority should be shown as necessary approvers or endorsers.
- Use titles, not names, to avoid repeated corrections.
- Procedures and policies which relate to these expenditures should be cross-referenced as footnotes.
- Specifically prohibited authority should, also, be listed, such as Pricing Policies, Credit Terms, Compensation Plans.
- A catch-all category, with low limits, should be provided to catch forgotten or omitted authority. Title it Miscellaneous or Various.

This procedure would include varied items of authority, based on the differing nature of each company. The procedure should include several pages of footnotes, referring to other procedures and policies which govern these expenditures, as set forth in other publications. It is also helpful if this procedure includes an introductory page which refers to the just mentioned footnote constraints, describes the use of the procedure in administering the Operating Plan and further advises that each limit is a monthly amount per invoice, or series of invoices related to the same transaction.

PHILOSOPHY OF MANAGEMENT

While the development of a management philosophy is an element of managing people, it is of concomitant importance in any financial manager's decision making. The Plan for control, described in the previous chapter, and the formulation of reporting policies should be shaped, in tone and style, by the financial manager's philosophy of management which will be attuned to that of the corporate hegemony, as it relates to his own field of control. There are three rudimentary requirements to developing a management philosophy—artistry, creativity, and excitement.

Any responsible manager must acquire, possess, and demonstrate a superb command of his craft—*artistry*. He will bring to his profession an educational background in finance, accounting, taxes, and management. He will hone this with continuing professional educational courses given by universities, management associations, and local accounting and financial societies. He will maintain his proficiency with extensive technical reading of current literature distributed by professional societies—i.e., the Financial Accounting Standards Board, the American Institute of CPA's, State Society of CPA's, the Financial Executives Institute, the National Association of Accountants, the American Accounting Association, the Securities and Exchange Commission releases, Financial Analysts Federation, monthly business magazines like Forbes, Business Week, Dun's Review, Money, Finance, and U.S. News and World Report, and business dailies like the Wall Street Journal or Journal of Commerce. The list is extensive, but each publication need only be scanned for special articles of interest, and those often can be sight-read for pertinent matter. This reading will serve the financial manager in good stead in thousands of ways—in creating new operating techniques and evaluating old ones. Technical proficiency is the color on the financial manager's palette with which he appoints the operating picture.

The artistry of the manager must express itself, not in a me-too approach to decision making, but with originality and *creativity*. One cannot copy systems, procedures, and operating techniques from other companies, even competitors. Every business is different, and every organization, composed of individuals, is different. The successful financial manager will use his artistry as a departure point from which to create a management climate which is unique and suitable to his company.

Lastly, the artistic and creative financial manager must engender an enthusiasm and *excitement* in his company which breeds success. He should hold a monthly staff meeting with his people to apprise them of plans and current developments, to keep them enthused and excited about the job everyone is doing. One-on-one meetings during the month aren't as good. They're usually too concerned with the specific operating details and exigencies of the moment. The enthusiastic manager, using the organizational techniques described on the previous pages, is surely as innovative and original in his planning and fruition of the corporate Plan as any novelist, painter, or film-maker.

MANAGEMENT BY OBJECTIVES

Without doubt, one of the most valuable tools for organizing for financial management is Management by Objectives. The responsible manager sets objectives for his personnel and measures their performance against these objectives. This can be a formal program, administered by the Personnel Manager, utilizing special forms designed for this purpose. In a formal program, the objectives start with top management's (the Board of Directors and/or President) goal or objective for the coming year, usually expressed in dollars of sales and earnings. This objective is passed down to those reporting directly to the President. They set their broad objectives, consonant with the President's goals. The Treasurer, for example, may establish a goal of improving accounts receivable turnover by 5 days, thereby increasing cash flow and decreasing interest costs on short-term borrowings by X dollars. These goals, in turn, are passed down to the next level. Second-level managers then set their objectives within the framework of their superiors; the Credit and Collection Manager, for example, to support his Treasurer's goal, may set his object of reducing 90-day past due accounts receivable by 20% or X dollars. Each manager also identifies trouble areas in his department which improve overall performance. An example, to reduce departmental turnover by x%, thereby saving X dollars in personnel recruitment costs. The department manager imparts his goals to his employees, receives back their suggestions, and creates his final objectives which have the input and support of his people. The entire company is thus involved in the attainment of the corporate objectives. Bi-monthly or quarterly reviews of progress are a part of the program, to monitor progress and allow for mid-stream correction. Annual evaluations give consideration to the success in meeting objectives.

An informal Management by Objectives program may be implemented quite simply by individual managers, using the same techniques above, merely dispensing with the use of any special forms, and with each manager being responsible for the attainment of objectives of those in his own department. Care must be taken that objectives are not set which are too easily attained. The Position Description, described earlier, defines the basic responsibilities of each employee. The objectives are the standards of performance by which his performance may be judged.

It is best to choose 5 to 7 key goals or results which the employee should achieve within a specified time. These should be specific, not merely restatements of the Position Description. Where possible, objectives should be quantified, as in "reduce the cost of model 750 by 7% by September 1st.". Unless the goal or objective is specifically defined, it will be difficult to determine to what degree it has been reached at the end of the specified period. Non-specific goals also result in a failure to properly appraise the magnitude of the job necessary to meet that goal.

Following are some criteria to help you analyze your objectives to determine whether or not they are specific.

Criteria for Judging Objectives

"Good" objectives are:

1. Stated in terms of end results.
2. Achievable in definite time period.
3. Definite as to the form of accomplishment.
4. Related to management of the business.
5. Important to success of the business.
6. Precisely stated in terms of quantities, where possible.
7. Each limited to one important commitment to a statement.
8. Those which require stretch to improve results or personal effectiveness.

"Poor" objectives are:

1. Stated in terms of processes or activities.
2. Never fully achievable; no specific target date.
3. Ambiguous in defining what is expected.
4. Theoretical or "idealistic."
5. Not of real consequence.
6. Either too brief, indefinite, long or complex.
7. Compound, covering two or more objectives to a statement.
8. Lacking requirement for improvement.

Although the objectives you list should not cover your entire job, they should cover those important or critical areas that will probably require your major efforts during the specified period. Do not list routine duties which are normal functions, and which do not require major efforts to bring about changes or up-grading. If your statement of objectives ends up describing the maintenance of normal performance in your area of responsibility, do not bother writing it.

Employees are individuals and different things motivate each one. How can we reach each person when everyone is so different? Does a common denominator exist? It does—it is INVOLVEMENT. All people are more productive when they experience *pride* and a *sense of accomplishment* in their work. People need to be *recognized* for their efforts, not only financially, but with *praise, status,* and even constructive criticism.

Through this technique, not only do we have a highly motivated, responsive work cadre, but we also have developed independent, capable workers whose personal desires more nearly align themselves with the desires of the company.

INTERNAL AUDITING

Having established an organization such that it may be financially managed, using the organizational tools described in this chapter, financial analyses may now proceed with confidence. But procedures are not always understood; employees turn over and replacements may not be properly trained; responsibilities and organizational relationships may be changed without proper documentation; top management, even the President, may implement new policies through implied direction, by-passing administrative or financial controls. Operational auditing control is required to tell you that what you think is happening, is happening; that the conceptual fidelity of the organization's control procedures is intact. A formal internal auditing function must, therefore, be established as an integral part of the financial management organization.

The auditing function is generally the responsibility of the corporate controller, although it is not uncommon for the audit manager to report directly to the President, the Board of Directors, the Audit Committee, or to another responsible administrative, accounting, or management information services officer.

In its broadest form, the audit function would overview the entire organization, verifying that Organizational Charts and Position Descriptions are kept current; that procedures are current and are being followed; that policies are not being violated; that forms and publications are current, controlled, and properly approved, that expenditures are being incurred in accord with the limits of established authority; that the coding and recording of expenditures is properly executed as specified in the Accounting Manual and Chart of Accounts; and, that responsible managers are setting and monitoring the goals and objectives of their subordinates.

The internal audit is, thus, another operating procedure, performed by company personnel, which is philosophically oriented toward monitoring the possibility of attainment of the organization Operating Plan and bottom-line objective. It does this, not through measuring and comparing actual results to the budgeted figures, but through evaluating personnel, operations, plans, policies, systems, procedures, and the tools of management (Procedures Manuals, Organizational Charts, and Position Descriptions). The internal audit, being concerned by definition with the evaluation of company operations, may evoke as its performance sphere any area or segment of the business. There should be no prohibitions on the divisions, segments, departments, committees, policies, procedures, personnel, or plans which the auditor may approach.

This authority should come down from the President in a stated Policy Manual release and be explicit in the Position Description for the auditor. Obviously, the one exception is the outside audit function, which would not be reviewed or audited by the inside audit group, it being performed by independent outside accountants on a fee-paid basis.

In addition to the broad corporate internal audit function, each line manager has a responsibility to audit his own department. In small departments, this is done by the manager, himself, in overseeing workers' operations. In large departments, a departmental auditor may be utilized to verify that procedures are being followed, particularly as they relate to work which affects other departments.

ORGANIZATIONAL CONCEPTS FOR FINANCIAL CONTROL

1. The financial manager operates in concepts, not details. These concepts include providing a framework for the operation of the enterprise.
2. The organizational framework includes Organizational Charts, so everyone knows where he belongs, and Position Descriptions, so everyone knows what to do.
3. Codified Standard Operating Procedures provide the "how to" and published Policies direct individual and group activities to conform to higher management's overall philosophies.
4. Publications such as Price Lists, Accounting Manuals, and Marketing Directives augment standard procedures, and published Limits of Authority are established to permit subordinates to exercise judgment in making expenditures.
5. Management Objectives and a Philosophy of Management needs to be developed to assure the attainment of corporate goals.
6. The entire organizational process is reviewed by internal auditors to verify that the management system is working, that reports are flowing which enable proper financial analysis to be performed.

Glossary of
Selected Technical Financial Terms

The following alphabetical listing provides definitions of various accounting and technical terms, most of which are used in this book.

Absorption Costing

This is a cost accounting method which applies both direct or variable costs and fixed or overhead costs to the product unit cost. Some companies have cost systems which employ the absorption costing method and value their inventories and cost of sales on this basis, but construct their cost calculation cards so that the variable costs can be readily separated from the fixed costs.

Accounts Payable

The amounts that the company owes to its regular business creditors from whom it has bought goods on open account. The company usually has 30, 60, or 90 days in which to pay. Sometimes, as an inducement to pay promptly, the suppliers give cash discount of perhaps 2%. Therefore, if an account payable is $1,000 with terms of "2% in 10 days, net in 30 days," payment of the debt within 10 days earns $20 (2% of $1,000), and thus $980 will settle the invoice of $1,000. If the money is owed to a bank or other lender, it appears on the balance sheet under Notes Payable, as evidence of the fact that a written promissory note has been given by the borrower.

Accounts Receivable

The amount not yet collected from customers to whom goods were shipped prior to payment. Customers are usually given 30, 60, or 90 days in which to pay. However, experience shows that some customers fail to pay their bills because of financial difficulties. Therefore, in order that the Accounts Receivable be stated at a figure representing the amount that probably will be collected, the total is reduced by an allowance for bad debts.

Accumulated Retained Earnings or Earned Surplus

Perhaps a good way to explain this item is to say that when a company first starts in business, it has no accumulated retained earnings. At the end of its first year, if its profits are $80,000 and dividends are paid on the preferred stock of $30,000, but no dividends are declared on the common stock, then the balance sheet will show accumulated retained earnings of $50,000. Let us go forward to a second year. Assume the profits are now $140,000, and that dividends paid are $30,000 on the preferred stock and $40,000 on the common stock. The accumulated retained earnings will be $120,000.

Balance at the end of the first year		$ 50,000
Net Profit for the second year		140,000
Total		$190,000
Less dividends paid:		
On the preferred stock	$30,000	
On the common stock	40,000	70,000
Accumulated retained earnings (At the end of the second year)		$120,000

Accrued Expenses Payable

The company owes, on any given day, salaries and wages to its employees, interest on funds borrowed from banks and from bondholders, fees to attorneys, insurance premiums, pensions, and similar items. To the extent that the amounts accrued are unpaid at the date of the balance sheet, these expenses are grouped as a total under Accrued Expenses Payable.

Back Order

An order filled when goods are out of stock, for shipment when the goods are again available. The customer is usually notified when and what items are back-ordered, and shipping dates are estimated.

Base Rate

The pay expressed in dollars per time period to which other considerations in wages are added, such as incentive premium, overtime, and shift bonus. The hourly rate of pay on which incentive earnings are based. Generally a guarantee. Also called Base Pay.

Bill of Lading

A type of contract in the form of an acknowledgment of goods received for transportation, usually by a common carrier.

Break-Even Performance

1. Under an incentive plan, the point where any improvement in performance would result in incentive premium.
2. The level of performance where there is neither profit nor loss.

Budget

A formal systematic plan of operations for the utilization of labor, material, and services for a future period of time expressed in financial terms. It includes an estimate or forecast of future costs, and provides for the control of most of the expenditures on a current basis. Known as the Operating Plan or the Profit Plan.

Capital

Capital is probably most often used in the sense that it represents the investment by the owners in a proprietorship, partnership, or corporation. It usually consists of the original investment plus the retained income (or earned surplus). This is often also considered as the net worth of a business enterprise. In a balance sheet, this figure plus all of the liabilities, short and long-term, should equal the total of all of the assets.

Capital Stock

In the broadest sense, this represents shares in the proprietary interest of the company. These shares are evidenced by stock certificates issued by the corporation to the shareholders. There may be several different types or classes of shares issued by a corporation, each class having attributes slightly different from those of another class.

Capital Surplus

The amount paid by shareholders over the par or legal value of the total shares. The balance sheet will show under stockholders' equity a breakdown between capital stock and capital surplus. Also called Paid-in Capital.

Commodity

Anything movable (except animals) that is bought or sold.

Common Carrier

A company which transports goods or people for hire. Usually thought of as truck lines, railroads, and airlines.

Common Stock

Stock that has no special privileges or rights, but that is entitled to whatever capital or income remains after any prior claims are satisfied. Holders of common stock are actually the owners of the company. It has no limit on dividends payable each year, as in the case of preferred stock. Therefore, in prosperous times when company earnings are high, dividends may also be high, with the result that common stock may be an attractive investment.

Correlation

The relation between the measurements of two sets of attributes attached to each of a group of objects, such that when one of the attributes is given, the other can be predicted with a varying degree of certainty. The greater the degree of certainty, the higher is said to be the correlation. When more than two sets of attributes are involved, the term "multiple correlation" is applied.

Cost-Plus

Actual manufacturing cost, plus an agreed profit.

CPM "Critical Path Method"

A scheduling technique to relate time and cost factors to individual project activities. Estimates are made on prior experience when possible. Usually prepared for analyses and determination in diagram form; should detect possible bottlenecks in sequential operations.

Current Assets

In general, current assets include cash and those other assets which in the normal course of business will be turned into cash in the reasonably near future, usually within a year from the date of the balance sheet. Total current assets includes, primarily: cash, marketable securities, accounts receivable, and inventories. These assets are usually working assets, in the sense that they are in a constant cycle of being converted into cash. Inventories when sold become accounts receivable; receivables upon collection become cash; cash is used to pay debts and running expenses.

Current Liabilities

Generally includes all debts that fall due within the coming year. It can be said that Current Assets are a companion to Current Liabilities, because they are the source from which payment of the current debts is made. The relationship between these two classifications is one of the most revealing things to be learned from the balance sheet.

Current Ratio

Current assets divided by current liabilities. Generally, companies that have a small inventory and easily collectible accounts receivable can operate safely with a lower current ratio than those companies that have a greater proportion of their current assets in inventory, and are selling their products on credit.

Current Value Accounting

The presentation of supplementary financial information, resulting from a method of measuring and reporting assets and expenses associated with the use or sale of assets, at current cost (or net realizable value or value in use, if lower) at the balance sheet date or at the date of sale or use.

Depletion

A term used primarily by mining and oil companies, or any of the so-called "extractive" industries. Deplete, of course, means exhaust or use up. As the oil or other natural resource is used up, a depletion reserve is set up to compensate for the natural wealth the company no longer owns. This reserve is set up in recognition of the fact that as the company sells its natural product, it must get back not only the cost of extracting it but also the original cost of the natural resource.

Depreciation

For accounting purposes, depreciation has been defined as the decline in useful value of a fixed asset due to wear and tear from use and passage of time; or, when not in use, by reason of action of the elements. Fixed assets may also suffer a decline in useful value from obsolescence because new inventions and more advanced techniques come to light, which make the present equipment out of date.

The cost incurred to acquire the property, plant, and equipment must be spread over its expected useful life, taking into consideration the factors discussed in the preceding paragraph. For example, if an auto-truck costs $10,000 and is expected to last five years, then, using a "straight-line" method of depreciation, it will decline at the rate of $2,000 each year.

Direct Costing

Direct costing is a cost accounting method which treats fixed manufacturing expenses as period costs instead of allocating them as part of the product unit cost. It also measures costs which are incremental to the project being studied, permitting a contribution margin (revenue minus direct cost) to be calculated.

Direct Labor

Those operations which are recognized as assignable directly to particular products, and which can be readily costed individually by product and operation. For example, labor that is applied to each piece or unit of product.

Discounts

There are many kinds of discounts, including discounted debts, bonds, securities, et cetera. This type of discount usually consists of an allowance given for the settlement of a debt before it is due. In this instance we are referring mainly to three kinds of discounts; cash, trade, and quantity. Cash discount is merely a small percentage allowed to be deducted from a bill to encourage prompt payment within a specified time allowance. Trade discount is usually a considerably larger percentage of the list or catalog price which is allowed to certain classes of customers before consideration of the regular cash discount. Quantity discounts are used to encourage a customer to order his needs in larger quantities, and hence less frequently. This permits lower manufacturing and handling costs by the manufacturer. (See Chapter 6)

Equity

Equity is quite simply the titled ownership, right, or claim to an asset or group of assets. On a balance sheet, equity is found on the *liability* side, because an equity holder is almost always a creditor, proprietor, or stockholder.

Escrow

A deed, bond, or other written contract delivered to a third party to be delivered by him to the grantee only upon the performance or fulfillment of some condition.

Fixed Assets

Property, plant, and equipment are usually defined as fixed assets. It represents those assets not intended for sale which are used over and over again in order to manufacture the product, display it, warehouse it, and transport it. Accordingly, this category will include land, buildings, machinery, equipment, furniture, automobiles, and trucks. The generally accepted and approved method for valuation is cost less the depreciation accumulated to the date of the balance sheet. This would be net fixed assets. Gross fixed assets would be before depreciation is subtracted.

Fixed Costs

A fixed cost is one that is usually incurred regardless of the level of activity and amount of production, within reasonable limits. It includes costs such as supervisory and clerical salaries, building repairs, machine maintenance, insurance, property taxes, depreciation, and others that might be said to be not "escapable" under normal operating circumstances. Most fixed costs fall into the category often referred to as "overhead."

GNP Deflator

A general price index, published by the U.S. Department of Commerce, Bureau of Economic Analysis, which measures change in the general price level from a base year.

Good Will

This is recognized mostly in connection with the acquisition of a going business, in which case it represents the difference between the purchase price and the value ascribed to the net tangible assets acquired.

Many companies have reduced the asset value of the intangible assets to a nominal $1. This indicates that these assets do exist, but the company has adopted a very conservative policy for the carrying value in its balance sheet.

Gross National Product

A measure of the total output of the national economy for one year. It is expressed in dollars and represents the total market value of all goods produced.

Hypothesis

The most likely answer in view of all present knowledge. After it is positioned, one sets about the task of gathering evidence to either substantiate or disprove it.

Imprest Fund

A fund advance for petty cash disbursements.

Indirect Labor

Work in connection with production which, however, does not change the quality or form of processed parts.

Industrial Engineering

The application of engineering knowledge and techniques to the study, improvement, design, and installation of: (1) methods and systems, (2) standards, including quantity and quality measurements, as well as organizational and operating procedures, and (3) controls whereby performances are measured against standards, followed by appropriate action, with due regard to the well-being of employees, in order to achieve better management chiefly in, but not limited to, industrial enterprises to the end that improved products and services may be had at lower costs.

Inflation

A rise in the general level of prices, or, equivalently, a decline in the general purchasing power of the dollar. A decline in purchasing power is traditionally ignored in the formal financial statements, and supplementary information, in "constant dollars" is required to show the effects of inflation. (See GNP Deflator)

Intangibles

Assets having no physical existence, yet having substantial value to the company. Examples are a franchise granted by the city to a bus company allowing exclusive use of certain routes, and a patent granted by law for exclusive manufacture of a specific article.

Interpolation

The estimation, approximation, or calculation of intermediate values within a range or collection of known data. (See Chapter 3, Exhibit 17)

Inventories

The inventory of a manufacturer is mainly composed of three groups: (1) raw materials to be used in the product, (2) partially finished goods in process of manufacture, and (3) finished goods ready for shipment to customers. The generally accepted method of valuation of the inventory is either cost or market, whichever is lower. This gives a conservative figure. Where this method is used, the value for balance sheet purposes will be cost, or perhaps less than cost, if, as a result of deterioration, obsolescence, decline in prices, or other factors, less than cost can be realized on the inventory. Cost for purposes of inventory valuation normally includes an allocation of production and other expenses, as well as the cost of materials.

Inventory Turnover

How big an inventory a company should have depends on a combination of many factors. An inventory is large or small depending upon the type of business and the time of the year. One way of measuring the size of the inventory for comparative purposes is in its relation to sales. Annual sales divided by inventory balance equals turnover. A more common method is to divide cost of sales by inventory to determine turnover. As a rule, the higher the turnover the better, although the actual number of turns should be compared to both the industry average and historical data within the individual company in order to establish a trend.

Leverage

A company which has a large proportion of bonds, long-term debt, and preferred stock in relation to the amount of common stock is said to have a high leverage factor.

LIFO

A method of tracing the flow of costs through inventory which assumes the last costs incurred are credited to inventory first, second from last, next, etc.—in reverse chronological order of their incurrence—until incurred costs for the number of units sold have been charged to cost of goods sold.

Liquid and Liquidate

The term liquid, in this book, pertains to assets. It represents cash in bank and on hand not committed for any other specific purpose other than to pay off current liabilities. Liquidation pertains to the ready conversion of other types of assets into cash or its equivalent.

Long-Term Liabilities

Listed debts due some time after one year from the date of the financial report.

Marketable Securities

This asset represents temporary investment of excess or idle cash, which is not needed immediately. Such cash is invested in stocks, bonds, and securities for the purpose of earning dividends and interest. In view of the fact that the funds so invested may be needed on short notice, it is essential that the securities be readily marketable and be subject to a minimum of price fluctuation.

Median

That value in any array which divides the number of items in half; *i.e.,* an equal number of items lie above and below this value.

Mode

In a statistical population, the category, value, or interval of the variable having the greatest frequency is called the "mode."

Model (*Statistical***)**

A model, as referred to in this book, would be a pattern, system, procedure, or postulation which relates functions and situations to a specific problem. It usually provides a more understandable concept or hypothesis, and lends itself to changes, plans, designs, et cetera, to visualize and analyze the results of simulated actions before costly actual steps or transactions are taken. A model could very well take the form of a standard or typical financial statement, or even an organization chart. It is a method of grouping facts and guiding thought in an orderly and logical manner.

Net Working Capital

The difference between the total current assets and the total current liabilities. The working capital or net current assets represent the amount that would be left free and clear if all current debts were paid off. The ability of a company to meet its obligations, expand its volume, and take advantage of opportunities could be at least partially determined by its working capital.

Nodes

Points at which subsidiary or contributory lines or directions join or intersect. Usually illustrated in network drawings as a small circle or dot. A graphic device to illustrate an event on a chart.

Operations Research

An approach to problem solving for executive management which is often simply defined as scientific common sense. Operations research is the application of scientific methods and modern mathematical and statistical techniques to the solution of complex business or operating problems. It provides analyses of relationships which determine the probable future effects of decision choices.

PERT—"Program Evaluation and Review Technique"

A planning and control device for defining and integrating activities, and the time needed for each to meet a complex objective. It is usually expressed in a network type of flow diagram.

Pooling of Interests

A business combination that involves a continuation of substantially all of the original ownership. A new accounting basis does not arise, and assets, liabilities, and surpluses, are carried forward and combined.

Population

The aggregate of statistical items is called the "population."

Preferred Stock

Means that these shares have some preference over other shares as regards to dividends, or in distribution of assets in case of liquidation, or both. The specific provisions with respect to any issue of preferred stock can be obtained from the corporation's charter. For example, to assume that the preferred stock is designated 5% cumulative, $100 par value each, means that each share is entitled to $5 dividends per year when declared by the Board of Directors before any dividends are paid to the common stockholders. The word cumulative means that if in any year the dividend is not paid, it accumulates in favor of the preferred shareholders, and must be paid to them when available and declared before any dividends are distributed on the common stock. Usually preferred stockholders do not have a voice in company affairs unless the company fails to pay them dividends at the promised rate.

Prepayments or Advance Payments

These may arise from a situation such as this: During the year a company might pay fire insurance premiums covering a three-year period, or a company may lease certain computing machines and, by contract, pay rental for two years in advance. At the balance sheet date, there will exist an unexpended item which will be used up in future years. As an example, two year's insurance premiums are still unused, and one year's rental value of the computing machines is still unused, at the end of the first year. If the advance payments had not been made, the company would have more cash in the bank. Therefore, payments made in advance, from which the company has not yet received the benefits, but for which it will receive benefits in the next accounting years, are listed as prepayments among the assets.

Present Value

The amount of money which must be deposited today, paying X% interest per annum, compounded, to enable the depositor to have X dollars at the end of a stated period.

Price/Earnings Ratio

The current price of a company's publicly traded common stock divided by its last four quarters of after-tax earnings.

Probability Theory

This is merely the belief, usually a logical one, that a future condition or event will occur. Statistically applied, it is a measurement of the likelihood of the occurrence of a chance event.

Process Costs (Often called Conversion Costs)

Costs charged to processes or operations and arranged over production units as distinguished from job costs where the costs are applied to the specific product. A manufacturing process where there is more or less of a continuous flow or chain of one process to another especially lends itself to this method. Each process or step in the total procedure adds an increment of value to the product, which presumably starts out as a raw material of some sort.

Production

Production or manufacturing is the series of steps or operations by which material is given new form in accordance with predetermined intention by the aid of machines, tools and labor.

Production Control

Comprises planning, routing, scheduling dispatching, and inspecting. These functions are organized so that the movement of material, utilization of machines, and operations of labor are coordinated as to quantity, quality, time, and place.

Pro-Forma

A term which is usually applied to a financial statement when the form or format follows the traditional and accepted information headings, but the figures themselves are either tentative, hypothetical, or predicted. This technique is often used in planning functions and also as statistical "models" to find out the effects of various changes or actions on the financial situation. It means "giving effect" to certain stated assumptions.

Prorate

To divide, distribute, or assess proportionately.

Quick Assets

They are those current assets which are quickly convertible into cash. This leaves out merchandise inventories, because such inventories have yet to be sold. Accordingly, quick assets are current assets minus inventories.

Net Quick Assets are found by taking the quick assets and subtracting the total current liabilities. Net quick assets provide a rigorous and sometimes important test of a company's ability to meet its current obligations.

Random

Usually used in selecting a sample lot for probability determination. A definite random pattern produces a smaller margin of error than either a systematic selection (for example, every tenth item in a lot) or an outright haphazard selection. A specific random type selection of a sample lot should improve the accuracy of estimates, predictions, and tests. There are numerous tables of random sets of numbers available. In simple terms, if you were to sample a population of one hundred items, instead of examining the first ten items, or each tenth item for example, under a random sampling plan you might examine the items in the following order: 2, 6, 9, 14, 27, 42, 56, 70, 84 and 98.

Return on Investment

The rate required to obtain the recovery of an original investment, by discounting the resultant cash flows from the investment back to the present value of the investment.

Securities

A general term to apply to any transferable certificate of ownership or indebtedness. They are usually thought of in connection with municipal bonds, government treasury notes, debentures, and high grade stocks.

Serendipity

An unplanned by-product.
Progress by serendipity is defined as making valuable and unexpected discoveries by accident.
Origin—The gift of finding valuable or agreeable things not sought for; a word coined by Walpole, in allusion to a tale, "The Three Princes of Serendip," who in travels were always discovering, by chance or by sagacity, things they did not seek.

Standard Cost

The predetermined cost of manufacturing a specific product. It is usually based on past experience when available and expected performance in the case of new items. It usually includes direct labor, direct material, and overheads. Standard costs are usually used to value inventories and obtain standard or normal cost of sales.

Statistical Quality Control

A form of "statistical inference"—judging an entire lot by examining only a sample. This is a broad field; for those who are interested, there are numerous excellent books and articles on the subject.

Stockholders' Equity or Net Worth

The total equity interest that the stockholders have in a corporation. This is separated for legal and accounting reasons into three categories: capital stock, capital surplus, and accumulated retained earnings.

Value Analysis and Value Engineering

A scientific method of obtaining the same or better performance and value from a specific product or product component at a lower cost. This is done by the step by step scrutiny and test of every part and every operation in the manufacture of a product.

Variable Cost

This category is also referred to as "direct" costs. It consists mainly of direct labor and direct material. As a general rule, all costs which contribute directly to the manufacture of, or conversion into, the finished product are variable costs. There are many borderline cost factors that are difficult to clearly categorize as fixed or variable. Many of them will have to be arbitrarily labelled by establishing set accounting policies in some areas. It would be wise, however, to be both scrupulous and consistent in this matter. In incremental analyses, it refers to those costs which would be eliminated if the project were discontinued.

Vertical Integration

The ownership or control by one organization of several or all stages of the productive process.

Weighted Average (Mean)

A mean is where the relative importance of each item is taken into consideration in the computation. In practice, each item is multiplied by some number (weight) representing its importance, the sum of such products being then divided by the sum of the weights.

Working Capital

Usually considered as that amount of capital in current use in the day-to-day operation of a business. It is probably best described as the excess of current assets over current liabilities—or net current assets.

Index

A

Absorption costing concept, explanation of, 117-120
  advantages, 120
  application using conventional standard cost system, 119
  definition, 269
  disadvantages, 120
Absorption product cost method, 132
Absorption vs. direct costing, 104-124 (see also "Costing, direct vs. absorption")
Accounting manual, 258
Accounting method, selection of, 105
Accounts payable, definition of, 269
Accounts receivable, 35-38
  cash discount for prompt payment, 37
  chart, 39
  definition, 270
  turnover, 35
Accrued expenses payable, definition of, 270
Accumulated retained earnings, definition of, 270
Acquisitions, evaluation of, 219-239
  compliance with regulatory government agencies, 221
  determination of price, 229
  for debt, 175
  possible results, 239
  reasons, 220
  selection of partner, 222
  statistical analysis, 222
Acquisitions in future, importance of, 24
Advance payments, definition of, 279
Advantages of absorption costing, 120
Advantages of direct costing, 115
Advertising in relation to selling expense, 133
"Aging" inventories by item, 41
American Institute of Certified Public Accountants, 105
Analysis, operations, vs. operations research, 213
Analysis staff, advantages of, 214

Anti-trust problems, avoidance of, in mergers, 221
Application of funds, 95-103
  cash flow defined, 95-99
  cash forecasting, 99
  cash management, 102
  two major sources, 96
Applied research as category of research, development and engineering plan, 210
Approach, non-technical, to discounted cash flow method, 64
Appropriation request, 79, 80, 81
Asset turnover, 203
Assets, important current, 33
  accounts receivable, 35-38
  cash, 45-49
  inventory, 38-45
Asset utilization, improved, financial analysis for, 34
  accounts receivable, 35-38
  cash, 45-49
  inventory:
    control by management, 38
    quantity levels, 41
    turnover, 42
  lock box system, 45
Assignment of responsibility for profit planning, 212
Audits, 88-93
  problems in, 90
  projects for, 89
  purposes of, 88-90
  responsibility for, 90
  timing of, 89
Authorization request for research project, 195
Auxiliary reports to primary financial report, 25

B

Back order, definition of, 270
Back-up reports, 22

Balance sheet, 22, 33-60
    accounts receivable, 35-38
    budgeting, 53
    capital budget, 56
    cash position, 35
    definition, 33
    fixed asset balances, 50
    gross assets, return on, 51
    inventory management, 38
    supporting statements, 34
    working assets, management of, 34
Balance sheet budget (chart), 57
Bank debt, 48, 162
Base pay, definition of, 270
Base rate, definition of, 270
Basic research, 197
Benefits obtainable from comparison analysis, 199
"Bias of the specialist," 32
Bill of lading, definition of, 271
Book value per share, 63, 243
Breakeven chart, 112, 113, 115, 121
Breakeven performance, definition of, 271
Budget, definition of, 271
Budgeting, 53, 241-252
    communicating, 244
    direct costs, 247
    organizational framework, 247
    profit center, 246
    reporting system, 249
    transfer pricing, 247
Burden costs, 107

C

Calculation of depreciation of capital investment, 71
Calculation of profitability rate in discounted cash flow
    method, 74
Capital budget, 56
Capital, definition of, 271
Capital expenditures in future, chart for, 59
Capital investment, 61
    calculation of depreciation, 71
    "discounted cash flow," 62
    estimated requirements, 61, 70
    importance of decisions, 61
    payback period, 72
    post-installation evaluation, 88
    profitability rate, 65, 78, 86
        calculation of, 74, 75, 79
    request for, 79, 80
        justification checklist, 79, 81
    sum of years digits, 71
    work sheets, 69, 70, 73, 80, 81, 85, 91, 92
Capital investment planning, 211
Capital stock, definition of, 271
Capital surplus, definition of, 271
Captive finance subsidiary, 173
Carrying charges vs. job change costs, 41
Cash balance, dwindling, as cause of company failure, 103
Cash discount, definition of, 274
Cash discount factors, table of, 76-77
Cash discount for prompt payment, 37
Cash flow, 65, 95-103
    defined, 65, 96
    diagram, 97

Cash flow *(cont.)*
    forecasting, 99
    illustrations of transactions providing, 98
    management, 102
    per share, 63
    two major sources, 96
    work sheet, 93
Cash flow back (chart), 73
Cash forecasting, 99
Cash management, 102-103
Cash position, 35
Cash regarding improved asset utilization, 45-49
Chart of Accounts, 257
Checklist, justification of investment, 81
Coding, 121
Color coding, 46
Comments as part of financial report, 28
Committed costs, definition of, 107
Commodity, definition of, 271
Common carrier, definition of, 272
Common stock, definition of, 272
Comparison analysis, 199
    benefits obtainable, 199
    charts, 200-202
    practical benchmarks, 203
    reasons for successes and failures, 204
    sources of data, 201
    time periods studied, 202
    value of, 199
Comparison, periodic, plan vs. actual performance, 213
Comparison sheet, financial, 200
Computer utilization, 177-191
    alternatives, 189-191
    binary, 180-181
    control, 188-189
    functional relationships, 179
    glossary of terms, 182-185
    organization, 185-186
Consolidation, 219
Construction of financial status report, 25-28
Content and form of post-installation evaluation, 90, 92
Contribution margin, 108
"Contribution theory," 109, 111
Control by management level of inventories, 41
Control of profits chart, 52
Controller, responsibility of, 31
    integration of staff functions, 32
Conversion costs, definition of, 280
Convertible bonds, 165
Convertible preferred, 236
Corporate surgery in profitability review by product, 142
Correlation analysis, definition of, 272
Cost analysis in profitablity review by product, 137
Cost-plus, definition of, 272
Cost reduction, financial analysis for, 145-158
    continuous organization required, 145-146, 155
    importance of right program, 146
    manufacturing budgets, 209
    operating budgets, 241-252
    opportunities, 147
Cost reduction:
    participation in programs, 146
    responsibility reporting, 246
Costing, direct vs. absorption, 104-124
    absorption costing, explanation of, 117

Costing, direct vs. absorption *(cont.)*
    advantages and disadvantages of absorption costing,
      120
    advantages of direct, 115
    application of absorption costing with conventional
      standard system, 119
    as affected by sales volume changes (chart), 114
    conclusions and recommendations, 121-122
    costs, definition of:
        committed, 107
        direct, 107, 111
        fixed, 106
        indirect, 107
        overhead, 107
        period, 106
        prime, 108
        product, 108
        semi-variable, 108
        standard, 109, 119, 281
        variable, 109-111
    disadvantages of direct, 116
    explanation of direct, 111
    gross profit margin, definition of, 109
    marginal income, definition of, 108
    selection of method, 105
    separation of fixed and variables, 109-110
    under absorption cost method (chart), 119
Costs, two kinds of, 126
CPM, 215
    definition, 272
Credit department monthly report (chart), 38
Critical path methods, 215
    definition, 272
Current asset, definition of, 272
Current liabilities, definition of, 273
Current ratio, definition of, 203, 273
Current value accounting, 29

D

Data, tabulation of, in profitability review by products, 136
Debt with equity, 165
    with warrants, 166, 167
Decimal factors, tables of, for sum-of-digits, 71-72
Decisions about capital investments, importance of, 61
Definitions of selected technical terms, 269
Depletion, definition of, 273
Depreciation:
    as fixed cost, 110
    as important source of cash income, 97
    definition, 273
Depreciation schedule (chart), 72
Detail, development in, as prerequisite of effective
    planning, 24
Determination of price in merger, 229-232
Development projects, evaluation of, 193-199
    (see also "Research and development projects,
      evaluation of")
Direct costing concept, 111-117, 247
    definition, 107, 273
Direct costing, explanation of, 111
    advantages, 115
    "Contribution theory," 109, 111
    disadvantages, 116
Direct labor, definition of, 275
"Direct to bank" remittance plan, 45

Direct vs. absorption costing, 104-124 (see also "Costing,
    direct vs. absorption")
Disadvantages of absorption costing, 120
Disadvantages of direct costing, 116
Discount factors, table of, 76-77
Discounted cash flow method, 62-93, 195-197
    factors slowing acceptance, 64
    non-technical approach, 64-65
    payback period, cash income and, 72
    post-installation evaluation, 88
    profitability rate, 65, 74
        calculation of, 17, 74, 75
    request for expenditure, 79
    work sheets, 69, 70, 73, 80, 81, 85, 91, 92
Discounts, definition of, 274
Discrimination in products for profit maximization, 143
Distribution cost control, 125-144
    cost reduction, 126
        for small order volume, 127
        for standard costs, 129
    definition, 126
    selling expense, 133
    specialization in small volume business, 135
Distribution of financial status report, 22
Diversification possible answer to problem product, 205
Dow Jones average, 204
Dun & Bradstreet report, 223

E

Earned surplus, definition of, 270
Earnings per common share, 203, 243
Economic order quantity, 41
Economic value of research and development projects, 194
Equity, definition of, 274
    cost, 160
Escrow, definition of, 274
Estimated capital investment requirements, 70-71
Evaluation, post-installation, of major capital investments,
    88
    form and content, 90
    problems, 90
    purposes, 88-90
    responsibility for, 90
    timing, 89
    types of projects for, 89
Exchange ratio, determination of, in merger, 229
Expenditure, capital, 61-93 (see also "Capital investment")
Expenditure, request for, 79, 80
Explanations as part of financial report, 28

F

Factory costs, 126
Failures in business, reasons for, 204-205
Financial analysis for improved asset utilization, 33-60 (see
    also "Asset utilization, improved, financial analysis
    for")
Financial analysis report, monthly, 21-32
    auxiliary reports, 25-28
    comments and explanations, 28
    construction of, 22
    distribution of, 22
    frequency of, 28

Financial analysis report, monthly, *(cont.)*
  three sections, 22
  timing of, 28
Financial compound interest and annuity tables, 66
Financial Executives Institute, 31
Financial Position, 35
Financial projections in long-range profit planning, 211
Fixed asset balances, 50
  definition, 274
Fixed asset spending plan, 211
Fixed costs, definition of, 106
  separated from variable costs, 109-110
Fixed expenses, 111
  definition of, 274
Flexibility essential in capital budget, 57
Flexible budget, 112, 115-116
Forecast, definition of, 242
Forecasting, 24
  on balance sheet, 54
Forecasting, cash, 99
  advantages, 102-103
Form and content of post-installation evaluation, 90, 92
Formalizing planning procedures, advantages of, 207
Frequency of financial analysis report, 28
Function of planning, 206
Fundamental and basic research as category of research, development and engineering plan, 211
Fundamental research, 197
Funds, source and application of, 95-103
  cash flow defined, 65-96
  cash forecasting, 99
  cash management, 102
  two major sources, 96
  statement worksheet, 100
Future plans, importance of, 23-24

G

General purchasing power, 29
GNP deflator, 29-30
"Good will" classification in merger, 229
  definition, 275
Government agencies, compliance with in mergers, 221
Gross assets, illustration of financial position in, 102
Gross assets, returns on, 51
  graph, 201
Gross fixed assets, definition of, 274
Gross profit analysis by products, 137
Gross profit margin, definition of, 109
Gross national product, definition of, 275

H

Historical cost, 104
Horizontal integration, 220
Hypothesis, definition of, 275

I

Idle money, elimination of, 45
Importance of right program in cost reduction, 146
Imprest account, 46
Imprest fund, definition of, 275
Inadequate accounting system, danger in, 205

Income and expense statement:
  comparison of absorption vs. direct costing, 104-124
  under absorption cost method, 120
Incremental costs, 108
Indexes, marketing, 134
Indirect costs, definition of, 107
Indirect labor, definition of, 275
Individual projects, budgets for, 57
Industrial engineering, definition of, 275
Inflation accounting, 28-31
Information system, factors important in, 21-22
Installment loans, 168
"Intangible asset" classification in merger, 229
  definition of, 276
Internal auditing, 252, 267
Internal Revenue Service, 105
Internal rate of return, 63
Interpolation, definition of, 276
Inventories, definition of, 276
Inventories to total current assets, ratio of, 34
  quantity levels, 41
    "aging," 41
  turnover, 42-45
Inventory management, 38
Inventory turnover, definition of, 276
Inventory turnover in comparison analysis (graph), 202
Investment, capital, 61 (see also "Capital investment")

J

Job change costs vs. carrying charges, 41
Job cost, 104
Justification checklist, 81

L

Labor, question of variables vs. fixed, 111
Lease, definition of, 172
Leverage, definition of, 277
Leverage leasing, 169
LIFO, 30
Limitations of operations research approach, 215
Liquid, definition of, 277
Liquidate, definition of, 277
Lock box system, 45
Long-range profit planning, 206 (see also "Profit planning, long-range")
Long-term debt, 30, 163
Long-term liabilities, definition of, 277

M

Management by objectives, 247, 254, 265-267
Management of research and development projects, 193-199
Management, role of, in inventory control, 41
Manufacturing budget, 209
Manufacturing cost, 126
Manufacturing gain and loss, 118-120
Manufacturing plans, 209
Marginal contribution, 108
Marginal income analysis, 111-115
Marginal income, definition of, 108
Marketable securities, definition of, 227
Marketing analysis, 125

Marketing, cost of, 125-144 (see also "distribution cost control")
Marketing plans, 208
Marketing research in regard to selling expense, 133
Materials requirement planning, 41
Mathematical methodology of operations research, 213
Mean, definition of, 282
Median, definition of, 277
Mergers and acquisitions, evaluation of, 219-239
    compliance with regulatory government agencies, 221
    determination of price, 229
    possible results, 239
    reasons, 220
    selection of partner, 222
    statistical analysis, 222
Methodology, mathematical, of operations research, 213
Methods of sales forecasting, 208
Mode, definition of, 277
Models, use of, in operations research, 215
    definition, 277
Monitoring of major capital investments, 88
    (see also "Evaluation, post-installation, of major capital investments")

N

Necessity for long-range planning, 206
Net fixed assets, definition of, 274
Net profit as major source of cash income, 97
Net quick assets, definition of, 280
Network techniques, 215
Net working capital, 278
Net worth, definition of, 281
Nodes in critical path methods, definition of, 278

O

Objectives, basic, of profit planning, 208
Operating budgets, 241-252
Operating procedures, 261
Operations analysis staff, advantages of, 214
Operations research and analysis, 213
    advantages of analysis staff, 214
    analysis vs. research, 213
    limitations, 215
    research, definition of, 278
    suggested procedure for research assignment, 214
        mathematical methodology, 213
        models, use of, 215
    value analysis, 215
Opportunities for cost reduction, 147
    value engineering, 148
Organization required for cost reduction programs, 155
Organizational charts, 155, 254-257
Over-expansion, danger of, 204
Overhead costs, definition of, 107, 275
Overhead expense in small order business, 127

P

Participation in cost reduction programs, 146
Partner, selection of, in merger, 222
Payback period, 62, 73
P/E ratio, 63, 64, 203, 230

Penalty in small order, 127
Performance auditing, 199-200
Performance rating, annual, with competition, 199-205
    comparison sheet, 200
    practical benchmarks, 203
    reasons for successes and failures, 204-205
    sources of data, 201
    time periods studied, 202
    value, 199
Performance statistics, 23
Period costs, 111, 114
    definition, 106
PERT, 32, 215
    definition of, 278
Petty cash, 47
Philosophy of management, 264
Plan performance statistics, 212
Planning, 23
    definition, 206
Planning procedure, suggested, 207
    sections, 207
    time period, 207
Policies, 261, 262
Pooling of interests, 175, 229
Population, definition of, 278
Post-installation evaluation for major investments, 88
    form and content, 90
    problems, 90
    purposes, 88-90
    responsibility for, 90
    timing, 89
    types of projects for, 89
Post-installation evaluation of major appropriation (chart), 91, 92
Preferred stock, definition of, 279
Premium on small special order, 132
Prepayments, definition of, 279
Present value, 64, 76
Price, acquisition, determination of, 229
Price estimating form, 130-131
Prime costs, definition of, 108
Probability theory, definition of, 279
Problems in post-installation evaluation, 90
Procedure, suggested, for operations research assignment, 214
Process cost, 104
    definition, 280
Process improvement and technical services as category of research, development and engineering plan, 211
Product analysis, 136
Product cost, definition of, 108
Product development as category of research, development and engineering plan, 210-211
Production control, definition of, 280
Production, definition of, 280
Products, profitability review by, 125-144 (see also "Profitability review by products")
Profit, analysis:
    by product and plant, 138
    by product and sales branch, 138-142
Profit and loss statement starting point for financial projections, 211
Profit contribution, 108, 137
Profit maximization through product discrimination, 143
Profit planning, long-range, 206

Profit planning, long-range, *(cont.)*
    advantages of formalizing, 207
    assignment of responsibility, 212
    budgeting, 206
    capital investment, 211
    comparison of plan vs. performance, 213
    definition and function, 206
    financial projections, 211
    manufacturing plans, 209
    marketing plans, 208
    necessity, 206
    planning vs. forecasting, 206
    purpose and objectives, 208
    research, development and engineering plan, 210
    suggested procedure, 207
    time period, 207
Profitability rate, 65, 78, 86
    calculation of, 74, 75, 79
        chart, 75
Profitability review by products, 125-144
    corporate surgery, 143
    gross profit analysis, 138, 139
    maximization through product discrimination, 143
    profit analysis by product, 138
        by product and plant, 138
        by product and sales branch, 138-142
    remedial action programs, 142
    sales and cost analysis, 128-129
    sales mix, quality of, 136
    tabulation of data, 136
    territorial return on investment, 141
Pro-forma balance sheet for merging companies, 228
Pro-forma balance sheet plan, 211
Pro-forma, definition of, 280
Pro-forma income statement for merging companies, 226
Program Evaluation and Review Technique, 32, 215
    definition, 278
Projection, definition of, 242
Projections of sales and profits, 24, 53-58
Projects, type of, for post-installation evaluation, 89
Prorate, definition of, 280
Publication control, 262-264
Purchase, 175, 229
Purpose, basic, of profit planning, 208

Q

Qualitative evaluation of research and development projects, 197
Quantitative evaluation of research and development projects, 196
Quantity, discount, definition of, 274
Quantity levels of inventory, 41
    "aging" inventories, 41
    carrying charges vs. job change costs, 41
    turnovers, 202, 276
Questions intrinsic to value analysis, 216-217
Quick assets, definition of, 280

R

Random, definition of, 280-281
Rate of return, 63, 65, 281
Reasons for competitive successes and failures, 204-205
Reasons for mergers and acquisitions, 220-221

Recommendations as part of financial report, 28
Reduction in distribution cost, 126
    for small order volume, 127
    for standard costs, 124
    selling expense, 133
    specialization in small volume business, 135
Regulatory government agencies, compliance with in merger, 221
Remedial programs for unfavorable "product mix" trends, 142
Replacement costs, 29
Reports, 27, 249-252
Request for capital expenditure, 79, 80
Requirements, estimated, for capital investment, 70
Research and development projects, evaluation of, 193-199
    economic value, 194
    qualitative, 197
    quantitative, 196
Research, development and engineering plan, 210
Research, operations vs. operations analysis, 213
Research projects, importance of, 193
Responsibility for post-installation evaluation, 92
Responsibility reporting, 31-32, 116, 246
Results, possible, of merger, 239
Retained earnings, cost, 162
Return on equity, 63, 243
Return on investment, 51, 74-79, 86, 243
    current assets, 83
    discounted cash flow method, 62
    for the entire business, 79-88
    internal rate of return, 63
    payback, 62, 73
    present value method, 62
    wasting assets, 67
Robinson-Patman Act, 132

S

Sale and lease back arrangement, 171
Sales analysis by number of customers vs. annual volume, 129
Sales analysis by order size vs. sales volume (chart), 128
Sales and cost analysis in profitability review by products, 137
Sales and income data, 23
Sales forecasting, 208
Sales mix, quality of, 136
Sales promotion in relation to selling expense, 136
Sales volume changes affecting cost (chart), 114
Scientific management, application of, 214
Scientific sampling, 215
Sections of plan, 208
Sections, three, of financial analysis report, 22
Securities and Exchange Commission, 28, 105
Securities, definition of, 281
Selection of cost accounting method, 105
Selection of partner in merger, 222
Selling expense, 133-134
    what it includes, 133
Semi-variable costs, definition of, 108
Serendipity, definition of, 281
Short-term funds, 48-50
Small order volume, reduction of distribution costs for, 126-127
    procedure for analyzing, 127

Small volume business, specialization in, 135
Source data for financial report, 25
Sources of data for comparison analysis, 201
Sources of funds, 95-103 (see also "Funds, source and application of")
Specialization in small volume business, 135
Spin-off, 233
Staff assistance to executive, 213
Staff communicator of information to management, 31
Staff meetings, 251
Standard cost card, 122-123, 130-131
Standard costs, definition of, 109, 281
Standard costs, reduction in distribution expense of, 132
Standard system in use with absorption costing, 118
Statement of changes in financial position, 95-103
Statistical analysis in evaluation of merger, 222-229
Statistical inference, definition of, 281
Statistical quality control, definition of, 281
Stock value, 87, 88
Stockholder's equity, definition of, 281
Straight debt, 163-164
Successes, reasons for, 204-205
Sum-of-years digits, 71-72
Supporting statements of balance sheet, 34

T

Table of discount factors, 83-84
Tables of decimal factors for sum-of-digits, 72
Tables of financial compound interest and annuities, 66
Takeover premium, 230
Tax effect of merger, 221
Tax-free merger, 232
Team effort, need for, in cost reduction programs, 146
Technical terms, definitions of, 269-289
Tender, 234
Terminology, technical, definitions of, 269-289
Territory analysis, 139-149
Time period for planning, 207

Time periods studied in comparison analysis, 202
Timing of financial report, 28
Timing of post-installation evaluation, 89
Trade discount, definition of, 274
Turnover, inventory, 202, 276

V

Value analysis, 215-217
    definition, 282
    questions, 216-217
Value analysis vs. conventional cost reduction, 216
Value analysis vs. value engineering, 216
Value engineering, 216
    definition, 282
Value of comparison analysis, 199
Variable costs, definition of, 109-111, 282
Variable costs separated from fixed costs, 109-110
Variable income statement, graphic, 123
Vertical integration, 220,
    definition, 282
Volume as important influence on costs and profits, 104, 111-112
Volume variance concept, 111-112

W

Walpole, 281
Wasting asset, 67
Weighted average, definition of, 282
Work sheet for cash flow, 100
Work sheets for capital investment decisions, 68-75, 90
Working assets, management of, 34
Working capital, definition of, 282

Z

Zero balance accounts, 46
Zero base budgeting, 251